Of the 1,690 U.S. [...] hind enemy lines in Korea, fewer [...] escaped capture and made their way unaided back to U.N. lines. Clay Blair tells the true, documented story of some of the most harrowing of these escapes . . .

Schinz

Shot down over the Yellow Sea, he led a Robinson Crusoe existence for thirty-eight days on an island.

Summersill

He plodded forty miles on frozen feet with his companion, Sawyer, across a mountain range in sub-zero weather.

Thomas

By living like an animal in a succession of burrows no bigger than a grave, he evaded Red troops for eighty-nine days.

Shadduck

The only U.S. pilot who successfully planned and executed an unaided escape from the hands of his Chinese captors.

BEYOND COURAGE

BEYOND COURAGE

Clay Blair

Foreword by General Nathan F. Twining,
Chief of Staff, United States Air Force

BALLANTINE BOOKS • NEW YORK

ISBN 0-345-30824-7

Printed in Canada

First Ballantine Books Edition: March 1957
Third Printing: February 1983

CONTENTS

"In the mould of this new profession, a new breed of men has been cast."

—ANTOINE DE SAINT-EXUPÉRY,
Wind, Sand and Stars

FOREWORD

Our nation has shown an intense interest in the fate of the Air Force officers and crewmen who became POW's in the Korean war. Tens of thousands of words, in news stories, editorials, magazine articles, and books, have been written about them. We in the Air Force have rather silently observed this attention come into focus. The accounts of how Air Force POW's were murdered, beaten, starved, tortured, thrown into dismal solitary confinement for months, and falsely charged with "germ warfare," provide new and vivid proof, if further proof is needed, of the evil, barbaric, and poisoned nature of Communism. For us it has been a bitter experience, but because of it, we can better equip ourselves to cope with this sort of thing in the future.

However, I believe that in all the words written a salient point has become somewhat obscured. It is the duty of every Air Force pilot or crewman who falls behind enemy lines to attempt to escape. In North Korea our men found this to be very difficult. The narrow peninsula held hundreds of thousands of enemy troops and Communist political agents. Climatic conditions, especially the bitter winters, and rugged terrain did not make for easy cross-country movement. Food and clothing were scarce. North Korean civilians were exceedingly reluctant to risk their lives aiding Americans. Particularly was this true after the Chinese Communists entered the conflict. There were almost no underground escape channels as in Europe in World War II. Worst of all, in a land of Orientals, a Caucasian was easily spotted. Daytime movement was almost impossible.

In spite of the odds, a small number of downed Air

Force pilots did succeed in avoiding capture and in one manner or another made their way back through the bamboo curtain to safety. Their exploits form a most fascinating and dramatic chapter of the Korean war. Here were the men of the Air Force out of their element, called upon to play strange and daring roles in a hostile land. For these men the chips were down, the stakes high, the results freedom, torture, or death. Previous training in the art of survival and the techniques of escape and evasion was vital to success. But there came a time when training could help no more, and only sheer courage, determination, and ingenuity enabled men to carry on.

Because it was necessary to protect escape techniques, routes, and the few faithful North Koreans who lent assistance, the majority of these stories remained untold during the war.

Now that many of them may be related safely, with minor omissions to protect our friends, the Air Force is grateful to Mr. Clay Blair, Jr., for his interest and devotion in shaping these accounts into a permanent record of courage.

I believe all fellow airmen and freedom-loving people everywhere will find in these stories a message of inspiration and faith in the moral, mental, and physical fiber of our combat air crews. I am proud that the American youth of today who patrol the skies against a ruthless enemy are the same breed of men who have defended the ramparts of freedom throughout our history. It is an honor to serve with them.

GENERAL N. F. TWINING
Chief of Staff, United States Air Force

The Pentagon
Washington, D. C.
8 April 1955

SURVIVAL!

COMBAT pilots, by their very nature, find capture distasteful. Ever since it first became an occupational hazard, they have sought to develop tactics and techniques to avoid it. There is an unwritten law among them that states that it is the duty of every pilot and airman, if captured, to try to escape. In World War I, it was entirely a personal matter. Pilots who crashed behind enemy lines operated strictly under their own steam and did as best they could. But in World War II, evading and escaping became a highly specialized art. In Europe, the allied governments created and maintained an elaborate underground, through which many airmen, both "evadees" and "escapees," returned to fight again. In the Pacific, where most of the battles were fought on islands and the people were Oriental, such an organization was not feasible. However, a fairly extensive Air-Sea Rescue Service was created, based around the flying boat and the submarine. In order to avail themselves of it, pilots in difficulty were advised to crash-land in open water whenever possible.

Very early in the Korean war, the need for an escape and evasion system became obvious. Though the enemy was not able to bring down many U.N. planes in aerial combat, his antiaircraft fire was accurate and plentiful. Losses were high among Air Force, Navy, and Marine Corps units flying propeller-driven planes close to the front lines. The Rescue Service that was eventually established was patterned along the lines of the one used in the Pacific in World War II. Pilots of disabled planes were instructed to head for open water whenever possible. Air Force amphibians and launches, patrolling

1

the peninsula, maintained a constant watch for friendly planes in trouble.

As time went on, the system was refined. Numerous islands along the east and west coast of the peninsula were captured by U.N. forces and cleared of Communists. These islands, designed to supplement the Air Rescue system, were designated as "safe" islands. Some had airstrips; others radar. Disabled planes were carefully plotted on radar and guided by radio toward the islands, where the pilots either crash-landed or bailed out. Later, helicopters were stationed on many of the "safe" islands to pull from the sea those pilots whose planes could not quite make it. The "safe" islands were easily defended, because the Communists had few or no naval forces and were not able to mount an attack against them.

Not all disabled planes were able to reach the seacoast. Many pilots were forced to crash-land or bail out directly over enemy territory. Some of those who crashed close to the front lines were rescued by short-legged helicopters of the Third Air Rescue Service, which were stationed immediately behind U.N. trenches. When an Air Force pilot went down behind enemy lines within reach of a helicopter, or "chopper," all air activity in the vicinity virtually ceased, except that directed toward the pilot's rescue. The other members of the downed pilot's flight formed a "Rescue Combat Air Patrol," or "RESCAP," and flew in circles over him, to keep enemy soldiers from closing in. Usually these planes were joined by scores more that were directed to the spot by the Fifth Air Force Joint Operations Center, and remained there until the helicopter—escorted by an additional armada of aircraft—arrived to snatch away the airman.

However, those who crashed deep in enemy territory, or at night, usually had to shift for themselves. There could be no organized underground; the North Koreans were untrustworthy and, besides, a Caucasian stuck out like a sore thumb among the Orientals. The only hope lay in virtually sneaking out, contacting a Christian family, most of whom were sympathetic toward U.S. airmen, or bribing the North Korean with money, barter items such as watches and fountain pens, or promises of a reward. In any case, the objective of all airmen who crashed under those circumstances was the same: to get to the seacoast and from there out to sea, either in an inflatable dinghy, which most pilots carried in their planes, or in a Korean boat.

Most pilots who flew in the Korean war were extremely "escape and evasion" conscious. They read avidly the secret reports of pilots who had crashed and had been rescued or who had escaped. They made sure that such equipment as their Mae Wests, dinghies, and parachutes were in top condition, that "emergency vests" or "Escape and Evasion Kits" were well-supplied with such essential gear as flares, paddles, small portable radios (an invaluable gadget called the URC-4), knives, signal mirrors, guns, and plenty of extra clothing in the colder months. In addition, they carried a "blood chit," which was a piece of oil-silk cloth, with a message in both Chinese and Korean promising a reward if help was extended to the downed pilot. Later, special "Barter Kits," containing wrist watches, fountain pens, money, etc., were developed for use in Korea.

Altogether, 1,690 Air Force personnel were brought down behind enemy lines, 1,180 as a result of direct enemy action. Of these, 175 were rescued immediately by helicopter or flying boat. It is known that 155 were killed when their planes crashed. Of the rest, 263 are known to have been captured; 248 were returned during Big and Little Switch, the prisoner exchanges, and 15 are still held by the Communists, in violation of the armistice agreements. Nine hundred and ninety-nine were carried as "missing in action" and eventually declared dead. The unlucky pilots who were captured sat out the war under miserable conditions in Communist POW camps. Many of them were made to suffer the torture of brainwashing. Others were beaten and starved until they signed phony germ warfare confessions.

Following in the tradition of the aviator, many Air Force officers attempted to escape from Communist POW camps. But it was not like Europe. Everything was against them. Most of the camps were located deep in North Korea, too far for a quick dash to friendly lines. The terrain was rough. Disease was rampant. The country was crowded with hostile people, agents, and Communist soldiers. There was no food, no clothing, no way of obtaining money with which to bribe. Moreover, the Communists had not signed the Geneva Convention; the North Koreans were quick to execute U.S. airmen who were caught escaping.

Only three Air Force pilots succeeded in returning to friendly lines after being captured. One of these, Captain William D. Locke, managed early in the war to escape during the confusion of a North Korean retreat. He hid under the floor of a schoolhouse in Pyongyang, where he had been temporarily interned, and waited there until U.N. troops had advanced to his position. Another pilot, Captain Ward Millar, walked out of an enemy hospital where he had been kept for three months and, with the help of a North Korean Army sergeant who had defected, managed to signal a U.N. plane, which later directed a helicopter in to pick him (and the North

Korean) up. One Air Force officer, First Lieutenant Melvin J. Shadduck, was shot down, captured, and then, entirely unaided, planned and successfully executed an escape from behind enemy lines.

There were almost a hundred Air Force officers who fell into a special category: they were neither rescued nor captured. Most of these men who crashed in no-man's land managed in one fashion or another to make their way back to friendly lines. About a dozen crashed deep in enemy territory, and some sneaked back through the Communist lines, unaided. Others made their way to the sea and eventually made contact with friendly naval forces or with the Air Rescue Service. Still others were assisted by Christians, or by North Koreans who wanted to collect the "blood chit" reward (the equivalent of a year's pay).

The fact that an Air Rescue Service existed in Korea was generally known. But its operating details and the stories of the men who had been rescued were among the best-kept secrets of the Korean War, and for good reason: any information about it would have been extremely useful to the Communists. As a reporter in the Pentagon, I knew vaguely of the Rescue Service and from time to time heard snatches of stories of men who had returned to safety. I did not learn in detail of these goings-on until one day in June, 1952, when I met an Air Force officer named Colonel Albert W. Schinz.

Schinz had just returned from Korea, where he had been deputy commander of the 51st Fighter-Interceptor Wing, flying F-86 Sabrejets. On the day I met him, he seemed nervous and ill at ease. He was unusually thin. His face was gaunt. I learned from other Air Force officers that Schinz had been through "an incredible ordeal," but they would not tell me what had happened. When I asked Schinz to tell me about it, he refused. "Everything that happened to me is secret," he said with an air of finality. Later, however, special arrangements were made whereby Schinz was permitted to tell me a portion of his experience, but only through careful security screening in Air Force Headquarters.

I shall never forget the day Schinz told me his story. We were locked together in a special room in the Pentagon. He still had a souvenir of his experience—a small diary in which he had kept a day-by-day account of his adventure. As he unfolded his story, he frequently consulted the book to check on some small detail or another. But the main outlines of the story were vividly implanted in his mind. He related them to me in an impersonal military manner. Later, I questioned him about his personal reactions, about what he thought, how he acted, what was the state of his emotions.

We talked for more than seven hours. As I listened, I realized that Colonel Schinz had indeed been through "an incredible ordeal." And, it seemed to me, he had been affected profoundly by the experience. To be sure, he had lost weight, and he was emotionally upset. But there was an unusual quality in his speech, in his manner, and the way he talked of God, to Whom he had turned for help during the darkest hours of his adventure. I promised myself that someday, when military security would permit, I would tell the full Schinz story.

Schinz soon moved from Washington to another Air Force base. After that, I took a more active interest in the Air Rescue Service and in the stories of Air Force men who had escaped from behind enemy lines. Little information leaked out about the system. But I learned enough to know that there were other Schinzes in the Air Force who had had experiences that were as incredible as, or in some cases even more incredible than, his. For security reasons, I was not able to write anything about the subject at the time.

A year after the end of the Korean War, feeling that by then, the security restrictions must be outdated, I went back to the Air Force to inquire. In Air Force Headquarters, I was surprised to discover that a staff officer, Major William J. McGinty had already cut through formidable barriers of red tape and secured the declassification of certain official Intelligence reports relating to these same stories. McGinty, a World War II fighter pilot who had served on the staff of the Far East Air Force in Japan, had met most of those in whom I was interested. He knew their stories from memory. Like me, he had been impressed. He was eager for the stories to be told.

After a number of conferences with Major McGinty, and other staff officers in Air Force Headquarters, I was given the declassified reports with the idea of trying to make a book. I discovered that the reports, originally prepared for official use only, were compiled by an Air Force captain named John Oliphint, who, during the war in Korea, operated a special "debriefing" center. For intelligence purposes, Oliphint made it his business immediately to get in touch with all U.N. personnel who, in one fashion or another, got behind enemy lines and then escaped. Oliphint's reports were finely detailed and, to say the least, fascinating.

As I read through the scores of individual reports, I relived the Korean War in an entirely new perspective. Suddenly, I was high over the Yalu River, MIG cannon shells slamming into my tail section. The next minute I was trying to open a parachute with a broken arm. Then I was on the ground, running from Communist soldiers with burp guns and grenades.

Or, I was hiding away in a damp cave, or trying to break an escape boat out of the ice, or tramping up the side of a mountain, fighting my way through a blizzard. From time to time, I was cornered and caught, beaten, humiliated, and starved by my Communist captors. It was hard to put these reports down. I studied them for over two months.

None of the reports lacked drama though naturally Oliphint's official accounts were devoid of personal emotions and such things as dialogue and motivation. After amassing an enormous collection of firsthand testimony through the use of a tape recorder, I sat back to reflect. In the end, I chose to write only four of the many stories. These were the stories that I considered from every point of view the "best."

As I came to know the other Air Force officers whose stories are contained in this book—Summersill, Shadduck, and Thomas—I saw in them the same strong qualities that I had first noticed in Colonel Schinz. There was the same extraordinary enthusiasm, the same selflessness, the same reticence and modesty. I found out in one way or another that these men possessed not only rare courage, but also an amazingly powerful will and a deep and immutable belief in God. I saw in their faces the radiant reflection of a great human and perhaps superhuman experience.

ROBINSON CRUSOE
OF MIG ALLEY

THE men of the 51st Fighter-Interceptor Wing had one main objective in the war in Korea, and that was to destroy more MIG's than the 4th Fighter-Interceptor Wing. It was as simple as that. To be sure, among these 150 pilots were grand strategists who could draw the distinction of the big and little war; there were also political theorists who could make sense—at least to themselves—out of containment, Korean style, and its relation to cold war and rice paddies. There were hard-bitten Communist haters; there were wandering idealists; there were those who had no feeling about the war, one way or another. But the glue that held together the diverse men of the 51st was that secret blend of competitive spirit and showmanship (and whatever else) that is common to all elite corps, whether made up of paratroopers, submariners or fighter pilots.

The aggressive, MIG-killing spirit of the 51st was personified in its leader, a strapping, black-haired colonel named Francis Gabreski. Gabby, as his men affectionately called him, was a terror to MIG pilots—a legend among airmen everywhere. He was an old man in terms of fighter experience. He had learned his trade early in World War II and later served under Colonel Hubert Zemke, the uncanny leader of the famous World War II 56th Air Force Fighter Group. Under Zemke, the 56th alone accounted for more than 1,000 Nazi aircraft. Gabby himself bagged 33½.

Korea was a new war and a new challenge for the old-school fighter pilots. Gabby soon found his way there and, like the others, went directly to the front lines, ready to outgun and outfly everybody, especially the men of the 4th Fighter-Interceptor. Gabby was a calculating killer. He never stopped devising new ways to shoot down MIG's. He sometimes sat all morning at his beat-up oak desk in the "headquarters" quonset hut, just thinking. Then he would hurry down to the flight line, get into a jet, and fly up to MIG alley to try out some new idea. Later he would spend all afternoon and evening discussing the idea with his men.

The Air Force had a term for Gabby and men like him: Tigers. The psychologists went to Korea to interview the jet aces to try to find out what a tiger had that ordinary pilots did not. They found out that tigers were usually shorter than the average American male, that they expressed themselves well, that they were friendly, soft-spoken, enthusiastic, loved competition, and were intensely alive. They usually came from large families, often broken by the death of one parent. As children, they liked hot rods and anything scientific or mechanical. They were active in sports in high school and liked to date girls. But it took more than a psychologist to find out what fundamentally made Gabby and the boys tick.

Gabby was always so busy thinking of new ways to keep ahead of the 4th Fighter-Interceptor in MIG alley that he did not have time for minor chores. Therefore, the details of operating the base—the administrative, supply, and personnel problems—were left up to Gabby's number-two man, a stocky, thirty-three-year-old colonel named Albert W. Schinz.

All of his adult life Schinz had been an Air Force officer. He was born in Ottawa, Illinois, and after graduating from high school, he spent two years in junior college and then, in March, 1940, joined the Air Force as a flying cadet. In January, 1942, after various stateside assignments, he went overseas with the 41st Fighter Squadron and flew 174 combat missions in the South Pacific.

After World War II, the Air Force sent him through college, and he obtained a degree in business administration. Later, in the years before the Korean war, he served routine tours of duty in the Air Force, largely of an administrative nature. In the second year of the war he was assigned to the 51st, straight from the Pentagon. Now he was trying to regain his tiger status but found it difficult, because he had to devote most of his time to administering the base and could only occasionally run up to MIG alley for a fight.

Schinz was a restless tiger though only a part-time one. He could never sit still. He especially did not enjoy sitting at a desk. He liked to get out of the office and walk around the base, and down to the flight line, to find out what "the boys" needed or might soon be needing. Often he jumped into his jet and flew to air bases in Japan to beg, borrow, or steal new equipment for his pilots, or to push personally one of his proposals through higher headquarters. Such energy and intensity led him to plan and build a handsome noncommissioned officers' club. When that was finished, he ordered plans drawn up for an officers' club. Always full of new ideas, projects, and unwavering opinions, Al Schinz was a fountain of talk and action.

These attributes made him an outstanding executive vice-president—for, in fact, that is what he was—of the 51st. Because he devoted his time almost exclusively to improving the base and the general welfare of the men, he was admired by most. But he was not all sweetness and light; he was tough when toughness was called for, and he was always ready to argue his point. In fact, there was little Schinz enjoyed more than a good, loud argument. It so happened that Gabby was of like mind. The two men spent many evenings pounding tables and trying to outshout one another. The tigers used to drop in to watch the show because more often than not it was informative: the subject usually concerned new ways to kill a MIG or improve the F-86 Sabrejet.

In four months and thirty-eight missions in Korea, Al Schinz had bagged one and a half MIG's, which was good, but not par for the course. He lagged behind his World War II record of four Zeros. One day in late April, 1952, he decided to let his base-improvement projects languish while he concentrated on building up his MIG score. Accordingly, he detailed himself to fly his thirty-ninth combat mission on May 1—May Day, a special Red celebration day when the Communists traditionally brought out MIG's in force.

On the appointed day, Schinz was up early. He banged out some necessary paperwork, then hurried down to the briefing room to set up the mission. Three other pilots met him there: Colonel Albert S. Kelly, the 51st Group Commander and two lieutenants. Kelly, an experienced World War II fighter pilot, was reporting for his first Korean mission. Schinz assigned him to fly his own wing, that is, fly slightly behind him to make sure no MIG's got on his tail. The other two pilots formed the second element of the flight.

The flight—code named Maple—was plotted with great precision. The planes were to take off and proceed toward the Yalu River, the northern extremity of MIG alley. As each flight neared the Yalu, it would turn sharply, and search the Communists' airfield at Antung on the other side of the Yalu for activity—or MIG's. The fiights would be strung out at five-minute intervals, in order to prolong the actual time on patrol at the Yalu. Schinz outlined special combat instructions and selected an escape course that the pilots were to follow if disabled.

Ten minutes before take-off time, Colonel Schinz, "Eagle Leader" of the flight, clomped heavy combat boots up the aluminum boarding ladder of his shiny, swept-wing Sabrejet. Carefully he squeezed his stocky frame into the cockpit. He checked out his equipment: the jet pilot's acceleration suit known as the G-suit, crash-helmet with radio and oxygen mask attached, a back parachute, rubber dinghy, and an escape and evasion kit containing money, watches, and fountain pens, as well as some Korean money. Unlike most of the tigers, he spurned carrying a gun and a knife.

When the equipment checks were completed, Schinz, via radio, contacted Kelly and the other two men parked in the jets on the ramp near him. "Start engines," he said. The quiet midday air was suddenly rent by the whine of jet turbines. Ground crewmen pulled the wheel chocks. Yellow generator carts were hurried out of the way. Then, one by one, the jets moved slowly out onto the taxi way. At exactly 12:30 Schinz and Kelly took off. The others followed at intervals as planned.

The "hot" area of MIG alley was a good half hour's flight from the 51st base at Suwon, South Korea. Although the F-86's were equipped with two wing-tip tanks to extend their range, the science of flying to MIG alley in an F-86 and then stretching fuel in order to have enough to last through a dog fight and still get home was an exacting one. The pilots experimented constantly in order to obtain the most favorable altitude and cruising speed. Often they were not successful; time after time, Gabby's pilots ran out of fuel on the way back from MIG alley and came home "flamed-out," making dead-stick landings.

Shortly after Schinz and Kelly reached the Yalu, they were joined by the second element of the flight. All seemed quiet as the jets cruised along at 30,000 feet, searching for MIG's below. But the peace was soon disturbed by a staccato radio report from one of the men: "Sun glints at two o'clock high." This was bad. The sun glints were MIG's. They were at 38,000 feet or more. When Schinz and Kelly looked up to confirm the report, they could see the MIG's clearly. There were 26 to 30 of them, and they were dropping their silver, bomb-shaped wing tanks, preparing for combat. They could tell by the flashes of red and yellow at the noses of the MIG's that the Communist pilots were already test-firing their guns.

Maple flight was in a bad position, cruising slowly under the MIG's and with wing tanks still attached. Schinz barked into his radio: "Clean 'em up." The F-86's toggled their tanks, and, at the same time, pushed the throttles to full power. It was too late. Four MIG's came in from above, nose guns flaming. Kelly, who saw them first, yelled over the radio: "Break right." This was a signal to Schinz to turn right sharply in order to get out of the path of the diving MIG's. Schinz and Kelly, now separated from the other elements, turned. It was then that Kelly noticed that his right fuel tank had not jettisoned. He pulled the toggle switch again, but the tank would not drop.

The Sabrejets leveled off, and at that instant Kelly spotted two more MIG's, below, at about 18,000 feet. He reported the fact to Schinz who immediately dropped the nose of his jet and dove toward the planes. Kelly followed—though the obstinate wing tank reduced his speed considerably. Schinz fired a few rounds at the two MIG's but they climbed skyward at a fast rate and were soon out of range. As the two F-86's made a wide turn to pick up speed, Kelly spotted two more MIG's beneath them. Once again, Schinz turned the Sabrejet toward the earth.

Confident that no MIG could "bounce" them while in such a fast dive, Schinz momentarily took his eyes off the MIG's below to make sure Kelly was in proper position. But in the split second required to make this check, he lost sight of the MIG's. Evidently he had pulled the nose of the plane up too far. He called Kelly on the radio: "Do you have them in sight?" Kelly did not; moreover, he had other news. Four more MIG's were now on their tails, with guns firing.

Kelly shouted, "Break right."

Schinz did not respond.

Kelly repeated his call.

Schinz returned, "Kelly. Is that you calling me?" By now, the airways were full of chatter and static.

Kelly said, "Roger. Roger. Break hard right, Al. I've got four right on my tail and they're closing fast."

Schinz replied, "O.K. I've got you."

The MIG's had closed to two hundred yards. Kelly was in trouble, a sitting duck with the hung tip tank. Both Sabrejets twisted into a hard right turn. They could not hope to outrun or outdive the MIG's, so they did the only thing they could do: tried to outturn them. The force of the turn was considerable. Schinz's head was mashed up against the side of the cockpit. He lost sight of Kelly. After a 180-degree turn, he called, "Are you with me?" He thought Kelly said, "I am right behind you," and he rolled out of the turn.

But Kelly was not behind Schinz. With his hung-up wing tank, Kelly elected to remain in the severe turn, in order to shake the MIG's. In fact, he flew in a complete circle three times. Meantime, the MIG's got to Schinz's tail, and Russian-made 37-mm. tracers began to rip into his fuselage and wings. Schinz turned the Sabrejet into a severe split-S calling on the radio, "Who is shouting at me?" He was upside down, and pulling through the maneuver when he noticed a light on the dashboard warning that the hydraulic system was out of order. This disturbing development was followed by an even more serious one: a dazzling red light signifying fire in the tail pipe lit up the cockpit. The question of just who was shooting at Schinz became academic; the aim was very good.

The jet dropped to 2,000 feet. Schinz said to himself, "Pull out and get some altitude before you lose control." As he rammed on full power, the jet spun crazily back up to 8,000 feet. At that precise instant, the rudder pedals became "Able Sugar" (completely useless), and the joy stick could not be budged either forward or aft. The jet was out of control; a fire was raging in the tail pipe. Al Schinz began thinking of escape.

Fortunately, the controls of the disabled jet had frozen while Schinz was heading south toward the sea, along the prescribed safety route. As he sped along through the air, the plane jerked violently up. Schinz put both hands and feet on the stick and pushed. Still it would not budge. The plane stalled; the nose dropped. Schinz tried, without success, to pull back on the stick. However, he discovered that by speeding up the engine, he could raise the nose. But he was unable to find a power setting at which the plane would level off, neither climbing nor diving. Consequently, he flew along as though on a roller coaster, dipping up and down.

At first, Schinz was confident that he could porpoise along in this fashion long enough to reach the Air Rescue Outpost on Cho-do Island, the planned escape procedure. Accordingly, he called on the radio, "Maple flight, this is Eagle Leader. I've been hit and I'm going to try to make Cho-do." There was no reply. He repeated the call. Again silence. He then switched to the D-dog channel and threw his IFF (Identification, Friend or Foe) from the stand-by to emergency position, hoping that the ever alert Air Rescue Service would hear the emergency broadcast and fix the location of the aircraft by radio. Too late, Schinz realized that all his radio equipment was out of order, and that in the confusion and speed of combat, the other members of Maple flight had lost him.

The jet yo-yoed southward over the Cholsan Peninsula, going nose-high into a stall, falling off, and then leveling again, as Schinz poured on the power. In each gyration, the jet lost about 2,000 feet altitude. After the second giant porpoise, he realized that he did not have sufficient altitude to

reach Cho-do. Quickly he changed plans: he would bail out
of the crippled jet near one of the islands off the coast; then,
when the search planes came, he would signal to them via his
small, two-way URC-4 radio. Schinz was sure of one thing:
he was not going down in North Korea and risk being captured.

Soon the jagged end of the peninsula passed beneath the
swept wings of the jet, and he was flying over the Yellow Sea.
He carefully searched the area below for an island that would
suit his purpose. He did not have long to look because by then
the jet had descended in stages to 1,500 feet. There was not
sufficient altitude to perform another porpoise. It was now or
never.

At that moment, the jet flew over a rather large island. In a
quick look, Schinz spotted a village on the northern end and
two reefs on the south that appeared to be unoccupied. He
decided to bail out over the deserted reefs. With the plane
climbing up on its last yo-yo, he put his feet in the stirrups of
the ejection seat, pulled the left-arm rest knob, then the right
knob. The cockpit canopy blew off. He glanced at the dashboard, noted that his altitude was below 1,000 feet. He fired
the ejection seat and hurtled out and upward into the air.

In the confusion, Schinz popped his chute before releasing
the heavy ejection seat to which he was still strapped. Ordinarily such an error is fatal, since the parachute is not strong
enough to withstand the initial shock of both man and seat.
Luckily, the parachue held, long enough for him to correct
the mistake. He watched as the seat fell away and splashed
into the water not far from the spot where the plane itself had
crashed. Then he realized he had not yet removed his helmet
and oxygen mask. These were discarded quickly as he made
advance plans to fall into the water.

Schinz was not worried. He knew that hundreds of successful parachute landings had been made in the water. Moreover, only a week before he had watched an Escape and
Evasion movie that told in vivid detail the techniques of such
a landing. He unsnapped the buckles on his parachute harness,
sat well back, and began opening the rubber dinghy. As he
spilled easily into the cool, but not cold, water, about one
hundred feet south of the island and precisely between the
two deserted reefs as planned, he was a model of preparedness.

Once in the water, Schinz inflated his yellow Mae West life
preserver. Noting that the bright orange and white parachute
billowed across the water, he decided to try a technique he
had seen in the movie and use the parachute as a spinnaker to
sail himself toward the island. He grabbed the top risers to
help fill the chute with air. But within seconds, Schinz's legs

were tangled in the bottom risers, a situation, the movie had warned, that should be avoided at all costs. The parachute collapsed and began to sink slowly, carrying Schinz under with it.

He fought his way up for a gasping breath, then went under again. As he tried to extricate himself from the tangle of shrouds he succeeded only in getting more deeply entwined. Then he thought of his dinghy again. He groped for the cord on the CO_2 bottle which if pulled, would inflate it. Five minutes later, after more dunkings in which he swallowed a considerable amount of salt water, Schinz located the Co_2 lanyard and gave it a pull. The dinghy inflated with a hiss.

Now survival depended on one strategy: getting into the dinghy. Schinz tried to climb aboard. Entangled as he was in the shrouds it seemed impossible. After several attempts he was ready to give up. Then he had a new idea: go in feet first. Slowly he maneuvered the dinghy into the proper position. Then he put his feet into the small end and carefully inched his legs upward. With a final lurch, Schinz pushed his buttocks up onto the edge of the dinghy. At that moment, the craft tipped over.

He plunged back under the water. The dinghy landed on top of him. Clawing his way to the surface, he managed to right the raft once more. This time he determined to go slower. Inch by agonizing inch, Schinz edged his legs into the bobbing dinghy. Most of the time, his head was under water. Finally, on the verge of losing consciousness, he made it. Quickly he buttoned up the kayak-like canvas apron; then put his head down and rested.

As he lay there thinking, he made two mental notes: one, henceforth, he would always carry a knife, and two, he would tell the escape and survival people that using the parachute as a sail was dangerous. With some justification, he concluded that a man should disengage himself completely from the parachute on hitting the water.

When he regained some of his strength, Schinz began untangling his legs and body from the parachute shrouds. After a few minutes he pulled the chute clear of both himself and the dinghy. Since he wanted to save the brightly colored chute as a distress signal, and did not have room for it inside, he tied it under the dinghy and let it trail in the water. Then he took an inventory of his rescue equipment. It included the URC-4 two-way radio, two night-signal flares, dye markers, and shark repellent, which were fixed to the Mae West. The Escape and Evasion Kit containing the things he might need most on land had not been fastened to his parachute harness, and it had sailed away when he bailed out.

Once settled in the dinghy, Colonel Schinz got out the

URC-4 radio, plugged in the battery, and extended the antennae. Confident that the planes in Maple flight were searching down the escape route, he called into the miniature speaker to try to attract them. There was no response. Was the radio damaged? Schinz tinkered with the insides, pulling and pushing the wires and tubes. It was completely dead. For the first time he began to worry. Now he had no radio to call the planes down to him, only a signal mirror. In vain, he searched the skies for signs of friendly fighters.

He then decided to paddle to shore. As he wedged himself into a comfortable position, he made an alarming discovery: the paddles that should have been provided with the dinghy were not aboard. Flailing his arms, he tried to propel the craft to the island. It was a losing battle. A strong tide was carrying him out to sea. The forgotten parachute dragging underneath helped the current to tug at him. An hour of this was enough to exhaust him. He collapsed and slept as the dinghy drifted away from the island and out to sea.

The sound of breakers woke him. It was dark, and his illuminated watch dial told him he had been asleep seven hours. Now the tide was flooding, and he was drifting slowly up to a rocky beach. He could not tell how soon the tide would ebb again and when the current would wash him out to sea once more. He remembered the dragging parachute and released it. In the process, he discovered that a special survivor's kit was also hanging under the dinghy. He pulled that into the dinghy and started paddling with his arms once more.

A short time later, Schinz heard the noise of airplane engines in the night. As the plane came closer, he could tell by the sound that it was an Air Force B-26. He began to have hope once more. It winged in low, right over him. He grabbed one of the flares and ripped off the top. But it fizzled and went out. The plane flew straight on over the horizon. He cursed softly to himself and began paddling again toward the dark land mass.

It took five more hours of arm flailing before Schinz and his rubber raft bumped onto the rocky beach of the island. At first his legs were so stiff from the hours of exposure in the cramped dinghy that he could not stand up. But he finally managed to stagger ashore, dragging the dinghy with him. Remembering the deep Korean tides, he climbed up rocks and cliffs until he reached the timber line twenty-five feet above the beach. He wedged the dinghy between some rocks, climbed in, pulled the canvas cover over him, and dozed.

The sun woke him from his damp, cramped sleep. For a long while he sat still in the dinghy, staring at the rocky beach below, watching the spray slap over the boulders and woosh in and out of the rocky caves. Above him rose the black heights of a cliff. He tried to keep his mind fresh and preoccupied by watching nature at work around him, but inevitably his thoughts turned to himself and his unenviable predicament. Was the island occupied by Communists? Was it inhabited at all? If so, could the rescue planes land safely and pick him up? Was there, on this barren spot, enough food and water to sustain life? Dare he light a fire to get warm and dry his clothes? How would his wife Lorayne, his young son and daughter feel when they received the "missing in action" report?

The last thought stirred Schinz into action. He had better get back to the base quickly, he thought, before his family had suffered unnecessary anguish. He unsnapped the dinghy cover and crawled out. The cold salt water rolled off his olive-drab GI trousers and shirt. He stamped his boots on the rocky ground, then took off his soaking flying jacket. He was shivering from head to foot, either from cold or exhaustion, or a combination of both. Would he become ill from it? Schinz decided not to chance it. He would build a fire and dry his clothes, even at the risk of alerting Communists who might be on the island.

Suddenly, he realized that he had no matches. Even if he had, they would have been ruined by the water. Then he remembered his Zippo lighter. He reached in his pocket and pulled it out. Salt water poured out as he snapped back the chrome-plated top. Schinz was heartsick. The lighter seemed ruined. He fell to his knees and sobbed. He was not a particularly religious man; but he broke into prayer. He asked the Lord to make his lighter work in spite of the salt-water dunking. Then he ran about picking up small twigs. He even found a piece of paper. He put the lot in a small pile, knelt down, and hopefully flicked the wheel of the lighter again; it burst into a long, yellow flame. "A miracle," Schinz cried aloud; and as soon as the fire had caught, he dropped to his knees and began praying all over again.

He took off his clothes and hung them by the fire to dry. Then he sat down and waited for the search planes. He was sure they would be coming over soon. He wondered if his small signal mirror would be adequate. He thought of gathering larger logs to throw on the fire to increase its size, but rejected the idea. Instead, as an additional distress signal, he pulled his dinghy out into plain view. He was so certain he would be spotted, and soon, that he did no further long-range planning. He just sat by the fire waiting, occasionally tinkering with the damaged radio or polishing the signal mirror.

No search planes came. By noon, his clothes were dry, so

he put them on and started a cautious exploration of his end of the island. It had been twenty-four hours since his last meal, and he was hungry. He found an old, almost overgrown path, and followed it up and down the rocky terrain, laboriously pushing his way through dense willow scrubs. He climbed over the brow of a hill, then dropped flat on the ground, and lay there, scarcely daring to breathe.

Ahead in a small clearing were four thatch-roofed huts. Schinz waited for a sign of life, friend or foe, but there was none. No smoke rose from the roofs. There was not a sound except that of a few birds in the scrub oak in back of him. He circled the huts warily, but still saw no evidence of activity. Finally, he walked straight into the village.

The huts were abandoned and littered with filth. Some were partially burned. The area around the village was dotted with slit trenches and abandoned gun emplacements. He poked through the huts. He found GI cans, punctured by bullet holes. The soldiers who had occupied the village were U.S. or Korean, he concluded. From the condition of the debris Schinz judged that the troops had been gone for several weeks or perhaps even longer.

By then, he was beginning to feel weak, so he made plans to camp in the abandoned village. He selected a small lean-to, cleaned out the filth, and covered the ground with cornstalks and grass from the nearby field. He named the lean-to "Headquarters." Then he gathered some wood and just outside "Headquarters" built a roaring fire. He stretched out on two empty rice bags that he had found while gathering the wood, and concentrated on regaining his strength. But he became very thirsty, and soon he was on his feet again, searching for fresh water.

He found a stream on the far side of the cornfield. Then he walked back to the village and searched for a vessel in which to carry the water. In one hut he found a rusty tin can. He took the can to the stream and meticulously cleaned it with rocks and sand. Then he carefully strained some water through his handkerchief and carried it back to the fire. He boiled the water for about fifteen minutes, to make sure it was sterile. Then he let it cool, sat back on his rice bags, and took a deep swig.

The water satisfied his thirst but did nothing for the hunger pains that were beginning to well up in his stomach. Soon Schinz was walking again, this time in search of food. In the cornfield he found a few unharvested ears of corn. Near the edge of the field he found a few spring onions as well as a patch of dandelion greens. He gathered up a handful of each and went back to the fire. He put the corn kernels, onions, and dandelions into the scoured cans and carefully boiled the lot into a crude succotash. The corn was bitter and hard, the onions tasteless, and the dandelions stringy, but it was his first meal in twenty-four hour, and it revived his body and spirits.

All the while, Schinz kept one eye cocked on the sky. He was puzzled by the lack of air activity. Where were the search planes? Where were the boys from the base? Had they left him to sweat it out alone, without even a cursory search? Then he began to worry again about the inadequacy of his signal equipment, and decided to make an SOS. The best he could do that afternoon was to fashion some chunks of red clay roughly into the shape of an SOS. But as he finished the work, he realized that it was so small and drab that it would never be seen from the air. His spirits began to fall once more. By nighttime, they were very low. No aircraft had come over the island all day.

Shortly after dark, Schinz took his two rice bags and crawled into the lean-to. He was very tired and anxious to sleep. He lay down, carefully spreading the bags over his shivering frame, but he soon found they afforded little or no protection from the cold night air. He slept for an hour, then got up and sat by the fire to warm up. Then he crawled back into the lean-to.

As the night wore on, the fire began to flicker and die out. Schinz took out his lighter to make sure that it still worked in case the fire went out altogether during the night. He was startled to discover that the Zippo would no longer light. An agonizing thought flashed through his mind: if he was to have fire at all in the future, he must keep the present one going. Quickly, he gathered a large pile of firewood and fanned the fire's smoldering embers into a bright blaze. To his other problems, Schinz now added that of maintaining a constant supply of firewood.

At daybreak, Schinz crawled out of the "Headquarters" lean-to, cold and stiff. He looked up at the sky. The weather was clear. The search planes were sure to come over soon, he thought. His mind turned to food; he had better try to find something more to eat. He stumbled down to the stream, filled his can with water, and on the way back to the fire picked a handful of onions and dandelion greens. While he watched his breakfast boiling in the rusty can, he conceived the idea of keeping a record of his experience. The information might later be useful to the Intelligence division. He pulled out a red grease pencil and scratched a few words in a small leather-bound notebook that he kept in his wallet.

After breakfast, Schinz went exploring again. He had begun to worry about the possibility of Communists on the island,

and he did not want to be surprised. He pushed his way through the thick underbrush and rough terrain. Soon he reached a point where he could see a large part of the island, especially the main village in the north. He watched the village for three hours. Satisfied that it also was deserted, he then hiked back to "Headquarters." On the way home, he stumbled across a magnificent treasure: three small packages of Army rations!

For lunch that day, his sparse fare of corn-onion-dandelion succotash was garnished by hardtack and crackers from the ration packages. He ate sparingly of the rations in order to stretch them as far as possible. That afternoon, his mind once again turned to signal devices. He polished his mirror and thought of ways to build an SOS distinct enough to be seen from the air. But none of his ideas seemed practicable. He examined his one remaining flare and wondered if it would fizzle like the other. Then an idea occurred: why not build a nighttime SOS out of grass and cornstalks which he could set on fire if a plane came over and the flare fizzled? He went to the clearing and gathered up a huge pile of cornstalks and arranged them in the shape of an SOS.

After the usual supper. Schinz crawled into the lean-to. Before going to sleep, he jotted down in his notebook: "It looks as though the whole island is vacated." But he was not sure. In the middle of the night, he jumped awake as a B-26 night intruder roared low over the island. Racing out of the lean-to, he fired his second flare. Three bright red balls of fire soared into the sky. The plane droned steadily off into the darkness.

Schinz began his fourth day on the island by watching a flight of planes passing over at very high altitude. He was certain that the B-26 of the night before had seen his flare and had reported the fact to Air Rescue. He was impatiently awaiting the arrival of a helicopter and jotted in his diary: "F-86's high overhead. Why no chopper?" After breakfast, while keeping alert for signs of air activity, he began his daily search for food. In one of the half-burned huts, he found a large pile of raw cotton. He was wondering what use he could make of the white balls when the thought suddenly occurred: "What a great SOS I could make with this!"

Schinz scooped up some of the cotton and put it in a wicker basket that he found in one corner of the hut. In a few minutes, he was on his way out to the cleared field. He dumped the cotton on the ground and then went back for more. Soon he had enough to begin the SOS. He sat on the ground, carefully stretched out each of the cotton balls and then padded them into the earth. It was tedious work. After a few hours, the letters measured about three by five feet. Satisfied, he went back to camp, cooked the usual meal, and, though his back and hands ached terribly, he comforted himself with the thought: "The chopper will see that with no strain."

That night as he rested in the lean-to, he heard the distant throb of airplane engines. He rushed from the lean-to, grabbed a burning stick from the fire, and ran to his cornstalk SOS in the clearing. He lit the first "S," and as it crackled into flames, he moved to the "O." But, by the time the "O" had caught the "S" had burned out. As the plane flew directly overhead, Schinz ran back to the first "S" and tried to light it again. While he was thus engaged, the "O" fizzled out. He ran to the last "S," lit that, and then relit the "O." Then both letters burned out rapidly. Schinz stood looking helplessly up into the sky as the plane flew on without a sign of recognition.

He walked slowly back to the lean-to, sat down, and wrote in his diary: "A hell of a good fire but a complete failure as an SOS." He then turned over in his makeshift bed and sobbed.

The next morning, after breakfast, he walked out to inspect his cotton SOS. Now it seemed very small. He took out his diary and wrote.: "I'm tired of you guys not seeing my SOS. I will build a new one with letters 25 feet by 15 feet. That should be big enough."

This was a formidable goal. Hauling the additional cotton from the hut, then sitting in the clearing hour after hour padding each small piece into the ground proved to be very hard work. But Schinz was a determined man. In the middle of the "O," he began to run short of cotton so, when completed, the "O" and last "S" were somewhat smaller than the first "S." As he finished the sign, Schinz jotted in his book: "I am beginning to learn the real meaning of the word 'patience.'"

In the afternoon, Schinz went exploring again. He made a happy find on top of a hill; there on a vantage point with a view of the whole island, somebody had left a decrepit but still comfortable old swivel chair. Tilting and swinging around on his creaking throne, Schinz smiled as he surveyed his little world. Across the water, he could clearly see the Communist mainland. But the island itself seemed to be completely deserted.

He liked the swivel chair so much that he heaved it to his back and stumbled down the hill with it. But his marginal diet had weakened him more than he realized; by the time he reached the lean-to with the heavy burden, he could hardly walk. Now he saw that he must husband his waning strength; he could not afford to waste it transporting luxuries like swivel chairs. Just the same, his diet of corn and dandelion greens seemed to taste a little better that night as he ate them while sitting in his comfortable chair.

After supper Schinz began to think again of his night-time SOS. He needed some means of signaling the aircraft that flew over in the dark. Perhaps the cornstalks would burn better if protected, he thought. He went out to the clearing and dug long ditches, roughly spelling out SOS. Into the ditches, he carefully piled more cornstalks. Later that night when another B-26 flew over low, Schinz ran out and lit the SOS fire. It burned satisfactorily, at least much better than the previous one. Moreover, the moon was bright, and there was a chance that the pilot had seen the white cotton SOS, too. Always the optimist, Schinz took out his diary and wrote: "A B-26 flew over and saw my sign. . . ."

He was up early the next morning, awaiting the chopper. None came.

Biting his lips in disappointment, Schinz sat in his swivel chair, staring sadly at the fire. What would he do? A thought occurred: perhaps it would be wise to move into the main village if it was indeed deserted. But then, what if Communists came over from the mainland? Would they not go first to the main village? Would he not be safer on this remote end of the island? What of the SOS that he had so painstakingly built? Had he not better stay near it in case it was spotted by friendly planes?

He thought about these things for a long while. He weighed them against certain realities he faced: a rapidly dwindling supply of firewood and an even more rapidly dwindling supply of food. Schinz had almost completely torn down all the huts in the village in order to keep his fire going. His three small packages of Army rations had lasted seven days, but now they were gone. Perhaps there were others in the main village. He was certain to find a supply of firewood.

At length Schinz decided he would hike over to the main village anyway, just to look it over. He might be lucky enough to find some food. He climbed up the rocky hills, slid down steep slopes, panting and sweating, resting often to gather strength. After a few hours of this, he came within a quarter of a mile of the village. He found a hill from which he could see the area plainly, lay down on the ground, and watched.

The village was larger than he thought. It consisted of about fifteen large huts or houses and one larger building that looked like a schoolhouse or a church. Off to one side of the village, he could see a field that had been under cultivation. There were cornstalks grouped together on one side of the field; dried-up cotton plants on another. Farther along, he saw a rice paddy. There was no sign of life in the village.

Schinz crawled closer. Again, for a long while, he lay on

the ground scrutinizing the huts. Finally, he cupped his hands to his mouth and shouted. He was surprised at the strength of his voice as it echoed through the village. He shouted again, but there was no answer. He saw no one come from the huts. He waited a few more minutes, then got up and walked into the town.

The village was completely deserted. The ground was littered with filth. It smelled of death and disease, so badly that for a brief moment, Schinz thought he would become sick at his stomach. He clamped his thumb and forefinger over his nose and pushed on in search of food and water. The huts seemed well built. Large timbers supported the thatch roofs. The walls were thick and firm. But the floors of the huts were covered with foul refuse, including the gaunt remains of several cats. Big rats scampered about when Schinz opened the doors. He reckoned the village had not been inhabited for at least six months.

Schinz could not remain in the village long. The stench was overpowering. Finding neither food nor water, he soon hurried out and began the long hike back to his "Headquarters" lean-to. He was now convinced that, if nothing else, the filth of the village was sufficient reason to keep him from moving there. He would just somehow make do at his original camp and hope that he could stay alive until the rescue planes spotted him.

He made some minor improvements at the "Headquarters" camp. The SOS sign was enlarged. He returned to the beach and dragged the dinghy back to camp. He placed it inside the lean-to and used it as a bed. It was not comfortable, but he could at least button up the cover at night and keep warm. The dinghy also yielded a surprise: a water-soaked package of cigarettes. Schinz spilled the tobacco into a can in order to dry it out, then with some Korean tissue paper "rolled his own." He rationed himself: one cigarette per day, which he smoked while sitting in the swivel chair in the evenings after supper.

Feeling the need for a weapon of some sort and having little else to occupy his time, Schinz set out one morning to make a slingshot. He cut a fork from a small willow tree and trimmed it to the right size. Then he ripped a piece of rubber from his G-suit, which he had found in the dinghy. The G-suit rubber turned out to be "inferior" as he noted in his diary. So he cut open a bladder of his Mae West. This rubber was more than suitable. From a pocket flap of the preserver, he tore a small piece of canvas to serve as the rock holder. The finished product was almost of professional caliber. It would come in handy later.

In his daily wanderings about the camp, Schinz had begun to collect a small inventory of usable junk and equipment. One day he found an old rusty shovel. Another day he discovered a knife. He uncovered a GI can that was not punctured by holes. He unearthed a few dishes, and an "A" frame, a device that Orientals strap on their backs to help carry heavy loads, which was very useful in collecting firewood. The most heartening discovery was made on the twelfth day.

While foraging the countryside for firewood and anything else of value, he came across a large bag of dried beans in a field. He put the bag on the A frame and packed it back to camp. Later, he found that by soaking the hard beans in water for about a half day, they became pliable and suitable for cooking. Afterward, Schinz put a few of the soaked beans in the tin can and boiled them for another half day. The result was less than sensational but for Schinz the beans added a new course to his monotonous diet of corn, dandelions, and spring onions. The "broth" or juice in which the beans were cooked was especially tasty.

On the fourteenth day, Schinz decided to take a bath. He hauled some extra water from the stream and poured it into the dinghy, which he had dragged into the sunlight. Then he took off his clothes and washed. After his bath, he poured out the water, then stretched out on the dinghy to bask in the warm sun. He looked down at his toes. In doing so, he noted with some alarm that he could not see his stomach. He stretched his hands around his body and discovered that his finger tips touched. He estimated that his waist, which was formerly thirty-six inches, was now about twenty inches, and that he had lost fifty pounds.

This discovery had a devastating effect on his morale. It was not that he was getting thin. He knew that all along, because his belt was getting loose. It was the actual dimensions of it that scared him. Fifty pounds! It seemed clear to Schinz that he was slowly starving to death. Lately he had been getting weaker and weaker.

The blow to his morale was particularly untimely because by now the firewood in the "Headquarters" village had been consumed. In order to keep the fire going, Schinz had to go on long hikes from the camp in search of wood, staggering all the way under the heavy A frame. Moreover, lately the wind had been blowing with some force, and his cotton SOS was frequently scattered across the field. He had to spend many hours gathering up the pieces and resetting the letters. It seemed to him that the weaker he got, the harder he had to work.

Two weeks had passed. An occasional plane had flown over,

but none reacted to his SOS. It was plain to Schinz that he was getting nowhere fast. If anything, he was losing ground. What could he do? He thought briefly of getting in the dinghy and paddling to the Communist mainland. With this in mind, he made two crude paddles. Later he discarded the idea: the thought of deliberately giving himself up was repulsive.

That afternoon, Schinz took a long hike in the direction of the main village. His spirit was broken; he felt weak, unable to go on. As he trudged along the trail, he unconsciously fell into prayer. He asked God to help him out of his dilemma. Then, within a very few minutes, Schinz came upon a large cave that he had not noticed before. He entered cautiously, and to his surprise, found that it was filled with bags of cotton! Enough to build a much bigger and better SOS, he thought.

That night after supper, Schinz sat in the swivel chair thinking. The discovery of the new batch of cotton, he decided, was an omen he could not ignore. In fact—coming so hard on the heels of his prayers—Schinz became convinced that God was now directing his destiny. Obviously, the only way out of his predicament was to build a bigger SOS. God had supplied the cotton, and it was up to him to do the work. Schinz was charged with renewed hope.

But the cave with the cotton supply was a long way from his "Headquarters" camp. It was, in fact, closer to the main village. Should he now reconsider moving to the village? Schinz remembered the dead cats, the rats, and the stench and instantly rejected the idea. But then he considered the great supply of firewood in the village. Perhaps somewhere in those many huts, there was some food he had missed on his first inspection; food that would give him strength to build the new SOS. But what if he was discovered in the village by Communists? To hell with that, he thought. Mere survival was now uppermost in his mind. Before going to bed, he wrote enthusiastically in his diary: "I am going to start all over at the new camp. And I am going to be home by June."

Having made the decision to move, Schinz was up early the next morning to get on with it. But it proved to be a much greater task than he had anticipated.

First, he gathered up all his equipment: the dinghy, Mae West, G-suit, a handful of corn, some old rags, his bag of beans, dishes, tin cans, tobacco, slingshot, and the G.I. can, and carefully strapped it onto the A frame. Then he knelt down and backed his arms into the A frame, and slowly staggered to his feet. As he was about to start out, he remembered the fire. He had no matches. How would he start a new fire in the village?

He put the A frame back on the ground while he pondered

the problem. The only solution that he could see was to transport a portion of the fire to the main village. In what? Could he carry the fire and the A frame at one time? Schinz thought not. But was he capable of making two trips back and forth to the main village? He was doubtful but decided to risk it anyway. Accordingly, he pulled a burning, six-foot branch from the fire, and began hiking toward the main village.

When he arrived, the brand was still burning. He laid it on the ground, then gathered more wood, and soon built a roaring fire. Then he started back for the "Headquarters" camp. Halfway home, Schinz began to feel dizzy and weak. He stumbled, fell, struggled to his feet, and then fell again. Finally, he crawled into camp. He plopped down alongside the fire, and was soon eating beans, dandelions, corn, and onions, which he had thoughtfully put on to boil before leaving for the main village. He drank the broth, then lay down and slept heavily.

Several hours later he awoke. He got up and looked skeptically at the A frame. Could he make it to the main village once more? Why carry all that stuff along? He convinced himself that for survival he would need every item. Finally, he got down on his knees, backed once more into the frame, struggled to his feet, and began the long, winding journey to the main village. He fell often, sometimes forward on his face. All through the trip, he prayed softly, repeating his small repertoire of prayers over and over. He covered the last half mile crawling on his hands and knees. When he finally reached the fire, he threw on a few logs to keep it going, then collapsed. As his mind drifted off into space, he wondered vaguely if he would ever wake again.

When Schinz awoke the following morning, he was so weak that he could hardly move. He believed that he was near death. When he finally got to his feet, he turned his eyes skyward and once more prayed. This time he asked God for food. When he finished praying, he held his nose and walked into the nearest hut. He could hardly believe what he saw: twenty-five bags of rice that, somehow, had not been devoured by the village rats. "Another miracle," he said to himself, and he thanked God. In one corner of the hut, he found a stone grinder and a sifter, and after fiddling with the devices a few minutes, he learned how to use them to separate the rice kernels from the husks. Soon he had all the clean rice he could possibly eat.

Now he needed water. Holding his nose again, he wandered through the stinking village. He found a stream, but it was dirty, and he was afraid to use the water. Once more, he appealed to God. Not long afterward, he came upon a burned-out hut that he had not seen before. He peered inside. There was a deep-water well. Almost delirious with joy, Schinz fell to his knees in prayer. Then he drew a bucketful of water and hurried back to the fire. From his A frame, he selected two cans, one slightly larger than the other. He put water in the larger can and then floated the smaller can on the water. The result was a crude double-boiler. Soon the rice was cooking. When it was done, Schinz ate like a pig. With his stomach full for the first time in two weeks, he slept soundly.

When he awoke again, it was late afternoon. Feeling much stronger, he got up and began making plans for a permanent camp. If there had been any doubt in his mind about the wisdom of remaining in the smelly village, the discovery of the rice had erased it. He decided to move into one of the huts. He selected the schoolhouse because it was the best built of the lot and had a very large fireplace. He cleaned out the dirt, moved his fire into the fireplace. Before going to sleep that night, he ate more rice.

The following morning, Schinz ate a rice breakfast and then, with his strength rapidly returning, set off on a pressing chore—cleaning up the village. He collected the remains of the dead cats, dragged them out of town into a field, and buried them. Then he swept other filth and refuse aside. He got a stick and chased many of the big rats into the fields. He worked especially hard on his schoolhouse living quarters, and soon the building, while not absolutely spic and span, acquired a military neatness, as Schinz carefully arranged the equipment from the A frame about the single room.

In the afternoon, he ground more rice. "This is recreation, not work," he noted in his diary. Then, with the stench rapidly abating, he went off in search of other food. In one hut, he found several strings of seed corn hanging from the ceiling. Then, curious about the neat shocks of cornstalks in the field, he went out and ripped one open. Inside, he found green stalks, laden with big, fresh beans. That night he cooked a veritable banquet on the schoolroom hearth: rice, corn, fresh beans, onions, and dandelion greens. Afterward, as he puffed on a hand-rolled cigarette, he wrote cheerfully in his diary: "In much better spirits."

Having regained his strength and self-confidence, Schinz now turned to the big job: building the giant-size SOS. He went to the cave and examined the cotton. He found it in excellent condition and estimated there was more than enough to build the SOS he had in mind. Then he climbed a small hill and surveyed the clearing between the cave and the village. He decided to put the letters "OS" in the clearing near the cave, and the other "S" on the opposite side of the village. He lost no time in getting to work.

As he had done so many hours before, Schinz sat patiently on the ground and unwound each of the small balls of cotton and pushed them into the earth. Hours, then days, went by, as he, little by little, created the giant-sized cotton letters. It was dull, monotonous, but necessary, work. He struck up a friendship with the birds that flitted back and forth across the field, chirping and tweeting. He chatted absently with one of the birds, which he believed was a cuckoo: "I might be cuckoo but at least my *name* isn't cuckoo. My name is Colonel Al Schinz, USAF." When the SOS was completed, the letters measured forty-five feet long and fifteen feet wide. Schinz was sure that his sign could easily be seen from the air and that he would soon be rescued.

Having completed the big job, Schinz set about making his life on the island more comfortable. He found a table and dragged it into his schoolhouse quarters. Oddly, he came across another swivel chair. It soon occupied his favorite spot on the hearthside. To his small collection of utensils he added a fork and a cup. Then, with a chisel and hammer that he found in one of the huts he cut a piece of aluminum from a B-26 drop tank and beat it into the shape of a spoon. One evening, he jotted in his diary: "Today I found a fishhook. I am going to try it tomorrow."

Next morning, Schinz poked around the village looking for earthworms. He found none. Finally, he collected a handful of corn and then trudged down to the rocky beach, looking for a likely fish hole. He baited the hook with a kernel of corn and threw the line into the water. He waited for a bite, but there was no activity. Finally, he became bored. He tied the hand line to a bush and began exploring the beach. Not far from the fish hole, he discovered three large oil drums that had washed ashore and were half buried in the sand.

Schinz ran to the drums and, brushing the sand away, read the English markings on the outside. He ascertained that one barrel contained 100-octane aviation gasoline, the others diesel oil. What a magnificent signal fire could be made with the oil, Schinz thought. What a discovery! He ran to the village, picked up his hammer and chisel and two earthen jars. Then he knocked a hole in one of the barrels of diesel oil and filled the jars. Back in the village, he poured the black oil into a GI can. He spent the afternoon shuttling between the village and the barrels. On the last trip, he brought back a jar of gasoline to use as lighter fuel, as an additive to his fire, and as a possible fuel for night signaling.

The following morning, Schinz collected a large pile of cotton and rags and doused the lot with diesel oil. Then, as if on cue, an airplane appeared in the distance. Schinz lighted the oil-soaked rags. Dense, black smoke billowed up into the sky. The plane turned toward the island and came closer. Schinz recognized it as an F-51 fighter. He jumped up and down, waving and shouting. The plane buzzed low over the island, circled, and then bore in again. Schinz waved his arms madly. The plane flew overhead and, to Schinz's utter amazement, dropped its two wing-tip tanks in the middle of the village. "Are you trying to kill me?" he shouted. The plane flew away and did not return. He cursed loudly, and that night he jotted in his diary: "Guess he thought I was a Korean working up a bunch of chow."

In the evening after supper, Schinz walked down to the beach to check his hand line. As usual, there was no fish on the hook. The kernel bait was intact and did not even seem nibbled. He dropped the line back into the water and then sat silently staring out to sea. A short time later, out of the corner of one eye, Schinz spied a shape on the water, coming around a rocky bend on the coast line. It was a sailing junk! As it came closer, he could see that there was only one man in it. When the junk was directly off the beach, Schinz yelled to the man. Then he jumped up and down, waving his arms and shrieking. The junk abruptly turned tail and sailed out of sight.

Later that night, tossing on the floor of the hut, Schinz cursed himself for shouting at the junk. If he had remained quiet, or hidden in the brush, he thought, the man might have landed on shore, in which case, he could have ambushed him, stolen his boat, and sailed south to Cho-do. What if he was a Communist? Had he recognized Schinz as a downed airman? Or did he think, as the F-51 pilot probably thought, that Schinz was just another Korean? He was very worried and wrote in his diary: "One man sailing junk passed within one block of the island. My hollering scared him away. Am sure he will report me to the Communists on the mainland." But, like the chopper, no Communists came.

As each day passed, Schinz became more optimistic about his chances of survival. For one thing, his strength had fully returned. His living quarters, while crude, were not unbearable. Every day he discovered an item or so that added to his comfort or general welfare. His signal devices had multiplied with the discovery of the oil. He now felt that he could easily lure aircraft toward the island in the daytime and that, once there, they would surely see the SOS. He was dissatisfied only with his night signaling devices.

On the morning of May 23, he felt unaccountably optimistic. Before breakfast, he noted in his diary: "I am due to be rescued." Within a few hours, he heard the sound of

aircraft engines. Once again, Schinz raced out and touched off
the oil-soaked rags, and again, dense smoke swirled skyward.
All day long, aircraft flew over the island. Schinz stood in the
clearing, waving a pair of home-made flags. "Lots of activity,"
he gleefully noted in his diary. He was so sure that he would
be rescued that day that he gathered up all the equipment that
he wanted to take back to the base and stacked it in the
clearing.

He poured more oil on the rags and waited patiently for
the chopper. But none came. He was dismayed. His spirits
plunged from the great heights to which they had been elevated to darkest despair. What in the world could the Air
Force be doing? he asked. When the sun went down and he
knew no chopper would come, he knelt on the ground and
prayed. Then, his forehead on the ground, he beat his fist in
the dust and sobbed.

The next morning Schinz reviewed the events of the previous day. Why had he not been rescued? What had he done
wrong? Apparently, his SOS was not good enough. Could he
make it any larger or plainer? He thought about it all morning, then an idea occurred: build a sign that spelled MAY
DAY, the standard international distress call, one used by
all Air Force pilots in trouble. That ought to attract some
attention, he told himself.

The new sign would require an effort far beyond anything Schinz had heretofore contemplated. He thought of
arranging the letters like this:

$$\begin{array}{c} \text{D} \\ \text{M A Y} \\ \text{Y} \end{array}$$

to conserve cotton, but even so, the sign had a total of five
letters. He decided to move into a hut near the field and the
cave that contained the cotton supply. It would be less luxuri-
ous than the schoolhouse but more convenient, since he would
not have to walk back and forth as much while building and
"policing" the sign.

Schinz cleaned out the new hut, moved his vital equipment
from the schoolhouse, and prepared to begin life anew in his
lesser quarters. For the next week, he painstakingly put the
May Day sign together. After more lugging of cotton, more
packing it into shape, and more cuckooing back at the cuckoos,
he neared the end of the job. It is a masterpiece, Schinz
thought as he tucked in the last bit of cotton and stood back
to admire it.

With the sign finished, his mind turned to other things. He
thought about his family. He thought about the Air Rescue
Service and muttered some unkind things under his breath.

He thought about Gabby and the boys, and wondered how many MIG's they had shot down by now. But most of all, Schinz thought about meat.

He had been on the island twenty-five days and had had nothing to eat but rice and tasteless vegetables. Some way he had to find meat. There appeared to be one survivor of the island's former cat population, a scrawny, moth-eaten tomcat that had slunk in and out of the settlement once or twice. Schinz conjured up visions of the cat roasted deep brown and flanked by piles of French-fried potatoes. He decided he would go after that cat.

Next morning, he awoke in bright, hungry spirits. He went to a stream near the May Day sign and dug out a small pool. The water was clear and cool. This was to be the refrigerator: once he caught the cat, he would dismember it, and store the uneaten parts in the cool water. That way, by Schinz's own careful reckoning, the cat might last a good three days.

He went back to the hut, got out his rusty knife and the slingshot. With great deliberation, he selected about fifty small, well-rounded pebbles for ammunition. Then he set out on safari.

Feeling not a little silly as he called, "Here, kitty, kitty, kitty!" Schinz tramped through the brush. The cat tentatively stuck its head out of a bush. Schinz tried to ease within grabbing range; the cat took off. The prey seemed actually to be enjoying the game. It would duck around an obstacle, then stick its head around as if to make sure the pursuer was still pursuing. Schinz would try easing the slingshot into firing poition slowly so as not to scare the cat. The cat would wait, with an expression that looked like a sneer, then duck nimbly aside. Schinz coaxed, wheedled, swore, cried. For three days this went on, the cat bounding happily around and around him until he staggered and stumbled home to his dinner of dandelion greens.

But then another possibility presented itself. One morning two confused birds flew into Schinz's hut. They hardly had time to realize they were under a roof before Schinz had streaked across the hut and closed the door. For forty-five minutes he crashed around the little hut, slamming his few pieces of furniture all over the room before he finally caught the birds. He wrapped them in a piece of cloth, took it out to his fire and left it there while he ran for a can of water. Hurrying back, he gingerly unfolded the cloth. The birds had flown.

To prepare for a possible recurrence of the bird incident, Schinz built a crude butterfly net from a piece of fishnet that he found on the beach. Luck was with him. The very next morning two more birds wandered into the hut. Schinz quickly snatched the birds out of the air, and as he noted in his diary later: "Hustled them down to the chopping block for an immediate head-chopping ceremony." He ate the birds, bones and all.

The taste of bird meat only whetted his appetite. Recalling that he had seen a few snakes on the island, he fashioned a fork out of a long—a very long—stick. Off he went, poking about in the brush and muttering over and over again to himself, "Snake meat is one of the world's greatest delicacies." But snakes are even nimbler than cats. After a futile day of snake chasing, Schinz resigned himself to his vegetable diet.

Then a baby wren fell out of its nest near his hut one day. Schinz grabbed it eagerly. The bird cocked its little head, studied Schinz with its big eyes, opened its beak, and chirped. Schinz couldn't do it, not to a baby. He put it back in the nest.

The next day the baby wren fell out again, and again Schinz put it back.

On the third day, the wren fell out and dropped right at his feet. Schinz looked down at the bird, then up at the sky. "Lord," he said, "I believe You want me to eat this little wren." So he did.

The last day of May, at which point Schinz had been on the island thirty days, was one of the toughest. The weather had turned bad, and Schinz had been working feverishly to get firewood under cover. He smoked the last of his carefully hoarded cigarettes and noted in his diary, "went on corn silk." May 31, he also noted down, is "payday."

With the weather bad, and no hope of aircraft coming over the island, Schinz dreamed up new projects to keep himself occupied. In the village several days earlier, he had noticed an Army cot minus its canvas. He dragged the cot frame to his hut and carefully dismembered it—no small problem without a screwdriver or wrench. Then he cut off the bottoms of three rice bags and slipped these onto the cot frame. He sewed the bags into place with some string, then put the cot back together again. He bounced up and down a couple of times to give it a comfortable sag, then lay down for an "operational suitability test" and discovered that it was "quite a sack," as he noted in the diary.

Next, he decided to make a mattress. In one corner of the hut, he found some cotton from which the seed had been removed. It was very soft and silky. He dumped that into the sagging cot, until it reached the level of the frame. He covered the "mattress" with some rags that he had sewn together to use as a sheet. Then he took four heavy pieces of cloth that he had found in the village and sewed them together. This served as a blanket. Finally, he took a large piece of burlap, doubled it over, placed a six-inch layer of cotton inside, and sewed up the open ends of the burlap. This was his comforter. As a crowning touch to his bed, Schinz added a new find: a mosquito net.

Schinz was extremely particular about his clothes and personal hygiene. He bathed often and boiled his clothes every third day. He was choosy about where he slept, and as a result, had thus far escaped lice and other vermin. He took good care of his shoes. He treated them every third day with the diesel oil. He kept his gloves repaired with a needle and rice thread that he had found in one of the huts.

One of the things that worried Schinz immensely was his beard and hair. Both were beginning to get very long and matty. Finally, when he thought he would go mad if he did not somehow find a way to shave and cut his hair, he stumbled across a pair of rusty scissors. Overcome with joy, he snatched the broken piece of metal, and held it skyward, thanking the Lord. He oiled the scissors and sharpened them on a whetstone. After two hours of happy hacking, he had his beard trimmed and his hair chopped off in a rough, mangy-looking crew cut. Just to get rid of the matted mass of filthy hair made his spirits soar.

On the morning of the sixth of June—Schinz's thirty-seventh day on the island—the weather cleared. Once again he was very optimistic. He noted in his diary before breakfast: "Today is it. I feel it in my bones." Sure enough, within a few minutes, Schinz heard the sound of aircraft engines. He ran out into the clearing as two F-51 fighters flew over low. He lighted the oil-soaked rags, waved his home-made flags, danced, shrieked, cursed. As the planes flew back and forth overhead, he began to have real hope. He had caught their attention! Then he ran back into the hut and dragged out the dinghy, the Mae West, the G-suit, and placed them in the middle of the clearing, pointing to them.

But soon the aircraft flew away. Worse still, no chopper came. It was the same old story again. What had he done wrong this time? Schinz asked himself. Perhaps it was his clothing. Instead of wearing his flight suit, he had on an old Korean shirt that he had found in one of the huts. Angrily, he wrote in his diary: "They must have mistaken me for a Korean. Can't I do anything right?" Then he added a postscript: "Get hold of yourself, stupid, don't crack up."

Later that afternoon, Schinz climbed to the highest peak on the island. For three hours he sat staring out at the sea thinking. He could not understand why the Air Force was deliberately ignoring him like this. Certainly the planes had seen the sign, the oil, the Mae West, and other items. What could they be thinking? Obviously, they thought he was just a Korean or perhaps a Communist. What could he do now? He thought of paddling to the mainland in his dinghy. Perhaps he could steal a sampan and sail south to Cho-do. He tossed the idea aside, and began drawing up what he called a "thirty-day plan." The main feature of the plan was the construction of a new sign. This time he would make it read:

I M
U S A F
P

meaning "I am a United States Air Force Pilot." That ought to convince the Air Rescue people, he thought.

On the way back to camp that afternoon, Schinz came across an old slit trench. As was his custom, he examined it closely for salvageable materials and was surprised to find three trip flares. "Just what I need for my night operations," he said to himself. He bundled the flares in his arms and hurried back to camp. He set one flare near the fire, pulled the safety catches and fuse. Then he waited for a plane to come over.

A few hours later, Schinz heard the familiar sound of B-26 engines in the distance. He pulled the trip wire, but nothing happened. He looked at the flare and said: "Why in the heck didn't you go off?" Then he decided to find out. He picked up the flare and fiddled with the trip mechanism. Suddenly it exploded in his face. He was blinded and deafened. Pain numbed his senses. His hands were bloody.

He thought he might stop the bleeding by putting his hands into boiling water so he blindly ran to the water can and put it on the fire to boil. Then he thrust his hands into the hot water. He could not feel a thing; his hands were numb. As he sat holding his hands in the water, his eyesight returned. Slowly Schinz screwed up his courage, then withdrew his hands from the water to see how many fingers he had left. He was surprised to see that they were all there. But he could see that his hands had been peppered by scores of schrapnel pieces. He still hadn't regained his hearing, so he stuck his fingers in his ears to check for blood; he found none. Within a few minutes he heard a bird singing; he knew he was not permanently deaf. He staggered to his bed and collapsed.

Upon awakening, Schinz saw that each shrapnel hole in his hand had turned into a small pocket of pus. Nervously, he searched for a red line of blood poisoning creeping up his arm. It was not there yet. After breakfast, he boiled more water and applied steaming hot rags to his hands. Then he got all of his needles together and, after carefully sterilizing them, dug into the pus pockets, extracting the shrapnel. It was tedious work, but Schinz knew that he could not survive with infected hands. It would have to be a perfect job. After three hours, he was satisfied.

That night he half-buried the other flares at a distance from the fire, and strung the trip wire into the hut, and tied it to the mosquito net bar. If a plane came over, he could trip the flare from his bed, with no danger of another explosion. Before going to bed, he examined his hands carefully, and though they were beginning to blister in a few places, he concluded that he had stopped the infection. The fact that he had the flares set raised his morale considerably, because heretofore his night operations had been slipshod and ineffective. It was likely that a plane would come over that night.

It was 2:30 A.M. when he awoke. A bright light shone in his eyes. For a minute, he thought he was having a nightmare. He blinked, then stiffened in terror as he saw rifle barrels aimed at him. Hands grabbed him and turned him over. Then he heard voices behind the light.

They were Koreans.

Schinz tried to speak, but no sound came from his throat. He turned over on his face and stuck his blistered hands up, waiting for the wham of the rifle and the impact of the bullet. He prayed quickly. Another hand grabbed his GI shirt collar, then moved to the silver eagles. A voice said in English: "American. American Colonel." On hearing the English, Schinz shouted: "I surrender, I surrender." But the Korean put his arm around Schinz, pounded him on the back, and shouted, "O.K., O.K., O.K., O.K.," over and over again. "We are friends. We help."

After Schinz had embraced each one of the natives in his delirious joy, he discovered how close he had actually been to death. The men were South Korean soldiers whose job it was to keep islands like Schinz's "safe"—free from Communist soldiers, so that fighter-pilots could bail out and be rescued from them. On a routine sea patrol, the Koreans had spotted the fire as they sailed by. Believing Schinz to be part of a Communist unit that had recently occupied the island, they had come to kill him.

The friendly South Koreans immediately began plans for evacuating Schinz from the island. They promised to take him to Cho-do. Within minutes, one of the Koreans set up a powerful two-way radio and called one Lieutenant "M," who Schinz later learned was the boss of the group, on another island. Lieutenant "M" and his assistant, Sergeant "D," owned a powerboat. When they learned of Schinz's plight, they promised to get under way at once for Schinz-do and pick him up. Six hours later—at 9:00 A.M.—they arrived.

It was risky business putting around in a slow sampan so close to the mouth of the Yalu River. The group boarded the craft and got under way immediately. As the boat chugged steadily southward through the Yellow Sea toward Cho-do, Schinz sat in the bow wolfing down Army rations that the Koreans had given him, occasionally exchanging a word with his rescuers. At a half hour before midnight that night, the boat pulled into Cho-do. Schinz went ashore after first gratefully thanking the Koreans and making sure they had proper papers with which to receive a reward. He watched as the boat turned and headed back in the direction from which it had just come.

Before going to sleep that night in a clean bed with sheets, Schinz shaved, bathed, weighed (he had lost forty pounds), and had a long chat with the men of Air Rescue. There were a lot of unanswered questions: Had they not seen his distress signals? The fires? The flare? What about the aircraft that had flown over time after time, didn't they report his presence? Had he been deliberately left to starve to death on this lonely island? Why hadn't they searched for him in the beginning?

In these conversations, plus later talks with men at his home base, Schinz learned that elaborate search procedures had been initiated after it was found that he was missing. The jets in his own flight had returned to base, refueled, then, joined by scores of other aircraft, had spent the remainder of the day sweeping back and forth over North Korea and MIG alley looking for his aircraft, or some sign of it. The following morning and the day after, more search planes combed the area, as well as the escape route that Schinz had suggested for disabled aircraft. It was then that Schinz discovered that he had not yo-yoed out of MIG alley along the escape route as he believed, but had veered west considerably. Thus, the area in which he crashed was not carefully searched.

The Air Rescue people had been watching his activity on the island with some interest for a matter of weeks. However, since no downed airmen were believed to be in the vicinity and since Communist agents were known to be inhabiting most of the islands, Air Rescue believed the activity to be that of a Communist, intent on luring innocent Air Rescue personnel into a trap. For months, the Communists had been attempting to capture a helicopter in this fashion. It was feared that a captured Air Rescue pilot might be persuaded by diabolical Communist techniques to reveal considerable valuable information about the underground and the safe islands, the backbone of the Rescue Service.

For these reasons, Air Rescue and the Joint Operations

Center had been reluctant to send a helicopter or seaplane into the area. However, when the distress signals persisted, and after the May Day sign was clearly discerned in aerial photographs, Air Rescue formed a commando party and dispatched them by boat with orders to investigate the island firsthand. When Schinz arrived at Cho-do, he learned that the party had already departed for Schinz-do the day before. Had he not been picked up by the South Korean soldiers, Air Rescue would have evacuated him the following day.

When Schinz arrived at his home base, all hands turned out to greet him. Gabby came, chomping on a big cigar, slapping the gaunt survivor on the back. Colonel Al Kelly was there anxious to find out what had happened in the critical moment of the dogfight when the two planes became separated. Colonel Joe Mason, Schinz's friend and boss of the Joint Operations Center, was there to explain the elaborate search that had been carried out. The chaplain came along, too, and as soon as he could, Schinz disappeared with him for more than an hour.

That night, the 51st Fighter-Interceptor staged a memorable party in the officers' club to celebrate Schinz's return. Beer and whisky flowed freely. Pilot after pilot came up to Schinz to ask what happened. Little by little, he told bits of the story. Finally, he decided to tell everyone the whole tale at once. He climbed up on the bar and waved his hands. Silence fell over the smoke-filled room. Schinz said, "Now I'm going to tell you all what happened. . . ."

For an hour and a half Schinz stood erect on the bar, talking. There was hardly a sound from the 150 officers, just an occasional cough or the scrape of a chair. Finally, Schinz came to the end of the tale of Schinz-do, and he shook his finger at the men and said, with some feeling, "Men, there is one thing that saved me, and that was God. When that dinghy started drifting out to sea, I prayed that He would bring me back to land. He did. When my lighter was full of sea water, I prayed that it would light, and He made it light.

"Then I got so weak I couldn't stand up, and I prayed that I would find something to eat, and I did. I found twenty-five bags of rice. When that flare blew up in my face, I prayed that my hands wouldn't get infected, and they didn't. When my hair got so I couldn't stand it, I asked the Lord to help me, and right after that, I found a pair of scissors!

"Now I want to tell you guys something. Everything I asked my God for, he provided. I dropped on my knees every morning and every night and said the Lord's Prayer and the Twenty-third Psalm. The good Lord is watching you guys, and me, and don't any of you tigers forget that for one minute."

A great cheer shook the officers' club. The men pushed and crowded the floor near the bar where Schinz stood. They shook his hands warmly. Tears filled his eyes. He got down off the bar and walked out of the club to his quarters.

The next day, Schinz was flown to a rear area base in Japan, where he managed to get through on an overseas telephone line to reassure his wife and children.

"Where in the world have you been?" shouted his wife, in a happy, wifely tone.

"Me?" said Schinz, running his hand through his chopped hair. "Why, I've been playing Robinson Crusoe—without Friday."

That night Colonel Schinz went to dinner. This is what he ate:

Two large shrimp salads, including the lettuce and raw-cabbage filler.

One double-sized *filet mignon.*

One mountainous order of French fries.

Two large salads.

Six eggs.

Two pots of coffee.

Four scoops of ice cream.

Two bananas cut up on the ice cream.

An extra-thick coating of hot chocolate that completely covered the ice cream and bananas.

Schinz returned to the United States shortly after his adventure and enjoyed a long leave at home with his family. Then he reported to the Pentagon in Washington, where he gave top Air Force officers, including those in Intelligence, the benefit of his experience. Later he was assigned for duty with the Tactical Air Force in South Carolina. He is currently assigned to the staff of the United States Air Force in Europe, with headquarters in Wiesbaden, Germany.

Schinz is still a restless tiger. He likes nothing better than to climb into a Sabrejet and lead his wing man through a series of six-hundred-mile-an-hour barrel rolls along the Iron Curtain. But somehow he always manages to be on the ground on Sundays. As Mrs. Schinz says, "I used to have to drag him to church, but now he leads the way."

COLD

CLINTON D. SUMMERSILL, a twenty-four-year-old Air Force fighter pilot, was stationed in Itazuke, Japan, when the war in Korea broke out in June, 1950. He was a stocky, happy-go-lucky bachelor, who flew F-80 jets and liked to pass his off-duty time in bars and night clubs. His blond hair was usually unkempt, and he was never without a cigar, the modern-day hallmark of the tiger. He was very friendly, anxious to get along with his fellow officers, and could tell an anecdote or story in a winning way. He had resigned himself to the belief that he would be killed while flying an airplane—or so he said —and spent all of his pay every month, chanting melodramatically, "Eat, drink, and be merry, for tomorrow we die."

Summersill—"Clem" to his friends—was from Penny Farms, Florida, an unusual little town since it was the home of about 250 retired ministers. Summersill's father was manager of a dairy farm that served the ministers and their families. Both he and his wife were very religious, and they raised their five children to serve God and country. Clem was the middle child, having two older brothers, both of whom served in World War II, and two younger sisters. He went to high school in Green Cove Springs, Florida, eight miles from home, and played second-string football. He did not particularly like the atmosphere in Penny Farms.

Summersill's great interest in life was flying. It began one day when a friend of his father's took him for his first ride in a Piper Cub. From that day forward, Summersill determined to spend his life in the air. He urged his father to allow him to

take flying lessons. The request was denied, but only because
the Summersill family could not afford the expense. Clem was
not thwarted; he hung around the nearby airfield and hitch-
hiked rides whenever he could. From time to time he was allowed to take the controls. He read every book, magazine
article, and newspaper story he could lay his hands on that
dealt with aviation. Finally he made up his mind that he would
join the Air Force.

In 1943, after graduating from high school, Summersill
applied for admission to the aviation-cadet program. The rolls
were temporarily full, so he entered the Air Force as an enlisted man to wait for a vacancy. He waited through 1944 and
1945, working in the meantime as a drill instructor at Air
Force bases in Texas and Wisconsin. To his great disappointment, the war ended before he was called to flying school.
Believing he might be more readily selected for the cadet program if he had higher education, he left the Air Force in the fall
of 1945, to go to college.

Two and a half years at the University of Florida at Gaines-
ville did not turn his head. Summersill was still haunted by his
love of flying. He reapplied for the cadet program and was
stunned to discover that he could not pass the physical examination—his eyes had weakened. With this bad news, Summersill then went back into the Air Force in the only way he
could—as a radio technician. Later, his eyes improved, and
he was accepted for pilot training; and in 1948, after a five-
year delay, Summersill arrived at Randolph Field, Texas, the
"West Point of the Air." A year later, a hot-shot fighter
"jockey," he was sent to Japan.

From the day the North Koreans marched into South
Korea, and the Air Force was alerted for action, Summersill
itched to get into the fight. But bad luck plagued him. First he
was transferred out of his jet unit, because his proficiency had
dropped. Then he was assigned to a ground job. Weeks later,
he wormed his way back onto flying status, but the best he
could get was a job flying big C-119 and C-54 cargo planes between Japan and Korea, hardly a satisfying way of life for a
fighter pilot when a war was going on practically under his
nose. Summersill kept his eye peeled for any kind of assign-
ment that would put him into the fight.

His chance came in late December, when a job in the
6147th Tactical Squadron opened up. The 6147th was a special Air Force unit that flew small "Mosquito" aircraft along
the front lines and directed close-support aircraft to ground
targets. The planes—T-6's—were old single-engine, trainer-
type aircraft that had been left over from World War II. They
had room for a pilot and an observer and carried smoke rockets

that were used to mark the ground targets. They were equipped with radios, so that the pilot could talk to the ground units and to the fighter-bombers, though most of the electronic equipment was worn out. But to Summersill, even this kind of combat flying seemed superior to flying transports.

By the time Summersill arrived in Korea, the war situation had gone from bad to good to bad again. General Walton Walker and his successor, General Matthew Ridgway, had rallied the Eighth Army and temporarily stopped the retreat after the initial Chinese attack had driven the U.N. forces back below the thirty-eighth parallel. But the Chinese were still pressing. They had launched another attack and had driven the Eighth Army even farther back down into South Korea below the Han River and were threatening to drive a wedge down through the center of the U.N. line and capture Pusan.

Most of the ground divisions had suffered heavy casualties. The men were exhausted, having been without adequate food and sleep for weeks. To stop the oncoming hordes of Chinese and North Korean soldiers, airpower was in greater demand than ever. Mosquito aircraft were particularly needed. Consequently, pilots of the 6147th flew two and sometimes three missions a day, remaining over enemy territory as much as six or eight hours. Mechanics worked around the clock to keep the battered aircraft in halfway-decent flying condition.

When Summersill joined the 6147th, he set up quarters in a tent and was soon winging his way in the "putt-putt" over the cold, rugged countryside. He had his troubles. He did not have proper winter flying clothing. His fleece-lined boots were sizes too large, and he could not fly the airplane while wearing them. He kept them stored in the baggage compartment and flew with only his paratrooper boots. The result was that his feet were numb when he returned from each flight. An hour and a half was required to thaw them out.

But worse than the cold was the worry of crashing behind enemy lines. Summersill learned soon that the Chinese Communist soldiers reserved a special sort of hatred for Mosquito pilots. They had a dirty word for the Mosquito planes that, translated, meant: "The little airplanes that drop the big bombs." It was the firm belief among Mosquito pilots and observers that to be shot down in enemy territory and captured meant certain death. Only one Mosquito crewman was known to have been captured alive. Presumably the Communists had shot the others on sight.

On the second day, Summersill was assigned a permanent observer, a thirty-three-year-old Army captain from the 2nd Division named Wayne Sawyer. He was married and had two small girls. Prior to World War II, he had been a bush pilot in

Alaska and Washington State. Before that, he had successfully created a flying paper route. He knew as much about flying a small airplane as Summersill, or perhaps even more. Certainly he was familiar with Mosquito piloting; he had flown more than 150 missions and wore three Distinguished Flying Crosses. He had crashed twice behind enemy lines, and each time escaped.

Sawyer had joined the Air Corps in 1939. In spite of his wealth of flying experience, he was washed out of the aviation cadets after failing to pass a physical examination. He transferred to the infantry and fought with the Army Ground Forces in Europe and the Pacific. He was fearless in combat. His nerves and voice were steady and controlled. He wore his hair in a short crew cut and kept himself in superb physical condition. Six years of combat had made him a moral, though not intensely religious, man.

On January 15, Captain Sawyer and Summersill were relaxing in their tent enjoying a day off. They had flown eighteen missions in nine days and were tired. They had just finished eating a big chicken lunch and planned to spend the afternoon and evening over a bottle of brandy. These plans were abruptly quashed when they received word from Operations that they had been assigned to fly a "fill-in" mission for a T-6 crew that had been unable to report for duty. As he pulled on his heavy winter flying suit, Summersill stared at the unopened bottle of brandy.

"Just our luck," he said to Sawyer.

The two men arrived on the flight line at twelve thirty, and checked the aircraft. Six smoke rockets were mounted under the wing. Summersill opened the baggage compartment and threw his big fleece-lined flying boots inside, slammed the door, and climbed up the wing into the forward cockpit. Sawyer crawled into the back cockpit and slid shut the "greenhouse" canopy. Summersill gunned the engine, and the silver plane bounced over the steel-mat taxi way to the end of the runway. Soon they were in the air and headed for the front near the thirty-seventh parallel, an hour and a half away.

At two o'clock in the afternoon, they arrived at the front and via UHF radio, Summersill got in touch with the ground controller. The latter reported the situation: there were a large number of enemy troops facing an equally large number of U.N. troops—mostly ROK's—along the front. A heavy firefight had been in progress all day. Word had been received that some three to four thousand Chinese Communists had been massing about eight miles behind the lines and were preparing a breakthrough. Could the Mosquito find the enemy troop concentration and then direct fighter-bombers toward it?

"Roger, buddy," Summersill answered.

He flew the T-6 toward the area where the Chinese troops were believed to be massing. As he sped northward over no-man's land, he studied the terrain below: it was the roughest he had ever seen. Jagged rocks and ridges, cut by deep ravines and canyons, poked skyward. Large patches of snow lay drifted in and among huge boulders, on the floors and hillsides of the canyons. Summersill shuddered and flicked on his intercom:

"It looks like the face of the moon down there, Wayne," he said to Sawyer.

"Right, laddie," Sawyer said. He was intently searching the ridges and canyons for signs of enemy activity.

A few miles behind enemy lines, the T-6 was joined by a flight of sixteen Navy Corsairs and attack planes (AD's). The fighters called Summersill via radio and asked for targets. Summersill explained the tactical situation and told them to stand by while they sought out the mass of enemy troops. The heavily armed planes climbed to a safe altitude—beyond enemy small-arms range—and circled lazily while Summersill pointed the T-6 toward the rugged earth below to look for the Chinese.

Flying in and among the ridges and canyons required great skill and constant attention. Sawyer did most of the looking. Suddenly, he shouted over the intercom:

"There the little yellow bastards are."

Summersill banked the plane so that Sawyer could get a better view. Then once more, he dove the plane toward the ground.

Sawyer said, "Clem, they're shooting at us. We better get out of here."

Summersill had allowed the plane to descend within two hundred feet of the ground. On warning from Sawyer, he pushed the throttles to full power and banked sharply around a rocky cliff. Then Sawyer spoke again:

"Clem. The manifold pressure's dropping."

In spite of full throttle, the engine was losing power. Summersill automatically reached down and checked his fuel switches to make sure the full tanks were cut in. He turned up the carburetor heat. Still the engine did not speed up. The T-6 was losing altitude fast.

Summersill then realized he had flown into a blind, horseshoe-shaped canyon. There was no way out except to climb, or turn and glide back to the open end of the horseshoe where the Communist troops were massed. He could not climb; he dared not turn around. In an instant, he realized he would have to crash-land the T-6 on the rough floor of the canyon.

Summersill tried to glide as far from the Chinese troops as possible. But the plane dropped fast. Within seconds, he was pulling back on the stick to dodge a huge boulder. The plane slid onto a large, upward sloping granite slab and skidded along for about a hundred feet. The belly tank ripped off and tumbled down the hillside, a mass of flames. Summersill's head smashed into the foam-rubber crash pad over the instrument panel.

The plane ground to a halt just short of a large rock. Summersill looked around. He saw Sawyer unfasten his safety belt and shoulder harness and climb up on the cockpit edge. With his parachute still strapped under his seat, he leaped into the snow, just forward of the leading edge of the wing. By then, Summersill was fighting his way out of the cockpit. Blood flowed down over his eyes and blinded him.

His parachute had somehow jammed. He knew he must try to save it because it would be useful in many ways: as a distress signal, as a sleeping bag, if necessary, as a tent, or as a waterproof cover for his boots. He was struggling to free it when he heard the flame crackling, and felt the heat. He knew the plane was on fire and that he must get out quickly. From a distance, he heard Sawyer calling, "Clem. Clem. Get out. Get out."

Summersill unstrapped his parachute harness and blindly crawled out of the flaming plane. As he left the cockpit, his left arm instinctively reached for, and found, the first-aid kit. He wrenched it from the fitting, jumped down on the wing, and slid into the snow alongside Sawyer. He wiped the blood from his eyes and looked at his observer. Then, for the first time, he noticed Sawyer's left leg.

It appeared to have been amputated or broken in the crash. Summersill looked back at the plane. He believed it would blow up any second. He thought: Shall I try to save Sawyer, or shall I run away and save myself?

Sawyer broke into Summersill's split-second reverie:

"My leg's broken through the ice. It's caught down between these rocks. Help me. Hurry! We've got to get out of here before the plane blows."

Wiping the blood from his face, Summersill knelt down in the snow and pulled on Sawyer's leg. He slipped and fell. Sawyer clutched his jacket, and the two men grunted, as they fumbled in the snow.

"Get out of the parachute," Summersill said.

Sawyer clawed his way out of the parachute harness. Summersill put his knee against the parachute pack, gave a mighty pull, and fell over backward as Sawyer's leg broke free from the trap. Water dripped from his trousers and boots; the hole into which he had slipped was a frozen-over puddle. His knee-cap was badly injured.

"I better get my fleece-lined boots out of the baggage compartment," Summersill said. He turned to run back to the plane. At that instant, one of the smoke flares, ignited by the heat and gasoline flames whooshed over their heads.

"Get out of here before we are killed," Sawyer yelled. Both men got up and starting running, Sawyer dragging his chute. Within a few feet, he dropped it in the snow.

"Forget it," he said to Summersill, "we can't get it up the hillside anyway."

Summersill nodded. The two men clambered over and around the huge boulders, stumbling and sliding on the slippery shale. "Where're we going?" Summersill asked. He could hardly see. "Follow me," Sawyer said, "I think I see a good hiding place up on the side of the ridge." Soon the men were plunging through a snowdrift. Sawyer sank in up to his thighs. Summersill followed behind, stepping in Sawyer's snow prints.

Sawyer had spotted a small group of trees covering a rock formation about halfway up the ridge. Now, as he plunged through the snow toward the spot, he could see that several of the rocks joined together to form a cave. Soon he was pushing his way inside. But the sloping ground was covered by a sheet of ice. Each time he crawled up, he slid back down. On the third try, he succeeded in pulling himself to the rear of the cave by his arms. He braced his feet splay-legged against two rocks. Then he extended a hand to Summersill, who slipped and slid up into the cave, grabbed a rock, and held on, only to slide completely out again. Finally, Summersill wedged himself inside.

In the rush to get away from the burning plane, neither man had had time to think. Now, as they sat crouched in the cave catching their breath, Summersill, not ordinarily a religious man, found himself praying at top speed. He turned to look at Sawyer and saw him make the sign of the cross.

"Give me the first-aid kit," Sawyer said. Summersill looked down and, for the first time, realized that he had brought the kit from the plane.

Summersill said, "Is it bad, Wayne?"

Sawyer looked closely at the deep cut in Summersill's forehead and replied:

"No, Clem. Just a few cuts."

"You're trying to make me feel good, Wayne. You know damned well my forehead is falling into my face. Isn't it?"

"No." He shook his head.

"Give me your signal mirror. I want to look at it before you bandage it up."

Sawyer got out his signal mirror and Summersill looked at his forehead. It looked worse than he had imagined. He would not live another two hours, he thought. He handed the mirror back to Sawyer. He said a few more prayers as the Captain bandaged his head tightly with gauze, and then slipped his wool knit cap back over his head.

Then Summersill remembered Sawyer's knee.

"Let's see the leg," he said to Sawyer.

They rolled up his trousers leg and looked at the injured knee. It was bleeding badly. The skin was severely lacerated. Summersill put a bandage on the knee while Sawyer got out an extra pair of wool socks, took off his fleece-lined boot, and changed the wet sock for a dry one. As he did so, Sawyer, who had had much experience in Alaska and Washington, gave instructions to Floridian Summersill on walking through snow:

"It's very important that our feet do not freeze," he said. "If you get frostbite, gangrene'll set in and you'll lose your feet and legs. If a foot gets wet, I have an extra dry sock here. Avoid heavy perspiration; otherwise, that'll freeze, too. And remember this: amid snow, man loses his instinct of self-preservation."

Summersill's thoughts turned only briefly to the physical discomfort caused by the subzero temperature. His feet were already so numb from the hour and forty-five minutes in the plane that he could not feel them. His hands were almost as cold. Both men had lost their gloves in the crash. But Summersill was much more worried about the Chinese Communists. He remembered an old fighter pilot axiom: Troops are always eager to meet the pilot who has been strafing them.

"What're we going to do, Wayne?" he asked. "The Corsairs didn't see us go down. No one's been alerted."

Sawyer was pulling maps from inside his jacket.

"The first thing we have to do, Clem, is get the hell away from the plane. Then we have to get away from this entire area as fast as we can. They are sure to search very thoroughly as soon as they discover that we were not killed in the crash."

Sawyer studied the maps.

"The Communists are here," he said, "and we are right here." He pointed with his bare finger. Not more than a mile separated the two positions. "They ought to be near the plane within a very few minutes."

"O.K.," Summersill said. "What are we going to do? We can't go south toward friendly lines. There are ten thousand Chinese between us and the ROK's." He did not say it, but he thought it: if they were captured, they would be shot on sight. Sawyer knew it too. "Why don't we head straight north," Summersill added. "The Communists would never think of looking for us in that direction."

"We might just try something like that," Sawyer said. He was carefully studying a map of the battle front. Summersill was quiet. Sitting in the cave was just like sitting on a block of ice in an icehouse, he thought. The temperature must be at least fifteen below zero. He thought he might be getting dizzy from loss of blood.

"Here's what I think we ought to do," Sawyer said, breaking the long silence. "Here. Look on the map. Over to the east here, there's an area where the Communist front is very thin. There are nothing but Communist guerrillas in through here, no organized front at all. That's because the country is so rugged."

"You mean here, right around Punggni?"

"Yes," Sawyer replied. "See, we can walk northeast, back into Communist territory as you suggested. Then when we get around right here, we can turn southeast, and infiltrate through the lines. I figure it's forty miles, maybe fifty, by ground because we have to go up and down. I believe that if we hide in the daytime and move on a forced march at night, we can make it. What do you think?"

"O.K., I'm with you," Summersill said. "But there's one thing I want to get straight: we're going to get out of here, and I don't mean maybe. There's no use trying to give up. If we do, the Chinks will clobber us for sure—especially the guerrillas. I know they never take POW's. I want it clearly understood that if they corner us, I'm going to shoot it out with them. The only way they will capture me is dead."

Sawyer had been on the verge of telling Summersill the same thing. He said, "You must be reading my mind, Clem."

Summersill added, "And another thing. If we get into any arguments, I want you to know that I will argue with you, but you'll have the last word because you're senior man. And listen to me: I'm going to hold you responsible for anything that happens to us, too."

They shook hands warmly. Then from a distance, they heard Chinese voices shouting.

"O.K., Clem," Sawyer said, "let's get out of here."

Sawyer let go and slid out of the cave. "Wait a minute," he said.

As Summersill watched, Sawyer took five steps through the snow up and around a rocky ledge toward a barren area. Then he backed down to the cave again, carefully keeping his boots within his original tracks.

"That'll send them off that way," he said to Summersill. The two men crawled back into the cave, and clambered out through a small crack between the rocks that opened to the rear. Then they plunged through deep snow, circling toward the top of the canyon wall. Suddenly Sawyer, who was leading, stopped. Summersill came up alongside him.

"What is that?" Sawyer said, pointing to indentations in the snow.

"Tracks," Summersill said. "It looks like a man and one dog."

"Right," Sawyer said.

"A searching party?" Summersill asked.

"Who knows?" Sawyer replied. "They might be Communist tracks. They might be the tracks of a Korean farmer coming to help us."

"How old are they?" Summersill asked. He was whispering.

"I don't know. But we better move on away from here," Sawyer said.

"If the tracks are fresh and the man and dog are nearby, why hasn't the dog barked at us?" Summersill asked.

"I don't know, let's get moving," Sawyer said.

They moved off through the snow as fast as they could travel, keeping one eye on the ground and one on the ridge tops and canyon walls for signs of Communist soldiers. Over an hour had passed since the crash. Though it was still midafternoon, darkness was being hastened along by a huge black cloud shaping up in the northeast. Soon the two men came to a thicket.

"Let's go in here," Sawyer said. "They'll never find us."

"Lead on, friend," Summersill said. The two men pushed their way through the thorny scrubs and bushes and, then, after a moment, sat down. They heard faint voices, coming from the area where they had left the burning plane; then, suddenly, an explosion.

"The plane," Summersill whispered.

"Yes. And I hope it got a few of them," Sawyer said.

Summersill nodded in agreement. Minutes later, they heard Communist soldiers moving up the canyon side toward the cave. They watched as the soldiers spotted the diversionary tracks and, falling for the ruse, set off in the wrong direction. Soon there was more shouting. Another soldier found the real tracks. The Chinese came toward the thicket, spreading out through rocks and snow, shouting and yelling.

Summersill pressed his lips close to Sawyer's ear. "They're coming this way. What are we going to do?"

Sawyer said, "Stay right here. It'll be dark in another half hour." He looked at the black cloud in the northeast. "Just hang on."

They waited twenty minutes. By then the soldiers were

very near. But it was getting dark very fast. The soldiers turned on flashlights. Summersill counted twenty lights.

"Don't you think we ought to move on?" he asked.

"Wait until you are sure you cannot see them any more— just the lights. Then we can be sure they can't see us, and we'll go fast. It won't matter if they hear us in the thicket. They won't be able to figure which way we went."

Before darkness closed in, the two men took a final look at the escape route on the map. It was plain that there would be many obstacles on the journey. The biggest was a sizable mountain, about 5,000 feet to the summit. They could see it plainly, towering over them in the northeast. It was covered with deep white snow. Climbing it would not be easy.

"Shall we go around it?" Summersill asked.

"I believe that if we try to go around it, we will run into Communists," Sawyer said. "There's fewer Communists on top of the mountain than any other place. It'll be tougher hiking, but safer."

"O.K., pal, I am with you all the way," Summersill replied.

As soon as they could no longer see the outlines of the Chinese soldiers, the two men got up and pushed out of the thicket, heading northeast toward the mountain. They moved quickly and quietly through the drifted snow, gradually drawing away from the dancing flashlights. They climbed one small snow-covered hill, passed over a low ridge, and then, about an hour later, came to the foot of the mountain. They stopped to rest.

"That's the tallest mountain I have ever seen," Summersill said. "What does it say on the map again?"

"Four thousand, seven hundred and fifty-nine feet," Sawyer said.

"Are you sure?" Summersill asked.

"Follow me and you can count them yourself," Sawyer said. He picked up a hefty stick, invited Summersill to do the same, then started up the long, white slope of the mountain.

The dark cloud had been warning enough, but they were really not prepared when the blizzard struck. They had moved about a quarter of the way up the slope. At first, the snow-flakes were harmless fluttering across the mountainside, a godsend, covering their trail. But then, the white flakes came in torrents, followed by heavy wind and sleet. Gloveless, bent against the driving cold, the two men moved slowly up the mountainside.

An hour later, they stopped to rest.

Summersill looked at Sawyer, who had been leading. His face and flying helmet were a mass of frozen ice and snow. Icicles hung from his nose. His eyes were glassy.

"Wayne, can we go on like this?" Summersill asked. He was unable to talk clearly. The sounds that came from his lips were mumbles. His face was half-frozen.

"Laddie, we can't stop. If we turn back, the Communists will get us for sure. If we stop here, we will freeze to death in two hours. It must be twenty or thirty degrees below zero right now. We have to keep going."

To maintain the discipline of the march, the two men drew up a "track" plan. Under the plan, a standard infantry procedure, one man would "lead" the other. The leader would set the pace, encouraging and urging on the other man when necessary. Under the plan, each man would lead for half an hour. The shifting of position would break the monotony of the steady dragging through the snow. It would give each man something to look forward to.

They marched off. About ten o'clock that night, eight hours after the crash, Summersill began to feel very gloomy. The trouble started in his feet. For hours, he had been plugging along in his paratrooper boots, plunging down in the white mass, which often came up to his waist. Snow had caught in his trousers leg, melted, and run down into the inside of his boots, where it froze. His feet had been numb all along, but now there was no feeling at all. He was unable to move his toes. He could just barely bend his ankles.

Finally he called through the darkness. "Wayne, Wayne, I think my feet are completely frozen." Sawyer stopped and waited for Summersill to catch up. "My feet," he repeated, "I think they're frozen."

Sawyer said, "What do you think we ought to do, Clem? There is no shelter around here. There is nothing we can build a fire with, even if we could get one started in this blizzard."

"There's nothing to do but push on," Summersill said. "But let me try to get something to put on my feet. Maybe I can make a pair of snowshoes from the branches of a tree."

Summersill pushed through the deep snow to a nearby tree. He cracked a few branches from the trunk. Even in the high wind, the sound of the brittle wood snapping was like the report of a rifle. Sawyer became worried. He hurried through the snow to the tree.

"Clem. Clem. Watch the noise. There may be Communists within a hundred feet of us. Don't break the limbs. Use your knife."

Summersill took a six-inch folding knife out of his emergency vest. One long blade was jagged, with full teeth, something like a saw blade. He drew the teeth back and forth across a frozen limb.

"How'll you attach the sticks to your boots?" Sawyer asked.

"What'll you use for string?"

"I'll cut off a piece of the emergency vest. Or, maybe I can use the mosquito netting. We won't need that here."

Summersill hacked away at the brittle limb. After a few seconds, he lost all feeling in his hand. He put his hand and the knife inside his jacket to warm. He did not want to fumble and drop the knife in the snow because he knew he would never find it again. But his hand did not thaw. Soon it became obvious to Summersill that his task was, under the circumstances, far too formidable. At length, he put the knife away, and the pair set off up the mountainside again, Summersill leading.

Not long afterward, Sawyer sensed that they had been going in circles. He had no proof, just the instinctive feeling of an infantryman. He took out his small flat compass and checked the direction. Sure enough, they were headed in almost the opposite direction that they intended, south— toward the Communists!

"Hey, Clem," Sawyer shouted through the wind. Clem stopped. Sawyer walked up.

"You're going in the wrong direction," he said.

For no good reason, the remark made Summersill angry. It happened that he was holding his compass in his hand the moment Sawyer came up. He had just checked his bearings. He looked at it again and saw that the needle pointed to NE, the same direction it had indicated all evening. Summersill spun around and jabbed the compass toward Sawyer's face.

"No, we're not," he said, "take a look at this." Then he noticed that as he turned, the compass needle did not swing. It remained steadily on NE, even though Summersill turned completely around.

Sawyer looked and shook his head. "The damned thing is frozen," he said.

"I believe you're right, Wayne," Clem said. He felt sheepish. "But this is kerosene in here. It isn't supposed to freeze unless the temperature is forty degrees below zero."

"Well, it must be forty below because it sure is frozen," Sawyer replied. "We had better keep one compass thawing inside our jacket at all times."

Summersill looked at Sawyer. He tried to laugh but the skin on his cheeks was too numb. "This is fantastic," he said.

Sawyer nodded.

The men continued. The slope became steeper. Two hours later, they came to a stand of small trees. They chose the spot to stop and rest because they could wedge their feet against the tree trunks and avoid slipping back down the mountainside. The wind was blowing at about forty miles per hour. It whipped the stinging snow into their faces. Summersill was in very low spirits. He was exhausted, and his feet were heavy and stiff. He told Sawyer he did not think he could go any farther.

Sawyer felt unaccountably good at the moment.

"Why don't we eat?" he said. Summersill perked up. "Fine. A good idea. The last thing I had was that chicken lunch, and that was twelve hours ago."

A quick search of their emergency vests disclosed that they had between them two cans of compressed beef—each can designed to provide one man with one meal—a few pieces of candy, cheese, and a few bouillon cubes. They had powdered tea, coffee, milk, and cream, but no means of making hot water because the flints that were supposed to be used to ignite the two emergency sterno cans were soaked in oil and useless. In order to stretch the rations as far as possible, they settled on opening one can of compressed beef and dividing it. Summersill took the first bite.

"This doesn't taste like home-cooked food but I guess we better eat it." He could hardly get the food to his half-frozen mouth. He handed the can to Sawyer, who ate stiffly.

Numb fingers probed around in the emergency vest. Sawyer pulled out a piece of cheese. He took a bite, then handed it to Summersill.

"Here have some of this. It's good."

"Be careful of the bouillon cubes," Summersill remarked. "They're wrapped in tin foil. The charm candy is wrapped in cellophane."

After eating the compressed beef, Summersill became thirsty. He reached down and scooped up a handful of snow. He was about to put it in his mouth when Sawyer slapped his hand, the snow spilling in all directions.

"Don't eat that," Sawyer shouted against the wind. "It'll dry the mucous membrane in your throat. You might get pneumonia. If you want water, take out the plastic water bottle and fill it with snow and then let it melt inside your jacket."

Summersill packed the plastic canteen with snow and shoved it inside his jacket. It was not very warm inside. Five hours passed before the snow melted.

The men pushed off once more into the blizzard. Sawyer led, and then Summersill. Most of the time, the men literally swam along in the snow, often armpit deep. Conversation was impossible except for the occasional "Come on, Clem," "Come on, Wayne," or "Are you there?" "How're you doing?" "Come along now," from the leader. They constantly had to wipe icicles and matted snow from their faces and eyebrows. Every half hour they stopped to clean the snow from their trousers.

All the while, they steadfastly followed a northeast course, moving ahead slowly, afraid to stop for long lest they freeze in their tracks on the mountainside.

About four o'clock in the morning, Sawyer, who was leading, noticed that the ground seemed to be leveling. The snow was not as deep, and there appeared to be a hard crust of ice underfoot. He turned and waited for Summersill to come alongside.

"Clem. Clem," he whispered, "I believe we have come to the top."

Summersill crunched wearily through the snow to Sawyer and stopped. His face was a cobweb of frozen ice and snow. He stared dully at Sawyer. The wind blew steadily out of the northeast. They turned their backs to it as they stopped to talk.

"The top, laddie!" Sawyer insisted. "I think we've come to the top."

Summersill was too weak to rejoice. "How do you know?" he asked.

"The ground has leveled. Look, the snow is shallow, and there is a hard crust of ice underneath. This must be the top. The crust was formed when the sun melted the snow and then it froze again."

Summersill looked at Sawyer, and then he stared blankly into the black void around them. He could not see more than a few inches through the slanting sleet and snow. "O.K.," he said, "O.K."

"The going will be much easier," Sawyer said.

He was mistaken. The wind came steadily out of the northeast. In the open, on top of the mountain, it blew with twice its former force. The noise alone was maddening; the sting of snow and sleet was almost unbearable. Like two forlorn cutters sailing into the wind, the men tacked back and forth across the mountain top, heading first due east and then northwest, in an effort to achieve a northeast course. They became so cold and exhausted that they could walk only with great difficulty in any direction. Summersill's frozen feet clumped against the hard frozen crust like two brittle stilts.

At length, Summersill, who was leading, fell into the snow. Sawyer came alongside and sat down.

"I can't go any further," Summersill said.

Sawyer nodded. Then, the two men sat in the snow, heads bowed. Suddenly, as if possessed by some superhuman force, Sawyer jumped up and violently beat his arms around his body. He shook Summersill.

"Get up, Clem. Get up. We'll freeze to death if we sit here. Get up."

Summersill jumped up. He looked at his watch. The crystal was clogged with ice and snow. "How long have we been here?"

"Two or three minutes," Sawyer replied.

"How about crawling?" Summersill asked. "That'll keep us going in the wind and probably keep us from freezing to death." He wanted to avoid walking on the hard crust.

"O.K., let's go," Sawyer said, "and watch out that you don't bump into any Communists."

They crawled off into the wind, heads down. Summersill remained in the lead. Every ten minutes he turned and shouted, "You O.K., Wayne?" Sawyer replied each time in the affirmative, but sometimes with only a grunt and a vigorous shake of the head.

Summersill realized that his mind had ceased to function in the normal fashion. It had focused on an imaginary point in the snow about six inches out from his nose. He could think of nothing except that in order to go on living, he had to get one numb hand out to that spot, pull himself along, then put the other numb hand in the same spot, and then drag two frozen legs behind him. He managed to pull himself along for more than an hour. Then he lost all consciousness and fell down in the snow.

Sawyer was struggling along in like manner only a few feet behind. He saw Summersill collapse, and then he stopped crawling. He realized that he had neither the will nor the strength to awaken Summersill or crawl around him. He got up on all fours, fighting to keep awake. But then, his strength drifted away, and, like Summersill, he fell face into the snow. The wind moaned across the white mountaintop, drifting snow against the two dark shapes.

Sawyer awoke first. He lifted his face off the ice and shook snow from his body. He noticed that the snow and wind had stopped and that it was getting light. Even though a heavy fog hung over the mountaintop, the visibility had improved considerably. He wiped a mat of snow from his face and glanced at Summersill. He was little more than a white lump. Sawyer crawled over and fell against him pawing at the huddled form with numb hands.

"Come on, laddie," he said. "Come on. We have to get out of here."

Summersill awoke with a start. He jumped up. Then, like a crazed animal, he walked round and round in circles. He tried to clear his head of sleep. Sawyer sat on the ice shaking his head violently. He watched absently as Summersill walked off in the direction in which they had been crawling earlier. Summersill had gone but ten steps when he became wide awake.

He stopped and stared dumbly ahead.

"Wayne!" he shouted. His voice was hoarse and raspy.

Half crawling, half running, Sawyer floundered through the snow until he reached Summersill's side.

"Look at that," Summersill said. Directly ahead, not more than five feet, the mountainside dropped away for several hundred feet, a sheer cliff. Sawyer stared down into the icy chasm.

"If we had crawled another fifteen feet—" Sawyer said.

Summersill nodded his head vigorously. "It looks like somebody has been watching out for us, buddy," he said.

"It sure does look like it," Sawyer said.

Summersill was profoundly impressed by the narrow escape. He began to think back over the events of the last fourteen hours. He remembered his prayers in the cave. Then he prayed again.

Dawn was not far off. Once they had fully regained their senses, the two men turned their thoughts to the matter of finding a suitable place in which to hide out for the day. It would be dangerous to move about enemy territory in the daytime. They took stock: Summersill's feet were completely frozen. Sawyer's left foot, which had broken through the ice into the puddle when he leaped from the burning airplane, was beginning to freeze, even though he had changed his socks. They were almost out of food.

While they discussed the dismal situation, they scanned the mountainside as far as they could through the fog. Once Sawyer thought he saw a small house. He walked a few feet in its direction, then shook his head. He said to Summersill, "I am seeing snow mirages, if there are such things."

"We better try to find a house someplace, because my feet are really in bad shape," Summersill said. "Maybe we can find some farmer who has a fire and will let us thaw our feet. We can hit him up for some chow, too."

Sawyer was looking at the map again. He was trying to ascertain their position. "I believe we're right here," he said to Summersill.

"You mean we've only come twenty miles?" Summersill asked, looking over Sawyer's shoulder at the map. Summersill grunted. He was discouraged. They were not even halfway to their objective. "We're averaging just a little better than a mile an hour."

"We better turn east now," Sawyer said, "I believe we are around the Commie flank now."

"O.K., Wayne, but let's look for a house and get our feet warm."

They set off in an easterly direction along the mountaintop. But they saw no houses along the ridges or the slopes below. Sawyer looked again at the map, trying to fix their exact position. Finally, he said to Summersill:

"Laddie, I don't think there is a house around here anywhere. This is desolate country."

"Well, let's don't just stand here," Summersill said.

While searching for a suitable hiding place, the men came upon a large evergreen tree. Thinking it might offer protection they crawled under it. "Just like home," Summersill said, burrowing his way under the limbs.

"Let's try to build a fire," Sawyer said. They took out their cigarette lighters. Both were soaked and would not work, so they began a careful search for matches. Summersill pulled out a package of cigarettes. "Getting warm," he said. The remark struck both men as hilarious, and they laughed loudly. But they could find no matches.

They had no sooner settled themselves under the tree than the snow fell from it with an earth-shaking thump. Then, as they shook the snow from their jackets and trousers, Summersill asked, "Any more bright ideas?"

As they walked farther along the mountaintop, it became light, even though the heavy fog still clung to the ground like a low-hanging cloud. After a while, Summersill said:

"Wayne, what do you say we push on and not hide during the day today?"

The thought had not even crossed Sawyer's mind. All his Escape and Evasion training had stressed that under no circumstances should an attempt be made to move through enemy territory in daylight. It was basic. Summersill broke in on his thoughts:

"The fog seems to be holding. It will afford cover and concealment. I think we ought to push on. If we try to hole up in this snow with no fire, we'll surely freeze to death before nightfall. I'm afraid I don't have a choice." Summersill was thinking of his feet.

Sawyer knew that Summersill was right. The latter had no choice. If he remained in the snow, without moving and without fire, he would die. The chances were also good that his own leg would get worse. He would not even consider splitting up.

"O.K.," he said, "let's go on."

He looked at the map again. "Look," he said, "we'll keep going east, and move down into this area. The map shows that a number of creeks originate here in this watershed. The creeks run east through the mountains and into the flatlands, and right into friendly lines. If we can pick up a creek and follow it out, we won't have to crawl up and down these mountains."

It was something to contemplate. Summersill looked at the map.

"You mean one of these creeks?" he asked. His numb forefinger mashed clumsily against the map.

"Yes," Sawyer said. "I believe it is all downhill to the source of these creeks, too. Walking ought not to be as tough today as it has been. We can stay right on the mountaintop, too—to hell with walking along the slopes. If we run into any Communists, we will fight it out."

"O.K., Wayne. Nobody captured, right?"

"Right," Sawyer replied.

They were hungry. They discussed eating but ruled against it, deciding to look for food during the day and save the rations. Breakfast consisted of a long swig on the canteen of melted snow. Then they were off walking along the top of the mountain. A few miles later, Sawyer, who was leading, stopped. He checked the map again.

"I think we ought to start down here," he said. "There should be a little basin—a sort of canyon down there where one of these creeks starts. We'll go down and try to pick it up and follow it out of the mountains. By then, we ought to be near the front and I believe we can slip through O.K."

They started down the steep face of the mountain. Walking was impossible. Sawyer sat down in the snow and slid for about one hundred yards. Summersill watched, and then slid down behind him. They got up, and slid another hundred yards.

"Great stuff, eh?" Sawyer said. "The mountain climbers call this glissading."

"Beats walking," Summersill replied.

On the next slide, Sawyer unavoidably built up a large ball of snow in front of his feet. The ball picked up speed, and then went crashing down the mountainside. Both men stopped and dug into the snow, trying to be as inconspicuous as possible, in case the thundering snowball had alerted the enemy. They lay still in the snow for almost an hour. Finally, when there was no sign of activity, Sawyer waved his hand, and they slid farther on.

The whole day was consumed descending the mountain. Much of the time, they glissaded. It was not easy. Moreover, it was dangerous. Once they almost slid into a deep crevasse. Their lives were in peril for an hour, as they clawed their way back up through the snow to safety. But most of the slow descent was made on foot, traversing slopes, cutting across ridges, walking along ice or snow through the incredibly desolate country.

By early afternoon, both men had reached a physical breaking point. Neither had ever walked so long, in so short a time, through such difficult and treacherous terrain. The lack of est, the absence of food, the numbing cold, the frozen feet, he almost psychopathic fear of being captured—all these factors began to exert a paralyzing grip on their senses. They blacked out for brief periods, or else their minds went off on sudden flights of fancy.

Summersill was the first to become delirious. It happened late in the afternoon. They were glissading down a steep slope, Summersill leading. Sawyer unavoidably cascaded another snowball from behind. It bore down upon Summersill, and reached him just as he slid under a log. The snowball smashed to pieces on the log. Summersill came out safe and unhurt on the other side.

He heard Sawyer hurrying down, calling, "Clem. Clem. Where are you?" Sawyer had not seen the log and did not realize that Summersill was lying safely in the snow on the other side. Sawyer clawed into the snow, yelling: "Clem. Clem. Can you hear me? This is Wayne. Clem. Clem." He believed that Summersill had been buried under the snowball.

Summersill knew that Sawyer was digging for him in the snow, but for some inexplicable reason, he lay there without answering. Sawyer dug for more than fifteen minutes before he uncovered the log and then found Summersill on the other side, resting comfortably, laughing.

Sawyer became very angry when he saw Summersill. "What the hell are you doing? I thought you had been buried. Why are you pulling a dirty trick like this?"

Summersill rolled on his side, shaking with spasms of laughter.

Sawyer screamed, "What are you laughing at, you idiot?" Then he caught himself. He sat down alongside Summersill and began laughing too. It was obviously time for a rest.

Soon they were off again. Within an hour, they could see, lying below them, the small snow-blanketed basin they had been seeking. It was very small, hardly more than three hundred yards wide. They could see that a double row of bushes twisted out of the basin in an easterly direction. They guessed that the creek, frozen over and covered with several feet of snow, lay between the rows of shrubs. At any rate, it tallied with the direction of the creek as indicated on the map. They started down the steep side of the basin toward the bottom.

Except for the crunch, crunch of their frozen boots in the snow, there was not a sound as they dropped down into the basin. Summersill was leading. Suddenly he stopped and raised his right hand in warning. He waited for Sawyer to catch up. He whispered: "There's a soldier up there along that little ridge. I just saw him adjust his rifle."

Sawyer shoved Summersill down, then he dropped to his knees. "Keep low," he whispered. The two men pulled out their .45-caliber pistols and lay, face against the snow, holding their breath, to keep the condensation clouds from giving away their position. After a few quiet minutes, Sawyer said:

"Are you sure you saw a soldier?"

"Positive," Summersill replied.

"Well," Sawyer said, "we can't lie here all day. Let's go get him. Show the way."

The two men crawled through the snow. It took them more than an hour to circle around and come up through a group of shrubs to the back of the ridge. They inched to within twenty feet of the place where Summersill said he had seen the soldier.

The ridge was bare.

"He's gone," Summersill said.

Sawyer believed Summersill was delirious again. But he said nothing. He was not sure of his ability to judge.

It was beginning to get dark when the two men headed back down into the basin once more. They had almost reached the row of shrubs that lined the snow-covered creek, when they spotted the tracks of a rabbit.

"Look at that," Summersill said. He was very hungry. During the day, they had chewed on a few twigs and had even tried without success to rip bark from a tree trunk, but this was the first sign of palatable food they had encountered. The trouble was that the rabbit was nowhere to be seen.

"We better not go look for it," Sawyer said. "We might get lost, and we don't have the strength to get lost."

They sat down, and in place of a rabbit for supper, they took a drink from the canteen. The sun was setting, casting a weird light through the fog. It played eerie shadows into the basin. In the last light, they surveyed the path of the stream and discussed new "track" procedures. The discussion turned around whether or not they should stay in the bottom of the canyon and walk along the creek bed, get up on top of the ridges, or walk along the side of the ridges as was the standard evasion procedure.

Summersill was very tired. The second wind that had carried him through the late afternoon was gone. His eyes ached. His back and legs were stiff. His mind kept wandering off, as though detached from his body. He said to Sawyer:

"Where do you think the Commies will be? On top of the ridge? Or along the canyon bed?"

"I think they will probably be on top of the ridges or along the creek bed. But, those ridge slopes are so steep, I don't think we can walk along them." They were whispering.

"I don't think I can even get up there, much less walk along in all that deep snow."

"Well, let's walk along the creek here until we bump into something."

"O.K., buddy," Summersill said. "Take off. I'm right behind you."

Even though the creek was covered over by a deep blanket of snow, it was easy to follow in the growing darkness. The twin row of shrubs delineated its course like two hedges alongside a sidewalk. Moreover, after about half an hour after dark, the clouds suddenly lifted. The sky became clear, the visibility extraordinary. The two men looked up in wonderment at the profusion of stars shining brightly overhead. On signal from Sawyer, they stopped.

"Look at that," he said. "We certainly have been having the breaks on the weather. It's overcast in the daytime when we need to hide, and clear at night when we need to see."

"Almost miraculous," Summersill said.

For the first time, the two men were able to get a good look at the surrounding countryside. As far as they could see, it was a mass of snow-covered mountains, peaks, ridges, and canyons. The creek alongside which they had stopped lay in the bottom of a canyon about three hundred yards wide and five hundred feet deep. The walls were steep, almost vertical in places, and covered by deep snowdrifts.

The stream itself, no more than ten feet wide, carved a course down through the middle of the canyon floor. It twisted and turned, snaking its way eastward down through the mountains. As it progressed farther from its source, it sank deeper and deeper into the floor, widening slightly, until it formed a sort of shallow canyon within a canyon.

"Just like a deep highway cut through the mountains, eh, buddy?" Sawyer asked.

"Well, I've seen better highways than this," said Summersill.

They looked at the stars for a moment.

"There's the North Star up there," Sawyer said, pointing.

"Right. I see it," Summersill said.

"We ought to keep an eye on it from time to time," Sawyer said, "to make sure we are approximately on course."

They walked on.

Not long afterward, Summersill suddenly began to cry. He did not know why, but he sobbed uncontrollably. Then he began to shout, "Wayne. Get me out of this snow. Get me out of this snow." He heard himself shouting insanely. He knew that snow covered everything for miles and that Sawyer was powerless to help. Yet he could not stop sobbing and yelling.

Sawyer tried to quiet him. "Clem. Be quiet. Be quiet. There might be Communists all around here. They'll kill us on sight if they get us. Do you hear? Shut up. You have to shut up." He wrapped an arm around Summersill. The two sat down in the snow. Then, as suddenly as he had lost his senses, Summersill regained them. To help restore his confidence, Sawyer said, "Why don't you lead for a while?"

Summersill took off down the stream, clomping through the deep snow. All at once, he stopped still. He blinked his eyes; then shook his head. He could not believe what he saw —two small mud huts. He stared at one of the huts for a moment, to make sure it was not a mirage.

Smoke, and an occasional spark, puffed out into the night from a small chimney sticking out of the top of the hut. Summersill looked at the other hut. It did not go away. It was obvious that both were real and both were occupied. Summersill turned slowly and walked back toward Sawyer, who had also seen the huts and was standing still. But Sawyer motioned for Summersill to turn around and keep going as before.

Summersill pulled out his .45 and walked back between the two mud huts. He moved very slowly, carefully placing each foot in the snow, digging in the toe and heel. Sawyer also had his pistol drawn. He crept along behind. When they had moved about fifty yards past the huts, they stopped to whisper.

"What was all that?" Summersill asked.

"Chinese one-man huts. They're like pup tents. It must have been a guard post. There must be a bivouac of some kind back over there." He swept his hand in the direction of the huts.

"I'll have to be more alert than that," Summersill said.

"Roger, laddie," Sawyer replied.

They pushed on through the snow. With the sighting of the mud huts, tension mounted; it was plain that they were now in an area occupied—and guarded—by Chinese troops. Tempers became short. They argued about the most inconsequential things—whether to stop and take leaves off a tree or whether to look through pebbles for worms and bugs. They fought over directions. Once, while Summersill was leading, he came upon a large boulder blocking the way. He started around the rock to the right.

"Don't go that way," Sawyer whispered.

"Why not?" Summersill asked.

"Because you'll fall into the creek."

"No, I won't."

"Yes, you will. Let's go around this way."

"Listen, I am leading, and I say let's go this way."

It seemed absurd. The rock was not large. Either way would have quickly led them around it. But the question of the routing had become a matter of principle. The two men argued for more than ten minutes. They had almost come to blows when Summersill finally gave in.

"O.K., you're senior officer. We go where you want to go. But I won't forget this."

They passed around the rock to the left, Sawyer leading. They were obviously on the verge of breakdown.

At midnight, the two men stopped by a rock to rest. Tempers were still short. A question of whether or not they should eat again was debated. It had been twenty-four hours since they had the first can of rations. They wanted, if possible, to save the little remaining food for emergency. But after a quick search of nearby bushes failed to produce even dead leaves, they agreed to eat the rations. Each insisted that the other have the larger share.

"Here, Wayne," Summersill said, "you need this. Eat it."

Sawyer was equally insistent: "No, Clem. *You* eat it."

After they had finished the can of food, divided about equally between them, Summersill decided that he would have dessert. He took a small square from the emergency vest, and thinking it was a "Charm" candy, pulled the wrapping off and took a big bite. He swallowed the bite before he realized that the square was not a "Charm" candy but a bouillon cube. The cube was very bitter and extremely salty. Summersill immediately became nauseous. He was worried that he would get sick and lose the food he had just eaten.

He got sick, but he did not lose the food; at least, not all of it. When he threw it up, he caught it in his hand and then swallowed it again. In a few minutes it came up again. Once more, he caught it and pushed it down. He did not want to lose the food. He knew he needed every scrap of energy he could get.

When they set off again, Sawyer led. Summersill trailed, alternately throwing up his food and swallowing it every few minutes. His stomach ached, his throat was raw. He did not complain to Sawyer because he did not want to become a burden.

The sickness soon absorbed the tiny remaining pocket of strength in Summersill's body. He felt he could no longer go on. But he somehow managed to, stumbling along blindly, following Sawyer. Vaguely, as though his voice were coming from millions of miles away, Summersill could hear Sawyer whispering words of encouragement: "Come on, Clem. That's the boy! Just one more step. Come on, boy."

From time to time, he blacked out entirely. When he awoke, he would look back along the path they had traveled, and try, without success, to recall having walked it. Once he went to sleep on his feet, standing erect in the middle of the snow. Sawyer walked a long way before he realized Summersill was not behind him. When he tried to wake him, the two men fell into the snow.

Summersill sighed. "Wayne, is it really worth getting up and going on?"

Sawyer replied, "I don't give a damn if I ever move again. I just want to sleep." They lay in the snow for several minutes.

Then, as he had done on many occasions before, Sawyer jumped up, stomping his feet, shaking his head, and slapping his arms around his body. He shook Summersill violently. "Get up, Clem. Get up. We've got to get out of here."

Summersill got to his feet. He was amazed to discover that his head had cleared and his stomach had stopped aching. He got out a piece of candy and put it in his mouth. Then he picked up a handful of snow and took a bite. He held the snow, along with the candy, in his mouth. The snow seemed to melt faster when mixed with the candy. He swallowed the mixture. "How good that feels on my raw throat," he said aloud.

They pushed on down the creekside, Summersill leading. Suddenly, the barking of a dog broke the silence of the night. Summersill stopped, his heart beating wildly. Both men looked around. It was difficult to determine the direction from which the barking came because it echoed through the canyon. Summersill looked at a patch of trees on the top of the right wall of the canyon, then he said to Sawyer:

"There they are, Wayne! See the flashlights up there?"

"Yes," he whispered, "I see them bouncing through the trees. They have dogs with them. They are after us."

"They must have spotted our trail back there in the bivouac. Let's get moving," Summersill said.

From some source, the two men obtained additional energy, which enabled them to run headlong in the snow. As they raced along, every fifteen or twenty seconds they looked back over their shoulders toward the forest on top of the hillside. They could see that the flashlights were still bouncing through the woods, seemingly coming in their direction. They had gone about half a mile, when Summersill looked around and stopped.

"Hey," he whispered, "look at that. Those damned flashlights have wandered off into space."

Sawyer looked around. It was true. The "flashlights"—in reality stars—were now clearly visible in the sky. From where they stood, they could see that the hillside sloped down slightly, "lifting" the stars out of the wood. Summersill could not believe it at first. He walked back some distance until the stars were "back" in the trees again. As before, they seemed to bounce and scurry through the forest. "I'll be damned," he said to Sawyer.

The "flashlights" were not the last objects that the two men conjured up in their imagination. Indeed, the remainder of the night was a nightmare of imagined objects: bridges, houses, enemy soldiers, flashlights, wild animals. The power of suggestion played a big role; every time one man spotted a bridge or tank, the other man instantly confirmed it. Many times they left the trail to clamber up the hillside to inspect a cave only to have it disappear into thin air.

About three hours past midnight, the men rounded a turn in the trail and came upon a deep gorge. Two eight-inch logs covered with snow and ice formed a bridge spanning the dark chasm. Sawyer looked at the bridge and asked:

"Is it real?"

Summersill kicked one end of the logs with his frozen foot. "Yep. She is a real one this time."

"Well, I don't think we ought to cross it."

"Well, what do you want to do, buddy? Sit here until daylight?" Summersill was getting angry again.

"Well, I guess you're right. I'll go over first," Sawyer said. He got up and started to walk across the logs.

"Wait," Summersill shouted. He pulled Sawyer off the log. "Let me go over first. I'm leading."

Summersill put his knees in the "V" between the two logs and inched along. Halfway across, he looked down. He could not see the bottom of the gorge. He shuddered. If one of them fell, he thought, what would happen? Suppose one broke a leg? Then what? Would both men stay together, or would one man go on? Summersill was greatly relieved when he reached the opposite bank.

"Come on across, Wayne. But be careful. It's very slippery and the gorge is very deep. Come on now. That's right. One knee in front of the other. Easy does it."

With only a foot to go, Sawyer stood up to walk off the end of the log. He slipped and fell. At the last instant, he blindly groped with numb hands for the side of the bank. Somehow, he found a handhold and stopped his fall. Quickly Summersill reached down and grabbed his clothing. As he did so, the .45 slipped from his jacket, struck Sawyer a glancing blow on the head, then clattered down—seemingly forever—into the icy gorge below.

Summersill braced a frozen leg against one of the logs, and

pulled Sawyer up on the bank. The two men lay on the ground for some minutes, breathing heavily. Finally, Summersill spoke.

"Wayne, what if you had fallen in the gorge and broken your leg?"

"That would have been very bad. I guess I would have been left behind, huh?" he said.

"No. I would have stayed with you," Summersill said.

"Is that the way it will be?" Sawyer asked.

"Yes," Summersill said, "it is the only way."

"O.K., so be it."

They pushed on, Summersill leading. By now, the creek had broadened considerably. Its banks, cut into the canyon floor, were steep and deep. Here and there, the ice coat had been broken, and water rushed against the rocks and boulders that littered the bottom. The men walked along a natural path that followed the lip of the bank. After a while, they came upon a boulder that lay across the path. The only way around it appeared to be a tiny ledge between the rock and the steep creek bank. Summersill was about to climb out onto the ledge when he noticed a black shape, seemingly crouched, on top of the rock.

"A mountain cat!" he said to himself. It seemed to be ready to leap. Summersill backed slowly until he bumped into Sawyer.

"Look, Wayne, a big cat!" he whispered.

"I see it," Sawyer said. His eyes were glued to the top of the rock.

"Give me your forty-five, and I'll shoot it," Summersill said.

Sawyer did not like that idea. The shot would alert every Communist for miles. "No," he said.

"Why not?"

"Because I want to keep it. You lost your gun. I want to keep mine."

"All right, then," Summersill said, "keep it."

He thought for a minute. "O.K.," he said, "I have an idea. I'll walk up to the rock. Just as the cat springs, I'll drop into the snow. Then, you kill the cat."

Sawyer did not like that idea either.

"No," he said, "I have a better idea. You just walk by like nothing happened, and maybe the cat won't notice you."

Summersill thought to himself: this guy is completely nuts. Here is a big cat blocking the trail, and he doesn't want to kill it.

"Very well," he said. "If it jumps, I'll kill it myself." He took out his knife and flicked open the cutting blade. Then, with his weapon held at the ready, he walked boldly toward the rock.

Suddenly, the "cat" vanished. When Summersill got close, he found in place of the cat, a big bush growing on top of the rock. He looked at it skeptically. Sure enough, the bush seemed to be in a "crouching" position. Sheepishly, Summersill put away the knife.

They trudged, stumbled, and crawled for another hour, always whispering encouragement to each other. Then through watery, half-closed eyes, they noticed that a faint light was beginning to glow in the east. Dawn! There was not a cloud in the sky. The day would be bright and sunny. They were sure the Communist soldiers would spot them if they remained on the open floor of the canyon. Once again, they began the search for a safe place to spend the day.

About ten minutes later, they came to a Korean house jammed in between the creek and canyon wall. The house did not disappear within a few seconds as all the others had. It was real. A light shone in the front window. Should they approach it? They stopped and held a whispered conference. The decision: to take a chance and try to make contact with the Koreans who presumably occupied the house. If, by chance, the Koreans were not sympathetic, perhaps they could buy protection. Since he had lost his pistol, Summersill was selected to walk ahead and make the contact. Sawyer would cover him from the brush.

Summersill walked straight up to the door of the house. He raised his hand to knock. Something—he did not know what—caused him to stop his fist in mid-air and back away from the door. He was suspicious. He crept to the window, stood back slightly, and looked in through the unfrosted pane. In one quick look, he counted six Chinese soldiers.

Though he ducked away into the darkness immediately, the scene inside the room remained vividly implanted in his mind. One Chinese soldier was sitting on a chair drinking a cup of tea. His head was bowed, his hands were wrapped around the cup. Another soldier was standing, smoking a badly rolled cigarette. He was talking to two other soldiers who were sitting on the floor. A fifth Chinese was sitting alone at a crude table playing cards. A sixth was lying on the floor asleep. There might have been others.

Summersill backed hurriedly toward the spot where he knew Sawyer was hiding. But Sawyer was gone.

Summersill thought: They have captured him quietly, and they are waiting to get me.

He pulled out his knife and switched the blade into position.

Then he walked around slowly in the darkness, calling very softly, "Wayne? Wayne?"

"Yes?" It was Sawyer's voice. He had moved to another bush. Summersill heard the click of the .45 hammer as Sawyer let it go forward slowly. The two men came face to face.

"It's a good thing you spoke up when you did," Sawyer said. "I thought you were a Chinese, and if you had taken one more step, I would have blasted your guts out."

"That's all right," Summersill said. "I was just getting ready to cut your throat."

The house, full of Communist soldiers, blocked the way ahead. The only way around it appeared to be through rushing waters of the creek. Sawyer and Summersill scrambled down the steep bank and plunged into the cold, ice-choked water, stumbling across rocks and boulders. The water was more than knee-deep. Summersill could feel it trickling down into his boots. In a matter of minutes, he knew, it would be frozen solid.

When they reached the opposite bank, they scampered up through the rocks. They found a trail that followed the lip of the bank and hurried down it, trying to put as much distance as possible between the Communist house and themselves before daylight. They had not gone far when, in the faint light, they saw a Chinese soldier walking up the opposite bank of the creek. They stopped and squatted in the shadow of a rock and watched him make his way toward the house.

When the Communist disappeared from view, Sawyer and Summersill got up and hurried on. They were rounding a bend when they spotted a second Communist soldier, this time on their side of the creek and coming straight up the trail toward them. Both men stopped, looked at one another and eased back into the shadow of a large tree. There was no need for talk. Summersill pulled out his knife. He made a signal to indicate he would tackle the soldier low. Sawyer took out his pistol, gripped it by the barrel. He motioned that he would knock the soldier on the head. It was important to avoid a big commotion that might alert the other soldiers.

The Chinese came steadily on. The airmen strained. They could see that he wore the standard green-quilted Chinese Communist Army uniform and carried a Russian submachine gun. When he was about thirty feet from the tree, he turned abruptly from the trail, climbed down the creek side, and skipped through the water to the opposite side.

"What the hell?" Summersill whispered. "Did he see us?"

"I don't think so," Sawyer said.

"That place must be a guardhouse or a trail block," Summersill said.

"Yes. I guess they are changing the guard right now. It looks like they have the whole canyon bottled up good. We'll have to be very careful."

"We'll have to hurry and find a place to hide because it'll be getting light very soon," Summersill said. He looked to the east.

"Remember," Sawyer said, "nobody gets captured."

"Right," Summersill said.

To avoid Communist soldiers who might be using the creekside trail, the two airmen cut off to the right and climbed halfway up the sloping canyon wall. It was rugged terrain and, therefore, less likely to be patrolled. They hurried on, searching everywhere for a cave. After a while, they realized that the ridges were not as steep. Ahead, the flat canyon floor seemed to blend in gradually with the ridge slopes. At last, they were coming out of the mountains into the flatlands!

The snow was thinning out. In some places, the earth was entirely bare. Summersill became aware of the transition in a painful way: while tramping through the relatively soft snow, he had felt little pain from his frozen feet. But, as the snow thinned, and they moved on frozen ground for long periods, the sensation of walking on stilts returned, and he felt as though he would go out of his mind. He said to Sawyer:

"Wayne, we have got to find a place and thaw out my feet. I just can't go on much farther like this."

"Well, maybe we ought to go back to the creek where the going is easier," Sawyer said.

The two men circled back down toward the creek—now a river more than a hundred yards wide—to pick up the trail. As they came down out of the ridges, they saw a Korean farm just ahead. They threaded their way through the frozen ponds of a rice paddy. Then Sawyer stopped. He whispered.

"Clem. Across the creek. Communist soldiers!"

"Where?" Clem asked. He seemed unable to focus his eyes.

"Right over there. About half a dozen of them. They have burp guns. They must be guerrillas. They seem to be headed back toward the mud house."

"Well, let's get the hell out of here," Summersill said.

"Wait! There's a potato bed. Let's try to get into it."

Sawyer led the way to a Korean potato bed, a large hole in the ground covered over by a thatched straw roof that protruded two or three inches above the surface. They pulled on the straw cover. It would not budge. It was frozen in place.

"We better keep moving," Sawyer said, "or we'll attract attention."

They struck off down the trail, one behind the other, bent over and walking slowly. Their clothes were dirty and torn.

Their faces were bearded and filthy. They hoped that from a distance, the guerrillas would take them for two old Korean peasants trudging down the path. Sawyer kept one hand inside his jacket on his .45 just in case the Communists became suspicious.

The ruse was successful. The guerrillas did not appear concerned. Soon they had rounded a bend and were out of sight. At the same moment, the airmen spotted a small, windowless mud house about one hundred yards up the slope from the trail. Both men turned automatically toward the house. If there were Communist soldiers inside, then they would fight it out. If it was inhabited only by civilians, they would ask them for help, hoping that they were not Communists or Communist sympathizers.

They paused briefly at the rear of the house; then split up, one going around the house one way and the other, the opposite. They met in front of the house. Then, with weapons drawn—Sawyer's .45 and Summersill's knife—they rushed through the opening that served as the door. They soon discovered the "house" was empty. There was nothing in it except a feeding trough. The "house" was actually a Korean barn.

They searched the dirt floor for something to eat. They found several kernels of corn but, otherwise, nothing. "The cheap cows even ate all the salt block," Sawyer observed, as he looked through the feed trough.

They sat down on the floor of the hut to rest. They talked for a minute, then Summersill proposed that they move on to the farmhouse itself, which they could see a few hundred yards down the trail.

"We can get warm and get something to eat. The Communists might find us if we stay out here. Or we might even freeze to death."

Sawyer was thoroughly exhausted. He did not want to move.

"I'm staying right here, Clem. I'm not moving another step. If the Communists come, I'll fight it out."

Summersill got up and looked out of the doorway. It was now completely daylight. He could see for miles across the Korean countryside. There was not a soul in view. Then, he said: "Wayne! There are some Communists in the woods over there. Look!"

Sawyer jumped up and whipped out his .45.

"Where?" he asked.

"Over there," Clem said. He pointed to a nearby patch of trees.

"Get back," Sawyer said, awake now, ready for action.

"What are we going to do, Wayne?" Summersill whispered.

"We'll watch them a minute, then try to break out of here. That patch of trees probably contains a command post. No use staying here. They probably walk right by this barn all day long going from the trail to the trees."

They waited a few minutes. Then, with Sawyer leading, they struck off down the slope toward the trail, walking at a slow pace, with heads bowed, posing again as Korean peasants. Summersill quietly congratulated himself for getting Sawyer out of the barn. He did not feel guilty about the lie. He sincerely believed that if they did not get to the house, they would both die. "I got Wayne into this damned mess and I am going to get him out," he said to himself.

They branched off the trail and walked up toward the thatch-roofed mud farmhouse. Summersill walked ahead. As before, he would knock on the door, while Sawyer covered from the rear.

"If there are Communists in that house, I think I can get three or four, and maybe five of them, before they get me," Sawyer said.

"I think I can get two of them before I go," Summersill said. There was no talk of surrender. They knew that if they were captured, they would be killed. It would be better to go down fighting, taking as many of the enemy as possible.

Sawyer ducked behind a large tree about forty feet from the front door; Summersill walked up to the side of the house and knelt down among several shocks of straw. He put his ear against the mud wall. He could hear voices inside the house, but he could not tell how many people were inside, or whether or not they were Communist soldiers.

After a few seconds, Summersill reached around the corner of the house and knocked on the door. Now he could hear the voices inside babbling in low tones, apparently discussing the knock. Finally, an old Korean with a white beard and a fez hat stuck his head outside. Summersill grabbed the man by the neck with both hands, and literally jerked him through the door and around the corner of the house. He forced him to squat down in the straw. Summersill did not want anyone inside the house to see him just yet, and he did not want to attract attention from the outside.

While the old man watched nervously. Summersill took out an Air Force "pointee-talkie," a device containing fifteen or twenty sentences printed in both Korean and English, to be used in such emergencies. Summersill jabbed a finger at the sentence that read: "I am here to help the Korean people."

The old man did not seem to understand. Summersill pointed to another sentence. It read: "I am an American aviator." The old man again looked blank. Summersill pointed to another sentence: "I am a Christian." Then another: "Are you a Christian?" But the old man did not seem to comprehend.

Summersill put the pointee-talkie aside and spoke to the old man in broken Japanese. The Korean's eyes lit up faintly. Then, half in Japanese and half in sign language, he explained that he did not know how to read. He told Summersill he would go back inside the house and get someone who could. Summersill immediately suspected a trap; the old man would probaby come back outside with Communist soldiers.

Summersill looked toward the tree where Sawyer was hiding. Sawyer was aware that something was amiss. He was alert and ready. Summersill asked himself: what can we do? The man certainly was of no use outside. If the Communists were inside, they would come out soon anyway to find out what had happened. After a few minutes, he turned the old man loose and then signaled to Sawyer.

Sawyer, with .45 held ready, stepped from behind the trees into the open, facing the door. He made signs to indicate that he would start blasting the instant the first Communist soldier came out. Summersill remembered what he had said: "I think I can get three or four, and maybe five of them, before they get me." He nodded, then waved his knife, indicating that he would rush from the side. Then they waited. Summersill could hear the voices inside the house jabbering excitedly.

After about five minutes—it seemed like hours—the door cracked open. Summersill tensed. A Korean of about forty stepped around the corner. He seemed friendly. Summersill put away his knife. If the man was sympathetic, he did not want to appear hostile. Unseen, Sawyer stepped back behind the tree.

Summersill took out his pointee-talkie again. The Korean looked at it, shook his head, then pointed to his eyes. He apparently needed glasses. He would go back inside to get them. Was it a trap? The old man had gone back to get someone who could read! Summersill let him go, then once more alerted Sawyer. The two men once again braced for a rush of Chinese soldiers. In a few minutes, the Korean came out alone —wearing glasses.

Summersill gave him the pointee-talkie and again jabbed at the sentence that said: "I am here to help the Korean people." The Korean nodded his head and smiled as he read the sentence in Korean. Then Summersill put his finger on the sentence that read: "I am an American aviator." At that the Korean became very excited. He slapped Summersill on the back, smiled warmly, and shook his hand violently. He made signs to show that he was sympathetic. Still Summersill did not fully trust the Korean; it could be a trap to lure them into a houseful of Communist soldiers.

The Korean stood up and pulled Summersill by the arm, motioning toward the door. Sawyer stepped from behind the tree and walked up, his pistol leveled at the Korean. The latter got a glimpse of Sawyer out of the corner of his eye and turned pale. He jabbered excitedly, and waved his arms high in the air. He was very frightened. Summersill said in Japanese, "*Tamadachi. Tamadachi* [friend]." The Korean was relieved. Sawyer slipped his pistol back in his shoulder holster. The Korean slapped Sawyer on the back, pumped his hand warmly, then urged both men to hurry inside before they were seen by Communist soldiers.

The Korean pushed open the door to the house and entered. Before going inside, Sawyer and Summersill once again took out their weapons. Then they rushed in, quickly looking behind the door, into each corner, and inside an adjoining room. They found no one else except an old Korean woman. Summersill heard the old man and the younger Korean laughing. At first he thought it was a trick, that they were trying to put something over on them. Then he realized the Koreans were chuckling signs of admiration and approval at the thorough way in which the two airmen had searched the house. They relaxed.

The airmen felt it was important for their safety to make it perfectly clear to the Koreans that they were not hostile, and that they wanted to become friends. As a first step, they sat down on the floor and, in accordance with the polite Oriental custom, started to take off their boots. When the Koreans realized what the two men were doing, they rushed forward, shaking their heads. They had seen what the tired airmen had not—the boots were hopelessly frozen. No amount of tugging at the laces would undo them.

The old Korean bent down and rubbed his hands over the ice-coated boots. Then he spoke to the woman. She disappeared into the other room and returned with a flatiron, which she placed inside the *habachi*, the charcoal-burning urn in the center of the room. When the flatiron was hot, the old man pressed it against the laces of the boots. Gradually the ice melted. Sawyer's boots came off easily. Summersill's were frozen to his socks and had to be cut in several places. The socks had to be "ironed" to unfreeze them from his feet.

Once the boots were off, Sawyer carefully inspected Summersill's feet. He could see ice crystals under the surface of the skin. There was no doubt that they were frozen solid. The brittle feet reminded him vaguely of two pieces of beef that had been in a freezer for a long time. He noted that the skin of one heel had been ripped off, apparently while rolling off the socks. He told Summersill to take two of the sulfa tablets in the first-aid kit, to guard against possible infection or gangrene.

The old man got a large bundle of loose cotton and a bottle of oil. He sat down and carefully spread the oil over their feet, then wrapped them with the loose cotton. Then he spoke in Korean to the old woman. She looked pained and hesitated. He barked at her sharply, and she fairly flew into the other room and returned with a brand-new, white Korean shirt. He promptly ripped it into bandages, which he wrapped around the outside of the loose cotton.

"These people seem to know a lot about frostbite," Sawyer said to Summersill. "I guess the cotton is to keep our feet warm and keep us from bruising them, which you can do easily while they are frozen. The oil is to keep the cotton from sticking to the frozen part."

"Pretty savvy, huh?" Summersill replied.

Meantime, the old woman had been preparing food. First, she brought the airmen two bowls of steaming celery broth. This was followed by two heaping bowls of rice and cups of hot tea. As they ate, they told the Koreans—through the help of the pointee-talkie and sign language—who they were and how they happened to have been shot down behind enemy lines. They stressed that they had been doing everything possible to try to rid the Korean countryside of Communist invaders.

Finally, when they felt that they had the confidence of the Koreans, Summersill pointed to the sentence on his pointee-talkie that said, "Please find someone who can speak English and who can help us." The younger Korean got up and nodded. He put on his coat and hat, and then he was gone.

"Do you think we can trust him?" Sawyer asked.

"I don't know, Wayne. But what else can we do? We are committed to these people now. I've had it anyway," Summersill said. His feet were beginning to hurt. Every muscle in his body ached. He was so sleepy that he could hardly hold his eyes open. Within seconds, he rolled over on the warm floor and was asleep. Sawyer sat against the wall facing the door with one hand inside his jacket on his .45—just in case. But several minutes later he, too, was sound asleep. The Korean woman covered both of them with blankets.

When Summersill regained consciousness, he heard the sound of gruff, Oriental voices. The first thought that flashed through his mind was: Communist soldiers! The young Korean has betrayed us! He was so frightened that he could not open his eyes. He lay on the floor waiting for the slam of the rifle bullet, wondering vaguely if there was a way out.

But after a few minutes, when no rifle bullet came, he opened his eyes. Standing over him were two soldiers dressed in GI field fatigues. Summersill blinked, and then recognized the soldiers as South Korean. One man was a first lieutenant, the other a sergeant. Each held a carbine slung over his arm. They were arguing in Korean. Summersill rolled over on his back and shouted: "Hey, boys. I thought you were Chinese." He started to get to his feet.

The South Korean lieutenant smiled, and said, "Hey! Take it easy." He pushed Summersill back on the floor and cautioned him not to try to get up.

"You might bruise your feet," he said.

Summersill knew he ought to be terribly happy, and, in a way, he was, but somehow he could not express it. He said, "Hurrah," but it sounded flat. He shook the lieutenant's hand warmly. His tired eyes said the rest. He fired questions: How did you get here, by foot, jeep, or helicopter? How many of you are there? How did you find us? How far are the front lines? By then, Sawyer was awake plying the sergeant with questions. But the sergeant did not speak English.

The ROK told this story: The young Korean who lived in the house had run twelve miles to the front and then had made contact with the ROK's. The ROK's set out immediately in a jeep through enemy lines toward the house. They traveled as far as they could in the jeep—eight miles—and then parked it and came the rest of the way on foot. The area was heavily infiltrated by Communist guerrillas. They had avoided detection on the way in. The lieutenant explained that he was very anxious to start back because it was getting dark.

While the ROK talked, the old Korean and the younger Korean made up two crude stretchers from quilts and poles. When Summersill and Sawyer were asked to lie down on the stretchers, they did so without hesitation. Then they bade farewell to the old Korean woman, on whom they bestowed a token present: the sewing kit from the emergency vest. She waved farewell, and then the group, joined by several friendly Koreans who had been waiting outside the house, set off toward the jeep, four miles away.

The younger Korean and a friend carried Summersill's stretcher. The ROK sergeant and another Korean carried Sawyer. The lieutenant walked ahead, watching for Communist guerrillas. He found them soon across the wide river. They fired burp guns and Russian rifles, but the aim was poor, the distance great.

The lieutenant waved the stretchers off the trail and, when the airmen were safely under cover, returned the fire. Soon the guerrillas ceased firing, and the party resumed its hurried pace. They encountered several more Communist guerrillas who fired random shots across the river. Each time, the Korean lieutenant skillfully returned the fire and dissuaded the guerrillas from taking further action.

Two hours later, the group arrived at the jeep, which had been parked off the trail and camouflaged. Summersill's stretcher was placed over the right-hand seat, with one end resting on the right side of the engine hood. Sawyer's was laid across the back seat. The lieutenant got behind the wheel, the sergeant, the young Korean, and the old one and their friends jumped on board, and soon the jeep was bouncing speedily along the trail. The Koreans hung on for dear life.

Just before dark, the jeep reached a U.N. outpost. It was an advance element of the 5th ROK Division. By then, both Summersill and Sawyer were heavily doped with morphine that the ROK lieutenant had brought along. However, they regained consciousness long enough to say good-by to the friendly Korean civilians. Summersill reached in his pocket where he had some 40,000 Korean won (equivalent then to about ten dollars). He got out the pointee-talkie and pointed to the sentence that said, "I will reward you." The Koreans refused to take Summersill's money. The airmen took their names and arranged for them to receive other remuneration.

Soon they were off again, bouncing along the bumpy dirt roads. At a ROK medical aid station, the airmen were taken off the jeep and placed on pallets on the floor of a building. Small Korean children came to look at the strange Americans. They gave them pieces of their candy and two eggs. Summersill tried to smile, but his face was drawn and ached. Then he mumbled in Japanese: "You're very kind; thank you very much." Tears filled his eyes.

An American ambulance was sent from the 187th Regimental Combat Team, a paratrooper regiment that was on the line alongside the Korean division. The ambulance ride was very bumpy. Alone in the back, on stretchers, Summersill and Sawyer alternately cursed the driver and laughed like maniacs. At a U.S. aid station in Punggni, they were unloaded and fed "homemade biscuits," beef sandwiches, and hot coffee. On the front nearby, a fire-fight was in progress. There were several wounded GI's in the aid station. One of the GI's came over to Summersill, looked him in the eye, and said, "Boy, Lieutenant, you look like hell."

Later that night they were taken to Andong and loaded on board a hospital train bound for Pusan. When they had been tucked in bunks across the aisle from one another, Summersill said to Sawyer, "Well, buddy, we made it."

"Right, laddie," Sawyer said. He was still clutching his map. He had obtained the exact location of the Korean farmhouse. "We walked forty miles in forty-three hours without stopping," he said.

"That's not quite a mile an hour," Summersill said.

"That's right, laddie, but what miles they were," Sawyer replied.

In Pusan, Sawyer and Summersill were transferred to the hospital ship *Consolation*, which was anchored in the harbor. Then, after preliminary medical treatment, they were put aboard a second hospital ship, the *Repose,* which took them to Tokyo, where they were confined to a hospital. Within a few days, Sawyer was up and about. He lost only a tiny piece of his left big toe. He was later assigned to an Army unit that specialized in briefing men on how to survive behind enemy lines. Summersill's case was more serious. He was put aboard an evacuation transport plane and flown back to Walter Reed Hospital in Washington, D.C. There, in order to save his life, both feet were amputated at the ankles.

Early on his journey back to the States, Summersill remembered a vow he had taken on the mountainside. On the first hospital ship, he called for the chaplain, a robust, gregarious man, who opened the conversation by saying jovially, "When are you fellows going to stop cracking up those planes and save the taxpayers a little money?"

Summersill forced out a feeble smile. Then he told the chaplain of his experience behind the lines. He finished the tale by saying, "I have a debt to wipe out. How can I go about doing it?"

"Son," the chaplain said, "that is a problem that you will have to work out yourself." Before long he found his answer in the Catholic Church.

The worst part about the experience for Summersill was the fact that with the amputation, he lost forever not only his opportunity to fly fighters, but also his right to serve as an officer in the United States Air Force. As he well knew, there were no double amputees on duty in the Air Force; certainly none had ever flown an Air Force plane. But the new warmth and insight he experienced in "paying off the debt," as he put it, gave him hope and courage. While still in the hospital, he began looking around for a civilian job to supplement the disability pension he would receive on discharge. In record time, he was hobbling around with new artificial feet provided by the Air Force Medical Service, determined to make a good show of it.

Not long after he received his new feet, a young Air Force aviation cadet was brought to Walter Reed. He was put in a private room. Summersill and his friends learned, through the grapevine, that he had been badly hurt in an automobile accident. Ever curious and eager to make new friends, one day Summersill pushed his way into the isolated room and started up a conversation with the cadet. With great astonishment, he learned that he was Hoyt S. ("Sandy") Vandenberg, Junior, son of the Chief of Staff of the Air Force.

As the days and weeks passed, Summersill and young Vandenberg became good friends. They talked of flying. Vandenberg hoped that his injuries would not—as Summersill's had—deprive him of flying status. Summersill told Vandenberg of his experiences and how badly he hated to leave the Air Force to go back to civilian life.

One night, several weeks later, Summersill, who by then was fairly proficient with his new feet and had taken to going out in the evenings on dates, pushed his way into Sandy Vandenberg's room, asking:

"Sandy, what time does the dining room at Bolling Air Force Base close? I have a date and I want to take her there."

He noticed that the door would not open fully. It seemed to be pushing against something. Summersill peeped around it and looked squarely into the face of Sandy's father, General Hoyt Vandenberg. He backed off and came to attention. For a minute, he felt about as tall as a pin.

"Dad," Sandy said, "this is Lieutenant Summersill, a friend of mine."

Vandenberg, who was wearing civilian clothes, put out his hand. Summersill shook it.

"Well, excuse me," Summersill said, "I have to be going."

"Come on in, Clem," Sandy said. As Summersill walked in and leaned politely against the hospital bed, the younger Vandenberg turned to his father: "Clem here was a Mosquito pilot in Korea. He was shot down and walked out through Communist lines in the snow. But he froze his feet, and they had to be amputated. He wanted to make a career of the Air Force, but now he must get out."

"You want to stay on in the Air Force?" General Vandenberg asked.

"Well, yes," Summersill said. "But there are no double amputees in the Air Force."

"Why don't you come over and talk to me?" General Vandenberg asked. "Make an appointment tomorrow."

"Yes, sir, I certainly shall." Summersill saluted smartly and backed out of the room.

Summersill called General Vandenberg's office, and an appointment was arranged for the following day. He brought along his cane. He was not yet too steady on his feet, but when Vandenberg opened the door to let him in, Summersill left his cane in a corner and walked, for the first time, without support.

Summersill sat in a leather chair facing Vandenberg's desk. The General offered him a cigarette, which he accepted, then he said: "Tell me all about what happened."

Vandenberg listened with great attention to Summersill's story. When he finished, the General asked:

"Well, why do you want to stay on duty in the Air Force? You can have a pension and probably make a pretty good go of it."

"Well, sir," Summersill replied, "I'm not looking for a soft touch. I like to fly. I like the Air Force. I believe I can still be of value to the Air Force."

General Vandenberg stared out the window toward the Potomac River for several minutes. Then he spun around in his chair and pushed three buttons on the squawk box on his desk. Voices answered crisply. "Come up here, will you please?" Vandenberg asked each one. Within minutes, three generals appeared in the office. By then, Vandenberg was dictating a special order, which, for the first time, permitted a double amputee to remain on active duty with the Air Force. Vandenberg turned to the generals, who were grouped around Summersill's chair.

"I want you to look around and see if we have a job for this man. As long as he can do his job efficiently and satisfactorily, he will wear an Air Force uniform."

The Air Force generals quickly found a job for Summersill, working on the Air Staff in the Pentagon. Not long afterward, he married a former Army nurse, and they set up housekeeping in nearby Arlington, Virginia. Summersill became so proficient in the use of his artificial feet that he could do almost anything, including flying an airplane.

CAVE MAN

THE twin-engine B-26 bomber sped southward. Beneath its stubby wings, the frozen North Korean countryside slipped to the rear. Ahead, the capital city of Pyongyang lay on the horizon. Captain Donald S. Thomas, a lean, twenty-eight-year-old Air Force navigator-bombardier sat in the copilot's seat, writing on a clipboard that was affixed to the knee of his heavy winter flying suit. His notes included such items as "one truck destroyed near Sinanju," "bridge strafed," "dynamite dump burned." He finished his report thus. "All ammo expended. 1/14/51, 0830. Checking K-24 for possible activity." In order to get a good view of K-24, an enemy airfield at Pyongyang, they approached the city at three-hundred-feet altitude.

When the first blast of small-arms fire struck the ship, it sounded to Thomas as if someone had thrown a handful of gravel against the fuselage. The firing kept up until the pilot pulled the B-26 up out of range, somewhere near the center of the city. But it was too late. The plane had already caught fire. The gunner who manned the rear-facing, top turret was first to notice it. He called Thomas and the pilot on the intercom. About the same time, they smelled the smoke. The pilot opened the plane's bomb bays and, over the intercom, asked the gunner if he wanted to bail out. The gunner did not reply.

The pilot climbed the burning plane to seven hundred feet. Then he unbuckled his safety belt and got ready to jump. Thomas laid a hand on his arm and said, "Hold on." Thomas did not want to bail out over Pyongyang, where they were sure to be captured and perhaps shot on the spot. He knew of an area near the west coast where a group of Christian Koreans lived. He had been told that they were friendly. If they could reach the area, they might get help. Thomas pointed to the spot on his map and the pilot nodded. He turned the flaming plane toward the coast. Then he told the gunner of the plan, but again, the gunner did not reply.

The plane was a mile from the coast and very near the Christians when the control wires burned through and it abruptly dove out of control toward the ground. Thomas jerked a bright yellow handle, and the overhead escape hatch jettisoned, and the pilot climbed out. When Thomas attempted to follow him, he discovered that he was caught in his seat. At that instant, a great flame whooshed up into the cockpit from the nose tunnel and burned the helmet and hair from his head. A second flame set his left glove on fire. He beat out his burning hair and yanked off the glove, only to find that skin hung down in shreds from the top of his hand.

Thomas had begun to pray because he believed the end was near. But suddenly, without knowing when or how, he was flung out of the plane. He bumped against the rudder and then floated quietly through the air beneath the white silk canopy of his parachute. He watched the plane crash into a rice paddy, then he looked for the pilot and gunner. They were not in the air. He could not see their parachutes on the ground. Then he realized that they had met with misfortune in bailing out, and he was alone.

Remembering that a parachutist ought to hit the ground in a limp position, Thomas tried to relax. It turned out to be an unnecessary precaution because the parachute caught in a small tree and held him, as if in a swing, dangling in his harness. He touched the quick-release button and fell to the ground. It was then that he noticed for the first time that his right hand was injured. It appeared to be broken, just behind the wrist. Thomas guessed that he had cracked it on the rudder. His left hand was severely burned, and many of the nerve ends were exposed. With some difficulty, he took off his yellow Mae West and tossed it into the bushes.

In the last minutes inside the burning plane, Thomas had laid out his plans for the immediate future. They centered around escape. He had made up his mind that, no matter what, he would not be taken prisoner by the Communists. Somehow, he would make his way back to South Korea. The first step, he decided, was to try to make contact with the Christians. He knew this would not be easy, since there were large numbers of Chinese and North Korean troops about. If he succeeded in finding the Christians, he would talk to them and see if they had any sort of underground or any ideas on how he could make his way through to friendly lines. He had money—about ten dollars—and an Escape and Evasion Barter Kit, containing a watch, ball-point pen, and other trinkets that would be useful in bargaining with the North Koreans. He also had his .45 in case he ran into any trouble.

The plane burning nearby was sure to bring Communist troops, so Thomas began walking away from it as soon as he got out of his parachute. It was very cold. The temperature in the air before they bailed out had been thirty-five degrees below zero. The ground itself was like concrete. But, except for his bare head and hands, Thomas was not at first uncomfortable. He wore seven layers of clothing, including two sets of underwear, wool shirt and trousers, a wool flying suit, an electric flying suit, a birdcloth flying suit, and great fleece-lined jacket and winter flying trousers. His feet were covered by two pairs of socks, GI shoes, wrap-around electric boots, and finally, large fleece-lined winter boots.

Thomas climbed a dirt dike that skirted the rice paddy in which the plane had crashed. From this vantage point, he planned his route through the labyrinth of ditches and mounds that formed the rice paddy. He selected a drainage ditch that led more or less toward the southwest, the general direction in which he wished to go, and slid down into it, holding his injured hands above his head. Then he was off, walking at a rapid pace away from the plane.

He had not gone far when he saw the faces of two small Korean children peering over the edge of the ditch. He stopped. He could see that they were very frightened. Before he could make a sign, they had run away—in opposite directions.

Thomas stood for a minute staring after them, not knowing what to do. They would spread the alarm, but he knew he could not go after both of them. He thought: Anyway I could not catch either one of them, weighted down by this heavy winter flying equipment. For want of a better plan, Thomas continued following the ditch. When he reached a point where the ditch turned north, he climbed out; and then he saw that the children had lost no time. A North Korean stood in each of the rice paddies around him. He was surrounded!

He ducked back below the lip of the ditch and with his burned left hand pulled his .45 from his shoulder holster. But he did not have strength in either hand to work the gun mechanism that would put a shell into the chamber. Since it was of no use to him at the moment, and he could not be sure whether the Koreans were friend or enemy, he put the gun away. Just then one of the North Koreans peeped over the edge of the ditch. Thomas raised his hands and climbed out. The North Koreans—about fifteen in number—gathered around him. One of them pointed toward the burning aircraft. He nodded.

Thomas silently cursed himself for the way he had conducted his evasion. If I had hidden away instead of trying to move in daylight, he thought, they would not have caught me. Surrounded by the fifteen men, he walked through the rice paddy toward a mud hut. The Koreans were unarmed, and they did not attempt to search Thomas. He began to wonder. Are they Christians? Are they friendly? On the way to the house, one of the Koreans put a fur-lined hat onto his bald head. Was this a friendly gesture?

Luck was with him. Once inside the house Thomas learned that the Koreans were indeed friendly. One of them produced a small can of salve with the word "penicillin" written on the outside, and dabbed the reddish paste across the top of his burned hand. Another Korean put cotton waste on top of the salve, and bandaged the hand with a piece of white cloth. Meanwhile, several of the men asked Thomas if he wanted to go to "Kyongsong" (Seoul). Thomas said, "Yes." He could see that they were very concerned about his presence and were anxious for him to move on. As soon as they had finished bandaging his hand, they opened the door and pointed southward, which as Thomas knew, was the direction of Seoul. Thomas returned the hat that had been loaned to him, waved good-by, and turned west toward the coast, walking as fast as he could.

The land between the Korean hut and the coast consisted largely of rice paddies carved out of reclaimed marshland. There were no houses in sight. As he threaded his way through the checkerboard of frozen irrigation ditches, dikes, and icy ponds, he kept low and stopped only to rest or to collect his bearings. Soon he began to perspire. In such cold weather, he knew this was dangerous, so he unzipped his jacket. This was an exceedingly painful operation because Thomas's hands were not only injured, but numb from the cold. When he stopped to rest, he cooled off rapidly—too rapidly—with the result that he had to close up his jacket again. Then, as soon as he began walking, he had to open the jacket again. And so it went. Each time he moved the zipper he suffered.

Long before he reached the coast line, Thomas had discerned the outlines of what appeared to be a massive wall. As he got closer, he could see that the wall was an earthen levee, specially constructed to keep the Yellow Sea from flooding the rice-paddy lowlands. He wondered if the wall, like the bridges in North Korea, was patrolled by Communist soldiers. He approached with extreme caution, keeping in the protection of an irrigation ditch wherever possible. There was not a soul in sight.

The back side of the levee was not steep. Thomas easily crawled to the top. He lay down on the frozen dirt and looked around. The levee stretched, in both directions, like an elevated road, as far as the eye could see. He noticed that about every hundred yards, a hole had been dug into the top. Thomas guessed these were gun emplacements that were manned during the summer months, to guard against possible invasion. There was no danger of that now; the Yellow Sea was frozen solid for almost a mile out. Soon Thomas began to shiver. The sweat on his body was beginning to freeze again. He realized he must push on.

He slid down the side of the levee, and zigged through a rice paddy. Farther south he entered a woods. He was glad of the concealment it offered. He darted from tree to tree, bush to bush, stopping only to adjust his clothing. He left the woods and came into a field that was covered by a thin blanket of snow in which his boots left enormous tracks, obviously those of a military man and not a Korean. He stopped and tried to take off the boots. But he was not able to unfasten the straps and buckles. He continued on, avoiding the snow whenever possible.

About one o'clock in the afternoon, he came upon a small village, tucked in behind the levee, which blocked his way ahead. For a long while, he watched the mud huts for signs of Communist troops. He saw none, but nevertheless, made up his mind to give the town a wide berth. He set off on a detour that would take him through woods behind the village, and then bring him out near the levee farther south. He was but halfway around the village when he saw a North Korean leave one of the huts and come in his direction. The North Korean carried a rifle.

Thomas was very frightened and angry. Once again, he berated himself for getting caught in the open. Hoping he might bluff his way to safety, he walked on hurriedly, watching the Korean out of the corner of his eye. The Korean came within three hundred yards, raised his rifle, took careful aim, and fired. When the bullet whizzed over Thomas's head, he did not flinch. He kept walking as if nothing happened. The Korean, apparently a policeman who felt he had done his duty in protecting his village with the one shot, tucked the rifle under his arm and walked back to his house.

Thomas was greatly disturbed by the incident because he was sure that the Korean would spread the alarm to the Communist soldiers in the area. The Communists would then know that an American had survived the plane crash and would have a good idea of his whereabouts. They would send searching parties into the area, and he could not hope to elude or outrun them. Where were the Christians? He knew that if he did not make contact with them soon, he would be in serious trouble.

He hurried on, trying to put as much distance as possible between the village and himself. Two hours later, he made his way back to the levee. He scaled the earthen slope and set off along the top, hoping that from his vantage point, he could see any houses—hopefully Christian—that lay among the rice paddies and distant foothills. He had made up his mind to stay away from the thickly populated areas. They were apt to be guarded by Communist soldiers, or police such as the one who had fired at him in the last village.

He had not gone far along the levee when, in the distance, he spotted a man coming in his direction. Thomas jumped down the side of the levee and made his way to a group of bushes, where he hid until the man had passed. Then he crawled into an irrigation ditch, and ran in the opposite direction at top speed. Several minutes later, he came up out of the ditch and was surprised to see a mud house wedged in behind the rear slope of the levee. He decided to approach it. It was still light and a poor time to make contact, but Thomas was anxious to get out of sight.

He watched the house for several minutes, and then he got up and walked boldly up to the front door and rapped loudly. An old woman opened the door and peered out. When she saw Thomas, her eyes became wide with fear. Thomas raised both hands, in a sign of friendship, and smiled. She seemed somewhat relieved but kept one eye on Thomas's pistol holster. Thomas took out his pointee-talkie, and gave it to the woman, pointing to the sentence that read: "I am a Christian." But the woman shook her head, indicating that she could not read. She nodded toward two other Korean houses about fifty yards away, suggesting that Thomas go there. But he did not want to leave, so she called out.

A boy of about fourteen years of age came out of one of the mud houses and walked toward them. Meanwhile, Thomas got out several other pieces of identification. One item was a three-by-five card with an American flag on the top and a message that said: "I am an American aviator. Please help me and I will help you." Thomas gave the papers to the Korean boy. He read them and became very excited. He made signs to indicate that Thomas should wait where he was for a moment. Then he ran back toward his house.

The old woman, meanwhile, had brought Thomas a bowl of water. He gulped it down and waited. Several minutes later, half a dozen Koreans of all ages and sexes came out and stood around watching Thomas from a distance. The boy came back and returned the papers. In no uncertain terms, he made it clear that Thomas was not welcome and that he had better walk south. The old woman concurred. She went back in her house and slammed the door.

The cold reception was a grievous blow to Thomas. It was apparent that he had picked the wrong house. The Koreans were obviously hostile. They were probably pro-Communist. He thought: How stupid! I have tipped my hand again. He climbed back up on the levee and hurried south as fast as possible. He knew time was running out. Within minutes, the Koreans would have notified the soldiers. He was very tired and confused and did not know what to do.

He had walked about a mile farther along the top of the levee when he suddenly heard shouts. He fell to the ground and stretched out, his heart pounding wildly. The shouting continued. He looked down the beach side of the levee and saw an old Korean hurrying along through the ice and snow. He was waving a black and white coat in the air, apparently trying to attract Thomas's attention. What was this? Did the Korean wish to talk? Thomas got up and walked back along the levee until he stood directly above the man. The man raised his hands as a sign of friendship. Thomas returned the gesture. He motioned for Thomas to climb down the levee.

When they came face to face, the old Korean grabbed Thomas's broken right hand and shook it firmly. Thomas almost doubled up from the pain, but he gritted his teeth and did not cry out. He was overjoyed to find a friend and did not want to complicate matters by seeming ungrateful. The Korean was very friendly. He drew a cross in the sand, and Thomas knew he was a Christian. Then he draped the coat around Thomas's shoulders, put a fur-lined cap on his head, and motioned for him to walk down the beach in the direction from which they had both come. The old man, hands placed on his hips Korean fashion, walked along the top of the sea wall to keep guard.

About a mile down the beach, they came upon a small sampan that was frozen in the ice. The Korean motioned for Thomas to climb in the boat and hide inside the cabin. Thomas hesitated. What could the old man have in mind? he asked himself. The ice was frozen for at least a mile out. Certainly the boat was not going anyplace. But the Korean seemed very worried about the Communists and kept waving Thomas on. Thomas opened the small cabin door and lay down on the deck. He did not know what the old Korean planned to do, but whatever it was, it certainly was better than anything he could devise himself.

He lay on the deck of the boat cabin for several hours. It was the first time since the crash that he had had an opportunity to think clearly. He thought about his wife, Margaret, and their six-year-old boy, who lived at an Air Force Base in Northern Japan. Soon they would receive the "missing in action" report. What would happen to them? Had he been a fool to re-enlist in the Air Force? The sales job in Birmingham was going very well. He had almost doubled his salary between 1945 and 1948. Another promotion was in the offing. Yet, he had given this up for the stripes of a buck sergeant. He had told Margaret he had "ants in his pants." It was more than that. It was some sort of indescribable urge to fly, to move around, to seek adventure.

He had been sent first to Guam, and then to Tachikawa Air Force Base, Japan, where he was stationed when the Korean war broke out. Although he was serving in peace-time as a sergeant, he had maintained his Reserve status as a commissioned officer. Thomas was "recalled to active duty" as a captain and assigned to B-26 bombers as a navigator-bombardier. This was a job he had performed in World War II, flying thirty B-17 missions against the Nazis, and later serving as an instructor in the U.S. He was an outstanding bombardier. Late in World War II, he had been selected to help work out the tactics and techniques of the dropping of the first atomic bomb.

After a month's refresher course in Japan, Thomas moved back into the swing of things. He flew his first two combat missions from Japan on September 1, 1950, when the U.N. forces were still trying to fight their way out of the tight Pusan perimeter. As U.N. forces drove the enemy back into North Korea, the bombers reached farther and farther to the rear, until some of Thomas's missions were six hours in duration. Often they returned to base in Japan with only a few gallons of fuel remaining in the tanks. They flew at night, bombing and strafing enemy supply lines, bridges, roads, trains, and trucks. Occasionally they flew in the daytime, as they had on this, his thirty-ninth mission.

It was completely dark when the Korean returned to the boat. He rapped on the outside of the hull, and Thomas came out of the cabin. Then, huddled in the dark, they conversed, using the sign language and bits of Japanese. The Korean explained that he lived in one of the two houses in back of the old woman's where Thomas had first stopped. When the young boy had brought the pointee-talkie to him, he wanted to help then, but he couldn't. The old woman was a Communist and very dangerous. If he had offered help to Thomas, she would have turned all of them in to the authorities.

He had let him walk away purposefully to deceive the woman. Once Thomas was out of sight and the Communist had gone back inside her house, the old man had come in pursuit, with the idea of offering help. He had brought the coat and hat as a disguise to hide his flying suit. He had hidden him in the boat until dark so that he could sneak him to his house without the woman or Communist soldiers being the wiser.

Thomas nodded to show that he understood. Then, to help cement the friendship, to let the Korean know that he understood he was helping him at grave risk to himself and family, he took a watch from his Escape and Evasion Barter Kit, and gave it to the man. The Korean took the watch, carefully wrapped it in a piece of cloth, put it in his pocket, then he motioned for Thomas to get on his feet. The two men crawled out of the boat, walked across the ice to the beach, scaled the levee, then slid down the other side.

After a roundabout journey, which took them on a wide detour around the Communist woman's house, they came to the rear of the Korean's house. The man, whom Thomas had named "Old Papasan," as a gesture of friendship, pushed open the door of the house, and they walked in. A Korean whom Thomas judged to be about thirty-seven years of age was sitting on the floor near the *habachi*. He got up, came across the room, and grabbed Thomas by the hand. Again, Thomas almost collapsed from the pain. But he held a smile on his lips. Old Papasan explained that the younger man was his son. The son seemed very concerned when he saw Thomas's wounds. He bade him sit down and take off his heavy clothing.

Like most Korean homes, the hut was small and sparsely furnished. In addition to the main room, there were two smaller adjoining rooms, a kitchen and a storage room. The big room had a solid mud floor, like concrete. In one corner there was a bookcase containing several battered books, one of which Thomas recognized as a Bible. A small crock stood in another corner. This, Thomas knew, was the toilet. A long chest occupied another wall. The room was warm, almost stuffy, and it smelled of cooked onions.

The old Korean's son, whom Thomas immediately named "Young Papasan," was very friendly. He introduced Thomas to his wife, a woman of about thirty, and his son, aged about eleven, and an older woman, whom Thomas judged was Young Papasan's mother. The wife—Thomas called her "Mamasan" —became very excited when she saw Thomas. She ran back into the storage room and put on a brilliant orange silk dress. Thomas realized that, in typical Oriental fashion, she was dressing in honor of the "guest." He tried to make the point that he certainly was not a "guest" in the traditional sense, and he hoped that she would not unnecessarily trouble herself. But he was unable to get across such a complicated message, and he finally let the matter drop.

While Young Papasan helped Thomas take off his boots, shoes, and jacket, Mamasan scurried about in her dressy costume preparing dinner. At length, she produced a sumptuous— for the Koreans—feast, including a plate of vegetables, a bowl of sweetened rice, a side dish of sea-gull meat, tea, and raw eggs. They sat down on the floor to eat, but when Thomas tried to manipulate his chopsticks with his broken arm, they fell out of control. Young Papasan examined the arm and shook his head.

Mamasan solved the problem by giving Thomas a big brass spoon. He ate everything except the raw eggs. After supper, they smoked and talked. Young Papasan and his wife seemed relaxed, but Thomas could tell that Old Papasan was worried that the Communist soldiers might be searching the area for the downed airman. Using the ballpoint pen to draw pictures, they asked him all kinds of questions: Where had he crashed? Where were the other crewmen? Was he married? Did he have children? Where did his family live?

As the evening wore on, Thomas began to feel dizzy. At first he believed it to be the effect of something he had eaten. But after a while, he realized that the trouble stemmed, not from his digestive tract, but from somewhere else in his body. He felt his forehead and found it was very hot. Was he coming down with influenza or pneumonia? He had had a slight cold when they took off on the mission and had been coughing throughout the day, but it had not occurred to him that he had fever. This could be a very serious handicap.

At length, they all ran out of small talk. Thomas then directed the conversation toward a subject that he had deliberately avoided thus far: his escape. What would he do? Where could he go? They talked about it a long time, about the large number of Communist troops between their position and the front lines. They talked about his wounds and about his developing fever. The old man advised Thomas to stop with them for several days or perhaps a week, until his hands were better, and until the fever had gone away. Then he could lay plans for the long walk south. The other Koreans nodded their assent.

Thomas was very grateful for the hospitality. He told the Koreans that God would bless them for offering protection to a fellow Christian. He also told them that the U.S. military forces would keep a record of the act of kindness, and when the war was over, or when it was otherwise possible to contact the family, they would receive a reward. Old Papasan made signs to indicate that they cared nothing for the reward. Thomas was a persecuted Christian among atheists. That was enough for him. He was willing to stake his life—and the lives of his family—to help him escape. In effect, the old Korean said, "The fraternity of God transcends political factions."

Old Papasan had one request to make of Thomas. He said: "You Americans are very impatient. It would be very bad if you became restless and tried to go on prematurely. If you were caught—which you almost assuredly would be—I, and my family, might become implicated. And that would be very bad for us. They would kill us all." He told Thomas that they could work out an escape plan after he was well. Meantime, to make sure he did not run away, Old Papasan asked that Thomas turn over his papers, his gun, and his GI shoes. Thomas felt this a fair bargain under the circumstances, but before giving the Korean his gun, he removed the cartridge clip.

When this transaction had been completed, Old Papasan motioned for Thomas to put on his fleece-lined boots. Apparently he had established a hideaway for Thomas, someplace outside. But Mamasan objected strenuously. She went to Thomas, placed her hand on his forehead, and shook her head. "The aviator is a very sick man," she told the others. "He had better be kept inside the house, at least tonight." But Old Papasan had other ideas, and a violent argument broke out. Finally, the argument was settled in favor of Mamasan. As Thomas came to find out, Mamasan was the guiding power behind the men. Her word was law.

Not long afterward, Old Papasan began yawning, and he said that he was going next door to his house and go to bed. Mamasan and Young Papasan thought that was a good idea. When the old man had gone, Mamasan went to the storage room and brought out several blankets and comforters, including an extra large one, which she gave to Thomas. Then the four Koreans and Thomas lay down, side by side, on the floor —warmed by the chimney flue that ran underneath—and put their heads on a hard, roll pillow. Soon, the Koreans were snoring soundly. Thomas experienced some difficulty in getting to sleep.

His fever had gotten steadily worse. His throat was parched, and his body ached from lying on the hard floor. He was lonely and began to worry. He had put his whole faith in these simple Koreans. Were they capable of seeing him through? Would he ever get back? If so, how? Friendly lines were still 115 miles to the south. He thought about his wife and son, and he could not sleep. Once, when Young Papasan got up to use the toilet, he asked for water. The Korean gave Thomas a package of

brownish powder, and told him to swallow it, but he was reluctant to give him water. Koreans do not believe in giving
liquids for fever.

Before dawn, Old Papasan returned to his son's house and
knocked on the door. Young Papasan got up, and after a hurried conference, shook Thomas, and told him to get up. By
then, Thomas was very ill. He tried to stand up alone, but his
legs were like rubber. The two Korean men helped him up on
his flying boots, wrapped the comforter around him, and half-
carried him from the hut. The early morning air was cold and
brittle. Thomas wondered vaguely where they were taking him.

About a half-mile from the house, the men turned into a rice
paddy. After walking a few yards down a drainage ditch, they
stopped and balanced Thomas on his feet. Old Papasan bent
over and picked up a piece of straw matting that lay on the
slope of a paddy dike. The matting had covered a hole in the
bank about thirty inches in diameter. Old Papasan crawled
into the hole and disappeared. Young Papasan handed his
father a few items through the hole, including some straw
matting, an old broken kerosene lamp, a bowl of rice, and the
comforter that had been draped about Thomas's shoulders.

After a few minutes, Old Papasan called out, and Young
Papasan helped Thomas into the hole. Thomas discovered
that the hole was a tunnel leading into a cave about three
feet in diameter and about six and a half feet long. This was
the hideaway. Old Papasan and his son had made it the evening
before while Thomas lay hidden in the boat. It was well appointed: the floor and sides were covered by straw matting held
in place by wooden pegs. Old Papasan hung the kerosene lamp
by a cord to another peg. He spread the comforter over the
floor, and placed a small basket full of apples in one corner.

Thomas lay down alongside Old Papasan in the cave, and
they conversed for several minutes. The Korean made it clear
that the cave was to be Thomas's new home—at least for a
while—and he was not, under any circumstances, to leave it,
either during the day or night. Old Papasan reminded Thomas
once again that there were numerous Communists in the area.
He was concerned particularly about the suspicious old woman
who lived nearby. It was important that she not have the slight-
est inkling of his presence. Thomas nodded to show that he understood. Old Papasan said he would return after dark, and
then he was gone.

The cave hideaway was far less comfortable than the
Korean house, but Thomas realized that it would be very
dangerous to remain so exposed. He was impressed by the
thoroughness with which Old Papasan and his son had planned
things. At least he could be assured that they would do nothing

rash, and that every precaution would be taken to keep secret the fact of his presence.

Thomas discovered that he could just barely sit up in the cave. He ate his bowl of rice with the brass spoon, then he munched on an apple. He took out a cigarette—he had about three left—lit it with a match Old Papasan had given him, took several drags and then snuffed it out. He knew he would have to stretch the cigarette a long way. He experimented with the wick of the lamp, turning it up and down to test the brightness, then he lay down to sleep. There was not much else he could do.

Sometime during the day, Thomas awoke with the feeling that he had been crying out. He felt his forehead. He was burning with fever and perspiring all over. He tried to take off his jacket, but his hands had both swollen to twice their normal size, and he could not pull the knitted cuffs over them. This fact led to further complications: his trousers were held on by suspenders. Since he could not get his jacket off, he could not remove his trousers, and thus he was not able to have a bowel movement. He rolled over and went back to sleep.

Later, Young Papasan came to the cave and pushed a second bowl of rice in through the tunnel. Thomas remembered that incident clearly, but little else. By then, he had become completely delirious from the fever. His mind was a whirling dervish of dreams and nightmares. He wept, laughed, coughed, moaned. Young Papasan took care of Thomas as best he could. Twice a day, in the morning before daylight, and evening, just after dark, he came to the cave with food and spoon-fed him. He gave him the brownish powders to help his fever.

On the third day—Thomas was still delirious with fever—Young Papasan became very concerned about his burned hand. It was still swollen and had begun to bleed. The Korean brought a pail of water from his house, crawled inside the cave, and soaked the wounded hand. Soon, the old bandage had loosened and he was able to remove it without tearing off too much skin. He doctored the wound with a milkish-white liquid that he kept in a sea shell, and then wrapped it in a new bandage. He examined the right wrist but did nothing about it because he believed it was only sprained.

Thomas awoke, and when he saw Young Papasan, he asked him to bring more water, so that he could wash his face. Half an hour later, Mamasan returned to the cave with a second pail and a rag. She rubbed Thomas's face. When she rinsed the rag in the water, she shook her head in wonderment; the water was black. The reason was that Thomas had not yet washed his face since the crash, and he was still full of soot and smoke smudge. The kerosene lamp had added its own layer.

The washing episode was but a brief oasis in Thomas's

desert of nightmares and fever. Soon he was delirious again, pawing at the comforter, babbling incoherently. His fever continued to climb until it seemed impossibly, even absurdly high. Thomas believed that he was dying. In the brief periods that he was awake—not insanely drifting out of his mind and body —he ate and then he prayed. His prayers were unconventional since he had never taken pains to memorize a large number. But, while conversational in character, they got the point across, and Thomas believed he had made peace with his Maker.

But Thomas did not die. He held on to his thin thread of life somehow, fighting the fever, without medicine, without hospital sheets, without anything, really, except an incredibly stubborn will to live. One morning he awoke, and his head seemed clear. He stared at the smoke-smudged straw mat on the ceiling of his cave for a long time, and then somehow he knew he had fought his way through. When Young Papasan brought his rice that night, he ate heartily and talked a blue streak. The Korean was relieved to see Thomas feeling better.

The next day a technical problem of significant proportions arose. The walls of the cave, once firmly frozen and solid, had begun to melt from the heat of Thomas's body. Thomas first noticed it when one of the pegs holding the side matting fell out. Then the lamp peg gave way, followed shortly by others. Large chunks of dirt fell on Thomas. When he told Young Papasan of the situation, the Korean became very concerned. A few hours later, he returned to inform Thomas that a new cave had been dug and that he was to be moved.

The new cave was located in the back yard of Young Papasan's house, about twenty feet from the back door and on a parallel with the outhouse. Strictly speaking, it was not a cave: Young Papasan had dug a hole in the ground about the size of a grave. He had placed boards over the top and then covered the lot like the remainder of the back yard, with a profusion of oyster shells. At one end of the hole, he had dug an adjoining "L." This was fitted with a trap door that served as the entrance.

On the way to the new hide-out, the Koreans carried Thomas inside Young Papasan's house for a visit. Although his head had cleared considerably, he was still so weak that he could not raise his arms. They laid him, still bundled in his heavy flying clothes and the comforter, out on the warm floor. Mamasan felt very sorry for Thomas, so she bathed his face and changed his bandage, made him a warm broth, and fed it to him with the brass spoon. She shook her head again and again to indicate that she believed Thomas to be a very sick man. Young Papasan stood by in the corner watching. Old

Papasan was very nervous. He could not relax when Thomas was inside the house.

Soon the visit came to an end. The Koreans picked up Thomas and carried him through the back yard to the trap door of the new cave. They lowered him inside and laid him out on the straw-mat floor; then they replaced the trap door and covered it with oyster shells. Once again, Thomas was overcome by the feeling that he had been sealed in his grave, buried alive. He lay for a long time watching the flickering wick of the kerosene lamp, thinking.

When it became daylight, Thomas was pleasantly surprised to discover that his architects had thoughtfully provided his cave with a picture window. It consisted of a small hole about the size of a half dollar that had been left open in the center of the roof. A bright cone of sunlight fell from the opening to the center floor of the cave. By squirming into one end of the cave, Thomas could get his eye directly under the hole, and after he had become used to the dazzling light, he could make out bits and fragments of clouds drifting by in the sky overhead.

Thus, he lay for the greater part of the day. He sent himself soaring above the clouds, bound for Tokyo and his home. From there, his magic carpet took him back to his wife's home in Birmingham, back to his childhood days in Pennsylvania, back to the farm, to the night of his father's premature death, to his mother's side while she taught school, to his uncle and grandmother's farm. All the places and events that had shaped his destiny and propelled him forward so that he could fight for his life and sanity on the floor of a cave in North Korea paraded before him.

From time to time, dirt fell through the hole into his eye, thus bursting the bubble of fantasy. Or else, the barking of Young Papasan's dog jarred him off his carpet. Sometimes it was the slamming of the door on the outhouse, or visitors crunching through the shells in Young Papasan's yard. Thomas became alert to every sound. He welcomed the intrusion, because it gave him something fresh to think about—new raw material for his mental gristmill. He was too weak to do anything but think.

Quite often his mind turned to thoughts of escape. He fully realized that the longer he stayed in one place, the greater the chance that the Communists would discover him. Sooner or later, he believed, someone was bound to make a mistake with a slip of the tongue, or otherwise accidentally make known his presence. He was particularly concerned about the children. While they had been specifically cautioned not to talk, there was always the chance that one might brag to one of his playmates. But there was nothing Thomas could do for the time being. It would be foolhardy, if not impossible, to push on without first recovering his strength and the use of his hands. Nevertheless, it required every bit of patience in his body to lie still in the cave.

Days passed. Thomas did little other than lie on his back and think or else sleep. The interminable confinement was broken only occasionally by the bark of the dog, or by the scratching of Young Papasan at the trap door with another meal. Mamasan realized that life in the hideaway was maddeningly dull so she did everything she could to help, especially in fixing the meals. One night she included a side dish of vegetables; the next, a little sugar for the rice; or a dish of onions or sea gull. Once, Thomas was surprised to find a side dish of meat, which had been cut into half-inch squares, broiled, and buried in gravy. He thought: beef. What a luxury! He ate every bit of it.

Then suddenly he remembered that there were few steers in North Korea. Young Papasan had certainly never owned one. Where could they have obtained beef? But if the meat was not beef, then what was it? With an appalling jolt, Thomas remembered that he had not heard the familiar barking of the dog all day! Had they slaughtered the poor beast in his behalf? Thomas was on the verge of dismissing the thought as nonsense when Old Papasan appeared at the trap door. He made signs to indicate that he had a new and wonderful present that would help Thomas keep warm. It was a brand-new, dogskin coat.

Thomas thought he might become ill, but he did not. He suffered no gastronomical bad effects from the experience at all. Psychologically, it was a different story. He had visions of the dog bounding about the back yard. He could see Old Papasan racing about trying to catch it. How had he killed it? Which portions had they saved? When he went to sleep that night, he pulled the new dogskin coat up over his shoulders. It gave him a peculiar feeling. He was certain that he was the first, and perhaps only, Air Force officer who had ever devoured an animal, and then, that very same night, slept under its fur.

Often during the evenings, or during the long days, Thomas's thoughts turned to his wife. He wondered where she might be, what she had done when she had received the "missing in action" report. Had she gone back to the United States or was she still in Japan? He wondered if he might contact her through mental telepathy. In the evenings, when he believed the atmosphere to be free of most disturbances, he lay on his back and repeated over and over to himself: "Margaret, I am alive and

safe. I'll be home sometime." This pastime soon grew into a
carefully prepared ritual that took place every evening. It was
a useful way to pass time.

The fever slowly got better, but try as he might, Thomas
could not stop coughing. Several times, Young Papasan came
to the cave in the evenings, extremely concerned about the
noise. They fed him sugar and water and several other home-
made concoctions to try to soothe his throat, but none of them
worked satisfactorily. Finally, Old Papasan came out one night
and told Thomas that they would have to move him to another
cave, one that was far away from the house. They could not
take a chance on Communist soldiers coming by and discover-
ing Thomas through his coughing. Thomas agreed that it was a
good idea to move. One by one, he passed his small collection
of junk, the lamp, the brass spoon, the basket of apples, the
comforter, up through the trap door.

With the Koreans pulling both his arms, he squeezed up
through the small opening. When he tried to stand, his knees
buckled, and he fell over. The Koreans helped him to his feet
and half-carried him through the back yard, across a field, to
the bank of an irrigation ditch about two hundred yards from
the house where the Koreans had dug a third cave. Thomas
crawled inside and lay down on the mat. He was breathing
heavily. He realized that he was still so weak that he could not
walk. He thought: How lucky I was to find these Christians.
Surely I would be dead by now if I had not.

The new cave was similar in detail to the others, with straw-
matted walls, a board ceiling, and a trap-door entrance. However, the Koreans were improving at their trade, the third cave
was much better built than the others. It was, in fact, practically airtight. Thomas learned this when, on several occasions,
he lapsed into a coma for want of oxygen. It was difficult to
keep the lamp lit. Thomas had finally to resort to keeping
the trap door propped ajar with a stick. That way he was also
able to get a little light during the daytime.

On the second day in the new cave, the tenth day since the
crash, Young Papasan brought a small bag of crushed wheat
and gave it to Thomas along with a pail of water. He explained
that the Communist troops had intensified their search through
the area. They had found his parachute and had pretty well
figured his route, after talking with the village policeman and
the old woman in the nearby hut. It was conceivable that because of the presence of enemy troops from time to time they
might not be able to bring him food. "In that case," Young
Papasan explained, "you mix the wheat with water and eat
that."

Thomas lay in the new cave for seven days. Then one night

Young Papasan came to say that he would have to move again; they had begun to wear a path to the entrance and it was a dead giveaway. Thomas packed his belongings again and moved to the fourth cave, which had been dug inside a rice paddy, some distance from the house. While he was not able to walk by himself, Thomas noticed that his strength had improved considerably. He hoped it meant that his general health was improving. He had no way to gauge, except through these short walks. Several nights later, when they moved him to a fifth cave, he was able to walk the entire distance by himself.

Then, all at once, Thomas's health seemed to improve rapidly. His coughing stopped, and his burned hand began to heal. His cracked right hand, which he had previously wrapped in an oil-silk aerial map, seemed to be getting stronger. This noticeable improvement in his physical well-being caused his morale to soar. He began to think in earnest about escape, and every night, when Young Papasan brought his rice, he engaged him in long conversations about the possibility. But Young Papasan would not hear of it. He would only say, "Be patient. Be patient." He did not believe Thomas was well enough to begin preparations for the escape. In the evenings, after Young Papasan had gone, Thomas stole out of his hideaway for several minutes at a time and did calisthenics to strengthen his muscles.

Thirty days passed. Meanwhile, Thomas had become fully fed up with his subterranean existence. One night, after getting nowhere with Young Papasan, Thomas became quite angry and demanded to see Old Papasan. The old Korean—on one of his rare visits—came out to the cave, and he and Thomas talked a long time. Thomas told him that he believed his health had improved sufficiently to permit him to carry out whatever escape plans the Koreans had drawn up. Thomas could see that Old Papasan was not ready, so he became very impatient and made it very clear that he was ready to be off. Finally Old Papasan gave in and promised Thomas that by the following evening, he would have an escape plan.

The next evening, as promised, Old Papasan returned to the cave with a plan that he had worked out in detail. He would go to Pyongyang, the North Korean capital, he said, and get a truck. He would bring the truck back to his house, load Thomas in the back, and they would drive toward South Korea, getting as close as possible to the U.N. front. Then they would abandon the truck and go the remaining distance on foot. Or, they might even signal a U.N. plane in some fashion. He drew lines on a map to show the route.

Thomas was very skeptical. The plan seemed impractical. Where would Old Papasan get the truck? How could they possibly drive through the Chinese or North Korean armies with-

out being stopped, or worse, strafed by U.N. aircraft? He
pressed Old Papasan for details, being careful not to seem too
skeptical lest the Korean become hurt or peeved and abandon
all idea of trying to save him. After some hours of talk, they
agreed to postpone the final planning for several days, until
Old Papasan could collect more information.

Before they had an opportunity to resume the conversations,
a naval vessel appeared off the coast and began firing large-
caliber shells over Papasan's house, at Chinampo, a city that
lay several miles inland. Both Young and Old Papasan became
extremely concerned about the firing—the shells literally
whistled over their rooftops all day long—and Old Papasan
forthwith canceled all plans to go to Pyongyang, or any other
North Korean city. The escape plan was put off indefinitely.
Old Papasan would not move from the safety of his house
until the naval vessel had steamed away. As he lay in his cave
listening to the shells rattling overhead, Thomas was suddenly
very annoyed at the Navy.

A week passed, and then another. The naval vessel—
Thomas could not tell from his cave what type it was—would
not go away. It lay off the coast day after day, lobbing incredible numbers of shells overhead toward Chinampo. Then
one day the thought suddenly occurred to Thomas: if he could
get out to the ship in some way, he would be rescued. He cursed
himself for not having thought of the idea sooner. That night
when Young Papasan brought his food, Thomas was very
excited and told the Korean to go fetch his father.

Old Papasan understood immediately when Thomas drew
a picture of a boat with himself standing in the bow, pulling
alongside the naval vessel. But he shook his head, and took
the pen and drew lines around the boat. What could this
mean? Then Thomas understood. The boats were all frozen
fast in the ice. But, he asked, couldn't one be broken loose?
The old man shook his head again. They would have to wait
for the ice to melt. How long would that be? About three
weeks, Old Papasan said. Then after careful deliberation, he
wrote the figures "10 March 1951," on a piece of paper.
That was his estimate of the day when the ice around the
boat would be melted.

Thomas was disappointed. He believed that if he had to
spend another three weeks in the cave, he would go out of
his mind. By then, the naval vessel might have sailed back to
Japan or South Korea, or the Communists might have discovered his hiding place. He asked the old Korean if there was
not some other solution. Didn't someone have a boat on dry
land that they could launch across the ice? The Korean shook
his head. Was there no other way to get out to the ship? Old

Papasan shook his head again. They would have to wait.

For several days, Thomas lay in the cave, listening to the steady blasting of the naval vessel's guns. Should he give up the idea, or should he try to break out and walk south? He tried to imagine what the Escape and Evasion Handbook would say. All of the lectures that he had attended urged fliers wherever possible to get in a boat and head for the open sea where they could be picked up either by friendly planes or by naval vessels. They had been cautioned to avoid, wherever possible, walking through enemy lines, or through places where the enemy was known to have large numbers of troops. The one word that had been stressed over and over and over through the lectures was patience.

But, Thomas thought, the men who had spoken of patience certainly had never endured anything like this entombment. True, he had been ill for four weeks, and he had not had much choice in the matter. But now he was well and able to take action. Was this really a time for patience? He might go on living in these caves for months. But was that worse than being captured by the Communists? Perhaps they would not shoot him, he thought.

And so it went, the little debate in the cave. In the end, Thomas decided that the Air Force officer who suggested patience was right, and that it would be foolish for him to leave his kind benefactors and try to make it south alone. He would wait for the ice to melt.

One evening not long afterward, Old Papasan came out to the cave in company with a strange man about sixty years of age. Old Papasan explained, by the usual pictures, that the friend owned a boat and that his boat would be available to carry Thomas out to the naval vessel when the ice melted. Old Papasan's friend was very amiable. He smiled a lot and, toward the end of his visit, produced from beneath his white coat, a large tin of corned beef, which he presented to Thomas as a token of friendship and trust. Needless to say, Thomas received the meat with great appreciation.

The days passed slowly. In the late afternoon of February 21—he kept track of the date with a homemade calendar —Thomas awoke with a peculiar feeling. He looked around the cave, and suddenly noticed that water was leaking down the sides. Rain! This caused him some concern, because he knew that his cave lay in a low point in the rice paddy and that all the rainwater would inevitably drain into his cell. As the minutes went by, the leaking became more profuse, and soon water was trickling in between the boards in the roof. Thomas pulled his blankets and clothes to one side, and did what he could to stop the leaks or to drain off the water. But the walls

of the cave, moistened by the water, began to break off and
fall to the floor.

By the time Young Papasan arrived with his evening meal,
Thomas was near panic. A vast quantity of the cave had fallen
in around him, and he was all but buried beneath the dirt, his
clothes and blanket soaked. Young Papasan's eyes widened
when he saw what had occurred. He dug the dirt from around
Thomas and then helped him bundle up the clothing and other
items. They hurried through the dark to Young Papasan's
house.

Thomas welcomed the opportunity to sit by the warm fire
and chat with the Korean family once more. It had been thirty-
eight days since he spent his first night in Young Papasan's
house. Where it had at first seemed drab and uninviting, it
now seemed like one of the coziest and most comfortable
places Thomas had ever seen. He stretched out on the floor,
wallowing in the luxury of space. Mamasan brought him
food and hot tea and then they all talked about the escape.
Thomas asked about the condition of the ice. It was melting,
gradually reaching back toward the boats. The tenth of March
was still the date, but it was two and a half weeks away.

Then they discussed where they should build a new cave
for Thomas. There were a number of problems. For one thing,
they were running out of building sites. The Communist troops
were still snooping about. There was the problem of moving
Thomas from the cave to the boat when the escape date approached. Suppose the Communist soldiers moved into the
area and blocked the way to the coast? After a long discussion
of these and other factors, the Koreans finally decided to build
the new cave down alongside the levee, just in back of the spot
where the boat was frozen in the ice. Thomas concurred in the
decision, since he thought it a good idea to be near the boat.

The new cave—his sixth—was dug into a field about fifteen
feet from the base of the levee, at a point twenty minutes'
walk from Young Papasan's house. It turned out to be much
harder to build than the others. For one thing, it was very near
the beach. When the Koreans dug down, they struck water,
and they had to line the bottom of the cave with boards to keep
the floor dry. Moreover, the cave was near a heavily traveled
area—the levee—and the Koreans were not able to work on
it for long periods at a time. In the end, more than two days
were required to complete it. Thomas was hidden in the shell-
covered cave in Young Papasan's back yard—near the outhouse—in the interim.

Early on the morning of February 24, Young Papasan
came to the trap door of the back-yard cave and scratched
away the shells. He motioned for Thomas to get ready to

move, and as usual, Thomas passed out his collection of furniture and equipment. Young Papasan loaded it aboard an A frame, and soon they were off, hurrying through the dark. On the way, the basket fell from the A frame. The lamp broke and spilled kerosene over a tiny bag of sugar that Thomas had used to sprinkle on his rice.

As soon as Thomas crawled into the new cave he knew he would not like it. He could tell that it was damp, and he worried about developing tuberculosis. But worse than the dampness was the fact that the cave was so shallow that he could not sit up inside it. He could just barely turn over. The cave was the nearest thing to a grave that he had ever seen. He pulled himself halfway out of the trap door, but Young Papasan made signs to indicate that he had better keep under cover.

They talked for some minutes through the trap door. Thomas complained about the size of the cave. Young Papasan was very apologetic. He explained that they had done everything possible to facilitate the escape, and that this consideration had outweighed comfort. After a while, Thomas could see that he was getting nowhere with the Korean so he resigned himself to the fact that he would have to stay where he was. He had lived underground for forty-one days under the most uncomfortable conditions. He made up his mind that he could stand anything for fourteen more—until the magical date of March 10.

Before leaving, Young Papasan was careful to explain that the cave had been dug in a heavily traveled area. Soldiers and civilians, he said, used the levee as a pathway both during the day and at night. Under no circumstances should Thomas come out of the cave. Even at night, it would be extremely dangerous. Thomas agreed to stay under cover, in spite of the fact that he knew his body would become cramped. Young Papasan reminded Thomas that he might not be able to get down to the cave every morning and evening. Then he went away.

Thomas squeezed back into the cave and stretched out on his back. Almost immediately, he felt the loss of the kerosene lamp, which at least had supplied light. Now he would face the next two weeks in utter darkness. He tried to eat his morning rice, but he found that in his position, it was difficult to swallow. He turned on his stomach. This was closer to a natural eating position, but his arms were still too weak to support his weight. Finally, he devised a position, half on his side, and half on his stomach, that he could maintain without undue discomfort during mealtime.

As in the other caves, daydreaming became Thomas's chief

preoccupation. He lay on his back most of the time staring up into darkness, thinking and planning. Every hour and a half, he smoked a cigarette—Young Papasan had given him a large supply of Korean tobacco—and ate one quarter of an apple. Occasionally, he broke into song. Singing was not a manifestation of happiness or joy, but simply a means of killing time. He sang every song he knew and after a while, composed his own. "Dixie," "The Marine Corps Hymn," and the Air Force song, "Wild Blue Yonder," were his favorites. They were stimulating and built up his morale.

Every evening Young Papasan came to the cave with two reports. The first was a report on the "State of the Ice." He would show, with pictures, just how far the ice had receded, and how much farther it had to go before the boat would be freed. March 10 was still the date. The other report was a brief summary of the war news. Old Papasan had a friend nearby who had a radio. He listened to the Voice of America broadcasts, then passed the information to Young Papasan, who, in turn, gave it to Thomas by way of a series of drawings.

These two reports usually contained enough material to feed Thomas's imagination throughout the remainder of the night. When he ran out of daydreams and tired of singing, he spent his time trying to make contact with his wife. Every evening, and often during the day, he repeated over and over: "Margaret. Margaret, Can you hear me? This is Don. This is Don. I am alive. I am alive. I will come back. I will come back."

To help pass time, Thomas kept two lists. The first consisted of a series of questions that he would ask his wife when he first reached her by telephone. He was worried about a number of things. What had she done with his uniforms? His pay records? Had she closed the bank account in Tokyo properly? This list, which Thomas kept on the back of a piece of paper in tiny print, quickly grew to 128 questions. The other list, written on another piece of scrap paper, consisted of gifts he would buy when he returned to Japan. These items included an ivory chess set for himself, a watch for his wife, and a toy boat for his son.

During the first several weeks of his entombment, Thomas had, through some miracle, avoided becoming infested with body lice. The only itching he experienced in the early days was that caused by his growing beard. Now, at last, the tiny vermin found him. To all of the discomforts of the new cave was added the maddening sensation of bugs crawling across his body. He tried not to scratch, but he could not restrain himself. He was not even able to search out the lice, or shake them from his clothing. He could only lie on his back and suffer.

This agony went on for six or seven days. Then one evening Young Papasan appeared at the cave with a blanket. He opened the trap door and said, in effect: "Move over," and he crawled into the tiny cell. When he had settled himself alongside Thomas, he explained that North Korean Army officers were in the area, looking for "draftees" for the Army. Young Papasan wanted to hide until they had gone. Thomas kept Young Papasan awake all night with his scratching. The Korean was very annoyed. Soon he, too, was scratching.

The following evening, he went back to his house to get some food, and when he returned, he brought a U.S. Army tin of DDT powder, which he said he had obtained from the U.S. Army when it had marched into North Korea in the fall of 1950. Thomas was overjoyed. He sprinkled the powder all over himself—not without some difficulty—the cave, his blankets and clothes. Thomas kept the precious can on hand, and thereafter he was not annoyed by the bugs.

The days of March passed with incredible slowness. More than once, Thomas made up his mind that he could not stand it any longer, that he would bolt the cave and walk to South Korea. Always at the last minute he changed his mind. One reason was that the ice continued to melt, just as Old Papasan predicted. It was only a question of time. As March 10 drew nearer, Thomas occupied himself by planning every step of the escape in minute detail. Then one morning Young Papasan came to the cave smiling from ear to ear. With great formality he announced that on the evening tide of the following day, they would put out to sea.

For Thomas the next twenty-four hours seemed an eternity. Finally Young Papasan came back. But when Thomas saw his face, he knew that something had happened to interfere with the departure. It turned out that nature had dealt Thomas a low blow. As Young Papasan explained it, the ice had been melting right along on schedule. Then, during the afternoon of the day before, the wind had suddenly shifted. Instead of a pleasant breeze from the southwest, there came a frigid blast from the north, straight out of Siberia. The Yellow Sea had frozen quickly, and all the progress of the last two weeks had been wiped out in one blow! It pained Young Papasan to relate this news. Thomas could not help himself. He wept.

How long would it take for the ice to melt again? Young Papasan had already consulted his father on the matter. Two more weeks, at least. Thomas broke down and sobbed again. Could he stand this subterranean existence for another fourteen days? What if the ice failed again? Should he not try an alternate escape plan? Was he out of his mind, lying in the caves day after day, week after week, month after month? The questions raced wildly through his mind as he ate his rice and apples. When he finished eating, he turned over and stared at the straw mat that covered the wall of his cave.

Old Papasan heard that Thomas had not taken the news well, so the following evening, he paid a visit to the cave. Thomas was still in very low spirits. The Korean tried to comfort him, but Thomas was in no mood for pity. He had reached the end of his rope and wanted nothing but to get out of North Korea. Old Papasan sat for a long while thinking. He became very concerned about the situation. He was especially worried that Thomas might pull some rash act and get himself captured.

Finally the old Korean spoke to Thomas. How much, he wanted to know, was the reward he would receive for getting Thomas back to friendly lines? Thomas explained that the "blood chit" was worth 200,000 won, the equivalent of a year's earnings. "But if it's money you want," Thomas said, in effect, "I can get you a lot more than that. I can get you all the money you need." But Thomas could see that Old Papasan did not want money simply for the sake of having it. He was not avaricious or greedy. He was thinking of something else. Thomas could see that a new plan was forming in the old man's head.

At length, Thomas learned what it was. Old Papasan believed that if he got enough people together, perhaps fifty good men, they might, with a concerted effort, rock the boat loose from the ice, then lift it up, and scoot it along until they reached open water. But such an undertaking would necessarily raise questions in the minds of the people from whom Old Papasan sought help. They might guess the truth. In due time, the Communists would discover what had happened, and there would be more questions. Old Papasan said he might try such a thing, but if he did, he would have to escape with Thomas, and take his entire family along. Otherwise, they would eventually be shot by the Communists.

Thomas was struck by the magnitude of Old Papasan's proposal. Was he willing to uproot his whole family, to leave his two homes, his farm, his country, simply for the sake of delivering Thomas to friendly lines? Yes, Old Papasan was willing, provided the reward was sufficient to re-establish himself and his family on a farm in South Korea comparable to his own. He did not want anything over and above that. Thomas hastened to assure Old Papasan that the reward would be ample for his requirements. He said that if it wasn't, he would give to him out of his own pocket. He would see that they obtained a new farm, new houses, and whatever seed and equipment was needed. Thomas was ready to promise the world to Old Papasan, but he was conservative. He did not want to disappoint him later. At length, it was agreed that within the next few days, Old Papasan would collect together a group of his friends, and they would try to break a boat clear of the ice.

Two days later, when he brought his breakfast, Young Papasan told Thomas that the big day had arrived. More than fifty men had been rounded up, and they were ready to try to free the boat. Several hours later, as Thomas lay in the cave trying to picture the scene that was taking place on the ice just over the levee, he heard aircraft engines in the distance. When they drew nearer, Thomas recognized the sound of the engines. The planes were friendly. Then suddenly, he heard the planes dive toward the ground. Machine guns opened up. For over half an hour, the air was filled with a fearful racket as the planes strafed along the beach.

At first, Thomas could not for the life of him imagine what they had been shooting at. But, by the time Old Papasan came to the cave after dark, he believed he knew. The Korean confirmed it: The planes had spotted the gathering of men on the ice alongside the frozen boat. Believing that some kind of military operation was in progress—the North Korean soldiers often disguised themselves as civilians—the planes had strafed the men who were helping Old Papasan. Fortunately the aim had been poor, and none of the Koreans had been hit. They had scattered like deer and run for the hills. But Old Papasan shook his head sadly. He knew he could never get them to return.

Another escape plan had been shattered! The irony of it, Thomas thought. He made a notation on his calendar. When he returned, he would certainly see that somebody got chewed out. Having attended to that, Thomas turned back to face the problem. There was no longer an alternative. Old Papasan could not risk himself and his family again. They would simply have to wait for the ice to melt, hoping that word of the strafing and unusual activity on the ice did not reach the Communists. Old Papasan set the new departure date at March 22.

Somehow, Thomas hung on for ten more days, lying on his back, staring blankly at the ceiling. But when March 22 came, Young Papasan produced a drawing to show that the boat was still held fast in the ice. Old Papasan set a new date: March 25. On that day, Thomas once more got all ready to leave. He was disappointed again. Young Papasan brought another picture to indicate that a shift in the weather had slowed the melting rate. Old Papasan reset the departure for 11:00 P.M., March 26.

At ten thirty the night of the twenty-sixth, Old Papasan and Young Papasan came to the cave and whispered for Thomas to come out. Thomas collected his clothing, cigarettes, papers, boots, and lice powder, and squeezed up through the opening, and for the first time in thirty days stood up and breathed the fresh night air. Young Papasan made signs to indicate "This is it!" and after a hurried conference, the three men ran through the dark to a nearby clump of trees. Thomas's legs were very weak, and his feet felt as though they were swollen so the Koreans helped him along.

Two other Korean men joined them in the trees. To Thomas's amazement, they proceeded to take off their clothes. One of the men motioned for Thomas to get on his back. When he was in place, the naked Koreans carried him piggy-back up over the levee, across the beach, and then waded through frigid water about seventy-five yards out to the boat. After everyone was aboard, the still-naked Koreans set two masts in place, raised a badly patched cloth sail, and soon they were headed toward open sea. For the first time in seventy-one days, Thomas breathed easily.

The sampan seemed seaworthy enough, although it leaked rather badly because it had been out of water for some months. It had two small holds. The forward hold contained a cook-stove, and Mamasan made it her headquarters. Thomas was put in the rear hold, which was not much larger than his cave, but deep enough to sit up in, a fact that seemed a luxury in itself. Altogether, including Thomas, there were thirteen people on board the thirty-foot craft. There was precious little food and water.

In conversation with Old Papasan, Thomas learned that he had brought all of his family except the old woman, who refused to leave, and only what clothes and possessions they could carry on their backs, including a photograph album. Old Papasan didn't want to leave pictures of himself and his family lying about, lest they fall into the hands of the Communists. The owner of the boat—the man who had earlier brought Thomas the can of corned beef—had brought along his son and several other Koreans to help operate the craft.

They began a search for the Navy as soon as the sampan's sails had flown full. The naval vessel that had been shelling Chinampo had long since steamed away. A debate broke out about whether they ought to head the craft north or south once they had reached open sea. Thomas voted to head di-

rectly south toward Inchon, or any other friendly port. Old
Papasan had another idea—he wanted to go north toward
Sinanju. He had heard that Navy ships had been shelling
that North Korean port recently, and he believed it could be
reached in less time than it would take to sail south. In the
end, Old Papasan had his way. They turned north.

The trip to Sinanju required two days. During the period,
they encountered no Navy ships. When they arrived in the
general area of Sinanju, there was still no sign of the Navy.
Thomas was becoming increasingly concerned, both because
they were almost out of provisions and because they were
moving farther and farther behind enemy lines. On the evening of March 28, Old Papasan, who had fished the waters
for more than fifty years and knew every rock and shoal, ordered the boat moored to a small, craggy island about four
miles off the coast.

The island was deserted. But, as Old Papasan knew, it contained a spring, and they went ashore and filled the water
casks. After dark, the Koreans sneaked up into the rocks
and grabbed several roosting sea gulls. That night Mamasan
prepared the birds for supper, and Thomas thought he had
never tasted anything so good as sea-gull meat. Since the
island had peaks that were taller than the deck of the sampan
and they could consequently search a wider area of water
for the Navy, the decision was made to remain anchored at
the island.

They remained on the island for two days without sighting a single ship. Thomas was very discouraged and quite concerned about falling into enemy hands. As if to confirm his
worst fears, late in the afternoon of March 30, two strange
boats came to the island and anchored. Thomas got his gun
from Old Papasan, then climbed high into the rocks to hide.
He remained hidden for a full day, until Old Papasan came
to report that he had made a "deal" with the owner of the
largest of the two junks to take them aboard. They moved
on board the new boat after midnight. It was much larger
than the first boat and had been in the water all winter and
did not leak as much.

Old Papasan took only his immediate family—Young
Papasan, Mamasan, their son, and his own younger son—
aboard the new boat. There were already a number of Koreans
aboard, and after they had settled down, Thomas counted fourteen besides himself on the craft. The following morning,
they cast off and sailed in a southerly direction.

They searched everywhere for the Navy, but without success. A day passed and then another. Then the owner of the
new boat became worried about sailing around in the open

sea. The year before, on the very same boat, his father had
been killed by strafing planes. They anchored at another island
to take on fresh water and sea gulls, and soon they were off
again fighting rough seas, lice—they were aboard the boat
in large numbers—cold, and a critical scarcity of food. Where
was the Navy? Where were they? Thomas could not answer
either question.

After they had wandered aimlessly in open sea for more
than a week, Thomas lost his patience. He approached Old
Papasan and told him that they must lay out a route that
would either intercept a naval vessel or take them in the
direction of Inchon. Old Papasan agreed. He was also concerned about the lack of progress. He immediately conferred
with the boatowner, but the latter refused to head for Inchon.
Moreover, he announced that he was ready to go back to the
beach and give up the whole expedition. Old Papasan relayed
the bad news to Thomas.

Thomas became extremely concerned. He made up his
mind that he would mutiny before he would sail back to the
mainland. He checked his .45, and put in a fresh clip. Then
he talked with the owner, but the Korean would not listen. He
had made up his mind that he was not going south to Inchon,
and that was that. Thomas went up into the bow of the sampan to think. He knew the time had come for a showdown.

Then Thomas had an idea. He scurried about the boat, collecting some old pieces of cloth and some flour, and made up
a batch of gooey paste. He spread it on a piece of black cloth,
then sprinkled some of the white flour over the glue. He
spelled out the message "American on board" in big letters.
Then he mixed a piece of charcoal with water, and painted
the same message in black on a white piece of cloth. When
he had finished, he called the owner and explained that he
would hang the signs on the mast stays, and if a plane came
over, the pilot would see the signs and withhold fire.

The old Korean shook his head negatively. He was not
convinced. Then Thomas played his trump. He pulled out the
$10.46, which he had been saving since he had crashed. He
showed it to the boatowner and told him it would buy 40,000
won, which Thomas would give him if he would turn the
boat toward Inchon. The Korean was obviously impressed,
but still he wavered. It was Mamasan who finally won him over
completely. She told him of Thomas's wife and child, and
insisted that the owner do everything within his power to help
reunite them.

By April 6, Mamasan had talked the owner into going all
the way to Inchon. But there was another delay; they had to
sail back to one of the islands near Sinanju for water. It was

a two-day journey. On the morning of the seventh, Thomas came up on deck to look around. They were only two hours' sail from the island where they would take on water and, if possible, sea gulls and then around and head south until they reached Inchon. Thomas was satisfied that everything, for once, was in order. He was just going back below to get an apple, when one of the Koreans yelled, *"Koonan! Koonan!"*

Thomas knew this meant ship. He hurried back up on deck. There on the horizon, coming in their direction, was a destroyer. The Koreans changed course and headed toward it. Thomas rigged his two flag signs, then he ran to the bow and began waving a white flag he had made for that purpose. Two Korean boys held his legs so that he would not fall. After an hour, the destroyer came within range, saw the junk, and hove to.

It was eighty-three days, almost to the minute, since the crash, when Thomas climbed aboard the destroyer, a British vessel, the H.M.S. *Cockade*. There are no words that can describe the joy he felt on being rescued. He opened his mouth to speak to the skipper and was embarrassed. A childhood speech affliction had returned. He could only stutter. He tried to explain about Old Papasan, Young Papasan, Mamasan, and the rest, but the words would not come. However, the British officer got the general drift and invited all fourteen Koreans to come aboard. The junk was taken in tow, and soon they were under way.

The ship's doctor took charge of Thomas immediately and examined him thoroughly. He discovered that Thomas's feet were swollen and explained that it was from a lack of protein in his diet. The speech affliction, he said, was a temporary emotional situation that would soon go away. The doctor also told him he would soon gain back the thirty pounds he had lost. Under the doctor's supervision, Thomas was given a bath and haircut; his magnificent red beard was cut off, and he was shaved. One of the British gobs furnished a set of bell-bottom trousers and a black turtle-neck sweater, and for the first time in almost three months, Thomas felt clean.

At ten thirty he was escorted to the captain's quarters, where he was treated like royalty. He sat down to what the captain described as "breakfast." It began with a full water glass of Scotch whisky, which oddly had no effect whatsoever on Thomas. He ate eggs, bacon, toast, and drank coffee. When he had finished "breakfast," the captain informed him it was lunchtime, so he sat right where he was and ate a full lunch consisting of two *filet mignon* steaks, French fries, vegetables, milk, and ice cream. Afterward, the captain escorted Thomas to the radio room. A message informing his wife that he was alive and safe was prepared. Then, on orders from the captain, the *Cockade* broke radio silence, and dispatched the message, via Fifth Air Force Headquarters.

The *Cockade*, bearing her usual cargo, set course for Inchon. Enroute, Thomas sought out Old Papasan, and gave him the "blood chit," as well as several other identification papers, which would enable the U.S. Government to provide him and his family with a reward. On arrival at Inchon, the Koreans and their boat were dropped at the refugee island of Tokchok-Kundo. With tears in their eyes, the Koreans embraced Thomas and said, "God's care." Thomas was taken to Fifth Air Force Headquarters.

As soon as he had completed the necessary Intelligence interrogations, and obtained new uniforms, pay, etc., Thomas was flown to Japan, where he immediately put in a long-distance telephone call to his wife, who had returned to her home in Birmingham, Alabama. After the initial exchange during which he discovered that his wife had never given up hope and had, as a matter of fact, only recently left Japan, Thomas took out his list of 128 questions. To the exasperation of his wife, who wanted to talk about his experience, Thomas ran through the entire list. The phone call cost him almost a hundred dollars. Afterward, he took the other list, bought the presents, and then flew to the United States.

The childhood stutter persisted. As a result, Thomas voluntarily requested relief from flying status. He was reclassified as a supply officer and assigned first to Maxwell Air Force Base, and then to the Northeast Air Command with headquarters in Newfoundland. When the Korean War was over, he learned that he had achieved the dubious distinction of remaining behind enemy lines without being captured longer than any other U.N. pilot.

Through an unavoidable accident, Old Papasan and his family were temporarily lost among the tens of thousands of refugees on Tokchok-Kundo. They were forced to sell the sampan in order to buy food. They were down to their last bag of rice when Fifth Air Force Intelligence Officers, after a relentless search, located them living in a hovel. The Air Force evacuated the fourteen Koreans to Pusan. There, they were awarded a vast sum of money—the equivalent of twenty-four years' pay for Old Papasan—two houses, and a new boat. Old Papasan established a fishing business and in the end he and his family fared well.

TIGER OF THE IMJIN

By April, 1951, the U.N. front in Korea had been stabilized roughly along the thirty-eighth parallel. The over-all objective of the war had been shifted from "gaining real estate" to "attrition," or killing as many Chinese soldiers as possible. U.N. troops were well dug in. Heavy artillery had been brought to the front. There were aircraft available for close-support missions. Each time the Chinese attempted a breakthrough, they were effectively dealt with. But the important battles were then being fought in the air as Far East Air Force bombers and fighters, under command of one of the Air Force's brightest generals, O. P. Weyland, ranged over North Korea, cutting the flow of enemy supplies and destroying MIG-15's at the rate of thirteen to one.

Under ordinary circumstances, the isolation of the battle-field in North Korea would not have been a difficult proposition for Weyland's Air Force. However, a political decision by the President had prevented his aircraft from crossing the Yalu River, where the Chinese maintained their major supply depots and rail centers. Thus, the Chinese were able to move supplies with impunity to distribution points just across the Yalu. From there, they were hauled the remaining short distance to the front at night, when Weyland's planes were operating at a disadvantage. The result was that in spite of all efforts of the Fifth Air Force, the Chinese were able to sneak troops into the battle zone and keep them supplied, at least with minimum equipment.

On April 23, word was received through Intelligence that

a large number of Chinese troops had been brought into North Korea, and it seemed obvious that the Chinese were building up for at least one final assault against the U.N. front. General Weyland was told to locate the Chinese concentration and destroy it, if possible, before the attack could occur. The big unanswered questions were: When would the attack come? And where?

Air Force First Lieutenant Melvin J. Shadduck, a Mosquito pilot based at Field K-6 about thirty miles south of Seoul, pondered these two questions as he sat in the quonset briefing hut on the morning of April 23, drinking a last-minute cup of coffee. Shadduck was twenty-seven years old. He was small and wiry, and he had tough hands and a bushy shock of hair. The Squadron Intelligence Officer gave him his instructions.

"You will fly with the U.S. Third Division. Report to Hazard Control as before." The officer pointed to the briefing map. The Third Division was strung out across the Chorwan-Seoul highway, the traditional invasion route to the South Korean capital. The Imjin River protected its left flank, ROK troops the right.

"We have an idea," the Intelligence Officer continued, "that the Communists might be massing in front of the Third for a breakthrough. Keep your eyes open. There will be plenty of fighter-bombers to work with you this morning."

Shadduck nodded. He knew the situation well, and he had flown over the area often. When he left the briefing hut, his mind turned to other things. He pulled out and read for the third time that morning a letter he had received from his wife. She was very ill, confined to a hospital in Chicago. The three children, all girls below the age of six, were living with his mother-in-law, who was not well either. He was needed at home. As he reached the wing tip of his plane, he folded the letter absently and put it back into the pocket of his green wool shirt.

He checked his T-6 aircraft over prior to take-off and once again began to worry about his wife and children. Through the Red Cross, Shadduck had previously been advised of the seriousness of his wife's illness; they had informed him that following an operation, complications had set in. He had applied for emergency leave, but the leave had been denied: pilots with Shadduck's qualifications were in urgent demand, and the war took priority.

However, the Air Force had made one big concession: it had waived the usual two or three months' tour at Fifth Air Force Headquarters following front-line combat. Shadduck had been told that in light of the illness, he could expect transfer back to the U.S. immediately after he had completed his hundredth combat mission. On receiving that word, Shadduck had launched an all-out program to complete his hundred missions. He had turned down the usual rest leaves and had been flying two and sometimes three missions a day, remaining over enemy territory for eight and nine hours.

As he climbed into the cockpit of the T-6, he was eager because it was his eightieth mission, and he had only twenty more to go. At two per day, he knew he could be out of Korea within ten days, and on the eleventh day he would be on the way to Chicago. He tightened his seat belt and shoulder harness and looked back at his observer, Technical Sergeant Jack E. Gauldin, a GI from the Eighth Army.

Shadduck said, "Hey. I thought you were supposed to be on leave?"

"Well, I was," Gauldin said, "I was waiting for transportation to Tokyo. The Operations Officer came up and said your observer couldn't make it today because he was sick, and he asked me if I would mind flying this mission while I waited. I said, 'O.K.'"

"You know you could have refused," Shadduck said. "Technically you are already on leave."

"I know it," Gauldin said, "but it's as good a way as any to kill time." He had just received several months' back pay, and he was stuffing the military scrip into an inside pocket.

As Shadduck gunned the engine of the T-6 and bumped out toward the steel-matted take-off runway, he thought about Gauldin. He liked the sergeant. He had a lot of spunk. He was one of the few GI observers at the base who was not afraid to fly with him. The others considered him a tiger. They believed he flew too deep into enemy territory and too close to the ground. On each of the last forty missions, he had returned to the base with bullet holes in his aircraft.

Shadduck did not think that he flew too low or too far behind enemy lines. He believed that he flew exactly as he should to accomplish what he was ordered to do, which was to seek out enemy troops and supplies and then direct fighter-bombers down to destroy them. He knew from experience that no Mosquito pilot could efficiently do his job while flying at three thousand feet. He had to keep down near the ground, even at the risk of getting shot down. Shadduck at least had the satisfaction of knowing that his reports were treated with great respect in Intelligence Headquarters.

When the T-6 finished its climb to altitude, Shadduck throttled back to cruising and unfastened his shoulder straps. He adjusted the trim tabs until he could fly the ship with his fingertips. Then, during the routine run up to the front line, he allowed his thoughts to turn once again to his wife and children. He was very concerned, because he was devoted to his family.

Shadduck was not ordinarily a worrier. In fact, like most Air Force pilots, he took pride in the rigid control he exercised over his emotions. He never got excited in combat. When he had been hit on his fifth mission and had been forced to crash-land—luckily behind friendly lines—he had flown his flaming plane with extraordinary precision and coolness. He was soft-spoken and moderate in his tastes, friendly and talkative. He liked to play with his children. Yet underneath, he was serious-minded and conscientious about his job, the Air Force, and his wife.

Shadduck was born in Sioux City, Iowa, the second son of a local policeman. He lived with his parents, brother, and two younger sisters in a modest home on the outskirts of town. Early in life he became interested in mechanical things, such as radios and motors, and he built model airplanes and joined airplane clubs. By the time he was fifteen, he had made up his mind that he wanted to be an Army Air Corps pilot.

When World War II began, his father entered the Navy, and the Shadduck family moved to Milwaukee, Wisconsin, where he was stationed. In order to complete high school with his friends, "Mel" Shadduck remained in Sioux City, living alone in the family house. He paid heavily for the privilege. He had to support himself, do his own cooking and laundry. He worked at night, first in a garage and then later as a janitor in a meat-packing house. In January, 1943, he graduated. Turning down an invitation from his father to join the Navy, he advised his local draft board to call his number early. By March, he was undergoing Army basic training.

After a short tour in the Signal Corps, he transferred to the Aviation Cadets, his real goal. He received flight training in Texas, and on graduation and commissioning as a second lieutenant, he was assigned as a ferry pilot, flying Air Corps planes around the U.S. Later, he was made a Communications Officer and an Aircraft Maintenance Officer at the Air Corps Gunnery School on Matagorda Island in the Gulf of Mexico, just off the coast of Texas. In 1946, Shadduck was released from active duty. He got married and went back to civilian life.

While on duty with the Air Corps, Shadduck had bought a small piece of land on a lake near Little Falls, Minnesota, about 130 miles due north of Minneapolis. After the war, he took his bride, a former WAC sergeant who had been a control-tower operator at one of the Air Force bases at which he had served, and moved to his lakeside place. Later they bought an adjoining 130-acre dairy farm.

When Shadduck's father got out of the Navy, he settled on the same lake, and soon the two Shadducks were busily engaged in building and selling summer cottages. In the evenings, Shadduck attended agriculture school, an extension class of the University of Minnesota, in order to learn the art of dairy farming. In his spare time, he engaged in a new-found love: living in the outdoors—hunting, fishing, and trapping.

But one thing distracted him. All day long, F-51 aircraft from the National Guard Base in Little Falls flew over Shadduck's lake. He was still fascinated. He used to put down his gun and traps and watch the planes for hours. All of a sudden he realized that he missed the Air Force and the military life, especially flying. Then, in 1948, he was surprised to receive an order recalling him to active duty in the Air Force. It seemed that the Air Force was short of communications officers, one of his special qualifications. He could have turned the order down, but he didn't. Returning to active duty, he spent three days in San Francisco and then, accompanied by his wife and two children, departed for Japan.

In October, 1948, he arrived in the Far East and was assigned as commander of a radar-warning installation in northern Japan. Later he was detailed to a supply school. Then he was put in charge of a large supply of radar and spare parts. He flew only part-time, fifteen or twenty hours a month, in C-46 and C-47 transports. When the war in Korea broke out twenty months later, he volunteered for action and was transferred to southern Japan to fly transports with the 374th Troop Carrier Wing.

It was rugged, monotonous work, flying back and forth between Japan and Korea, eight and ten hours a day. After he had logged more than 150 flights, the Air Force nominated him for a supply job in Korea. But Shadduck did not want the job—he wanted to go to Korea and fight. The quickest and surest way to achieve his aim, he thought, was to volunteer for T-6 duty. He was accepted. In January, 1951, just before he went over to Korea to join the Mosquito outfit, he put his wife and family (by then they had a third child) on a ship bound for the U.S.

The T-6 passed over Seoul, winging northward toward the front. Below, Shadduck could see thousands of U.N. troops dug in along the highway and on the hilltops. Tanks and large artillery pieces were embedded on the slopes, their long rifles and guns pointing toward the north. Shadduck had flown over the area more than 150 hours. He knew every ridge, every gully, every stream by heart. Soon he dove the plane toward the ground and "buzzed" the Third Division Ground Control Unit bunker.

When he was directly over the trench, Shadduck slipped open the "greenhouse" cockpit canopy and tossed out a message dropper attached to a streamer. The leather pouch, used for communicating when radios were out of commission, contained a completely unauthorized item: a two-ounce bottle of bourbon whisky. Shadduck had made up the package before leaving the base. He had wrapped it in toilet paper on which he had scrawled a message: *"Shadduck's Special Cure All.* Take for any disease including 'Battle Rattle,' the Common Cold, or Sore Feet."

Then via radio, he contacted the unit, "Hazard Control." He received a grateful thanks for the streamer package, then orders to patrol the area directly north, five to ten miles behind enemy lines. He flew northward to relieve the Mosquito plane that was still working in the area. When the pilot of the latter spotted the incoming T-6, he wobbled his wings and turned south toward the base. Shadduck wobbled his wings in return, and then he turned his mind to the business at hand: locating the enemy.

In contrast to the area behind U.N. lines, there was seldom an enemy soldier in sight behind Communist lines. Trucks, guns, trenches, and bunkers were very skillfully camouflaged. Only experienced pilots who flew close to the ground could detect the enemy through his clever disguises. Shadduck, as was his custom, put the T-6 down close and began looking. Within a very few minutes he was astounded by what he saw.

The ground was literally crawling with thousands of Chinese troops. He could see men dug in everywhere. Off to the sides, hidden under trees and bushes, he spotted trucks, guns, stacks of ammunition supplies, and food. "This is it!" he said to himself. This is the enemy build-up! In the rear cockpit, Gauldin was rapidly taking notes. Soon they were on the radio to "Hazard Control" to report the discovery. Hazard Control acknowledged and told them to be on the lookout for three flights of fighters that were coming into the area to work with them.

Shadduck searched the skies. He spotted four Navy Corsairs and flew straight toward them, trying to contact the planes on his radio. He could not raise them; apparently they were not monitoring his channel. To attract their attention, he flew in front of them and wobbled his wings. The Navy planes turned. Shadduck wobbled his wings again, then flew for a moment in the direction of the enemy positions, then wobbled his wings once more. Finally the flight leader broke away and followed the T-6.

Shadduck flew low over the ground, then fired smoke rockets into the midst of the enemy troops, marking their exact location. He turned, made a run on a hillside, and fired another rocket. The Navy pilot, meanwhile, had climbed overhead, was circling and watching while Shadduck marked the targets. At length, Shadduck flew the T-6 to one side to get out of the way of the attack. But the Navy planes flew away. Apparently they had a prebriefed target and were planning to return to the area later.

He continued to fly around over the enemy positions, providing valuable intelligence information to "Hazard Control" via radio. Then suddenly, a vicious burst of enemy machine-gun fire ripped from the ground. Shadduck wheeled the T-6 to one side and made a note of the position. At about that moment a flight of Air Force F-80 jets came along. With his last smoke rocket, Shadduck pin-pointed the gun. The jets flew over the slit trench and splattered the area with napalm. Suddenly all was quiet. Shadduck counted thirty-five dead enemy troops.

An hour passed as the T-6 buzzed around waiting for more fighters. Shadduck had yet to direct an attack on the main enemy troop concentration and the bulk of the machine-gun emplacements. Finally, a group of four Navy Corsairs came along. He called them via radio and reported that he was out of marker rockets but that he would buzz the positions. Without waiting further, he dove the plane, pointing out the troop concentrations, the large nest of machine guns, and then the antiaircraft gun emplacements on the hillside.

The T-6 was at 1,800 feet in a tight bank when Shadduck felt a thump under the cockpit, near his belly gasoline tank. Within a second, he heard a small explosion. Fire broke out around the base of the control stick. The flames spurted up and burned the right side of his face. He was momentarily blinded. The flame died for a moment and Shadduck saw that the plane was in a tightening spiral, diving toward the base of a hill. He struggled to right the ship; to keep it from stalling. When he got it under control, he was too low to bail out, so he put the plane in a steep climb, heading toward friendly lines to the south.

Flaming gasoline sloshed around the floor of the cockpit. Shadduck's right leg and right hand, which was holding the control stick, were literally frying in the flames, but he could not move or let go. As the plane climbed, the gasoline ran back along the floor into the rear cockpit. Gauldin yelled,

"We are on fire, we are on fire!" Shadduck reached for the radio to sound "May Day," the distress call that would alert Air Rescue, but the mike and cords were burning furiously.

Since he was not able to use the radio, Shadduck flew directly in front of the Corsairs to attract their attention. Then he chopped the throttle, turned around, and yelled to Gauldin, "Get out of here." Gauldin immediately opened his cockpit canopy, stood up, and bailed out. Shadduck threw back his own canopy, unfastened his safety belt, crouched for a moment in his seat, then leaped out. His chute opened with a jolt. He waited for the whine of enemy ground fire: he was a Mosquito pilot and the parachute was a perfect target. But none came. He looked at his right hand and saw that it had been burned to a crisp. Pieces of it hung down in shreds. He thought it smelled like burned chicken feathers.

Shadduck landed in a deep canyon alongside the Imjin River, about fifteen miles directly north of the thirty-eighth parallel. The canyon walls rose steeply to about four hundred feet. He knew that he was in the middle of a Chinese Army, so he moved with speed and caution. He took off his parachute and ducked behind a bush. From his concealed position, he watched the plane, which had crashed farther down the canyon, burn. Then he turned attention to his right hand. He had no first-aid kit; not even a handkerchief. He jerked off some of the sensitive pieces of skin and threw them away.

He looked for Gauldin. He thought it would be better if they were together when the rescue helicopter arrived. There would not be much time for maneuvering in this heavily populated "Chink" country. He edged his way along the foot of the brown rock canyon wall, softly calling Gauldin's name. He did not want the sergeant to mistake him for an enemy soldier. He had moved only a few feet when he heard Chinese voices on top of the cliff. They were yelling and talking loudly, obviously about the airplane which had crashed below.

Shadduck quickly retraced his steps until he reached a crevice, the entrance of which was covered with scrubs and bushes. He crawled inside; then using his left hand, he dug out a pile of dirt, and pushed it down over his legs and feet to camouflage them as much as possible. His trousers and socks were badly burned. He was afraid that the smell of the burned cloth if nothing else might give him away.

He could see what was going on outside through a small opening in the grass. He watched the four Corsairs dive-bomb and strafe the targets that he had pin-pointed. This worried him considerably. The planes should have been flying "CAP" (Combat Air Patrol) over the two downed airmen, keeping the enemy soldiers off until the chopper arrived.

"They couldn't have missed seeing us," he thought. Both men had bailed out almost alongside the other aircraft. The plane itself had crashed only five hundred yards away. He did not want to believe the planes had not seen them.

Directly above, on top of the cliff, a Chinese 20-mm. gun fired steadily at the attacking Corsairs. Shadduck made a note of the position. Then he heard more 20-mm. guns firing from the hill toward which he had previously directed the F-80 jets. Then suddenly, the firing ceased. The four Corsairs flew away. The attack was over. He realized that the planes had somehow not seen the crash. They must have been studying their shoelaces or something, he thought. Escape and rescue now consisted of what he could make of it.

Like most pilots who fly over enemy territory, Shadduck had always had the feeling that "it can't happen to me." He was especially confident after he had been shot down the first time. He had thought that it certainly couldn't happen twice. He was not mentally prepared for his misfortune. He lay in the crevice a long time thinking about it, about how suddenly it happened. How one minute he had been flying along through the open sky, thinking about what the cooks would have for lunch when he got back to the base, and then the next minute, he was burned and wounded, lying in a cave in the bottom of a canyon far behind the front lines, surrounded by enemy troops.

He began to think about being captured. In the four months he had been in Korea, he had heard of many T-6's that had crashed behind enemy lines, but he had never heard of any pilots or crewmen who had been taken alive. The Communists did not admit officially to any captured pilots. The presumption was that they were all dead. It was likely, he believed, that if he were caught, he would be executed on the spot.

While he was thinking about this, Shadduck examined his hand. He could see that it was severely burned. It occurred to him that the wound was so bad that he would be immediately eligible for transfer back to the United States. He would not have to fly the other nineteen missions—if he could only get back to friendly lines. He would be on his way to see his wife in a matter of hours. It was a challenging alternative to capture and death. Suddenly Shadduck felt an intense desire to escape.

A few minutes after the fighters had gone, he spotted two Korean men, dressed in civilian clothing, wading across the river toward the crevice. While he held his breath, the two men picked up his parachute, folded it under their arms, glanced around for a minute, then waded back across the river. They were joined by two other men carrying another parachute. I must be Gauldin's, Shadduck thought. He watched the men until they disappeared beyond a hill.

Shadduck was on the verge of crawling out of the crevice when he heard Chinese voices accompanied by the rattle of pebbles and stones. He looked out and saw that several of the soldiers were making their way down the steep canyon wall. Some time later, he saw them again—about eight in number —spread out in pairs searching along the riverbank. The soldiers peered into almost every bush. One of them came within twenty-five feet of Shadduck's crevice, stared directly at it for a moment; then, apparently satisfied that the bushes were undisturbed, walked away.

Several minutes later, Shadduck heard the crack of a forty-five pistol. Gauldin! The shot was quickly followed by shouts and a volley of rifle fire. Gauldin has been trapped, Shadduck thought. He is trying to shoot it out with the Communist soldiers! There was a little he could do from his position to help, so he remained silent, and soon the firing stopped. But Chinese soldiers searched the riverbank off and on for the rest of the afternoon. Shadduck did not stir from his hiding place.

While he lay hidden in the crevice during the afternoon, he had ample time to plan his escape. There was one thing in his favor: he had flown over the area so many times and was so familiar with the terrain that he did not even have to take out his maps. He knew that the Imjin River, alongside which he had crashed, flowed almost directly south, and that if he followed it long enough, he would eventually reach friendly lines. Almost without further consideration, he adopted the river as his main line of escape. He briefly considered Gauldin, but decided that it would be dangerous to try to make contact with him. If he were still alive and uncaptured, he could make his own way to safety. He knew the area as well as anyone.

Shortly after dark, Shadduck crawled from the crevice and stretched his arms and legs. The cold, April air whipped up the canyon and caused him to shiver. Then he started walking southward along the rocky riverbank. He had not gone more than one hundred yards when he heard a terrible commotion: Chinese voices chattering, whistles blowing, and trucks grinding gears. Then he saw the reason for it: just ahead a road joined the riverbank. The Communists had established a check point at the junction.

Shadduck remained in the shadows, listening and watching. He could see that not more than ten or fifteen feet separated the check point, which was manned by several Chinese M.P.'s, and the river's edge. Could he get by on the riverbank without being seen? He soon concluded that he could not, so he slipped quietly into the rushing river. The water, mostly melted snow from the mountains, was ice cold. He sank in up to his chin, and was swept along by the current, half-floating, half-swimming. He kept his face turned to the opposite bank as he passed by the check point.

Several hundred yards farther, Shadduck swam back to the riverbank and crawled out. His teeth were chattering wildly. He gritted his jaws together to stop the noisy clatter. Then he ran along the riverbank, crouching to keep out of sight of the hundreds of Chinese soldiers who were clogging the road. He could hear many of the soldiers laughing and shouting. One was playing a flute. Shadduck believed they were marching into battle, that the Chinese offensive was about to start, if it had not already. This thought lent wings to his feet. If the Chinese broke through and pushed south, he knew he would have even farther to go to reach U.N. lines.

Suddenly, out of the clear of the night, Shadduck heard a long, low whistle. A Communist soldier! He stopped and ducked in the shadow of a tree. Then a short distance away, he heard a second low whistle. Another Communist! They are signaling to one another. They have spotted me and are closing in, he thought. He plunged back into the icy river water and sank in over his head. The current pushed him along at a fast clip. Every few seconds, he stuck his head above water to breathe.

Several hundred yards south, satisfied that he had bypassed his pursuers, he climbed out of the river once more. Again he heard the whistles. He squatted for a moment on the riverbank, listening carefully, then walked on. More whistles! He stopped again. He noticed that the whistles were without pattern, and finally, he realized that the "signals" had been made by some kind of bird. He cursed himself for being so stupid. Nevertheless, every time one of the birds whistled, he jumped.

About three hours farther along, the river flowed out of the hills into a small valley. The moon was now shining brightly. Shadduck hesitated for a moment, then struck out boldly across the open country, walking alongside the river. He had almost crossed the valley when he spotted a peasant on the bank ahead. The Korean watched as Shadduck approached. Shadduck walked on boldly, not missing a step. For some strange reason, he found himself counting his paces. Exactly twenty-three feet from the point where he had first seen the man, Shadduck passed abreast of him. Neither spoke. The peasant turned and walked slowly toward the road where the Chinese soldiers were marching. As soon as he was out of sight, Shadduck ran south as fast as he could.

A few miles farther, the Imjin River made several curves, roughly in the shape of an S. Rather than follow the river through each maneuver, Shadduck laid out a route that took him straight across the wide, sandy beach that lay between the curves. He knew it was dangerous to leave the river but he was in a hurry. He had come within U.N. artillery range, and a distracting barrage of 155 mm. was falling into the area. From the noise of the battle, he became convinced that the Communists were attacking. He wanted to take advantage of the confusion and move south before the U.N. lines had been pushed back beyond reach.

He was crunching along through the sand when he spied a Chinese foxhole immediately ahead. He ducked to one side and almost stepped into another. Then he realized that he was practically surrounded by enemy troops: he had wandered into a company area without even realizing it. Fortunately, most of the soldiers, unconcerned about the artillery, were asleep. Shadduck threaded his way through the foxholes, walking on tiptoe and keeping in shadows. As quickly as possible, he made his way back to the riverbank. Once he reached it, he swore he would never leave it again.

The river flowed from the sandy flatland back into a steep canyon, and Shadduck hurried on, confident that he would be as safe from artillery fire in the canyon as anywhere else. I can get hit as easy standing still as I can moving, he thought. But very soon the canyon wall became vertical, plunging directly into the river. There was no path. The only way to move on appeared to be to get into the water. But it flowed particularly fast through the canyon and was choked with rapids. Shadduck was afraid he might not be able to negotiate it.

He examined the canyon wall. Though steep and rocky, it was dotted with niches and cracks. Could he climb it with only one good hand? He decided he would have to. Pulling himself up with his left hand, wedging his toes in among the rocks, he started the ascent, with his right arm hanging loosely at his side. He fought not to look down. Once he did and almost fell.

The canyon wall was about 150 feet high. After an hour's climb, Shadduck had come within a few feet of the top. There he found that the wall sloped up, like the roof of a house. The slope was very slippery, and there were no handholds. He lay flat and crawled along slowly, pulling gently on small shrubs.

He was within five feet of the top when he began sliding backward toward the edge of the canyon wall. He grasped desperately with both hands at roots, small shrubs, rocks, dirt—anything to stop the sliding. He lay flat against the ground, pressing his ear and cheek in the dirt to try to brake himself. Three feet from the edge he grabbed a small bush with his injured hand. It held.

The pain from his hand was maddening. But he lay there, not daring to move lest the bush pull out and send him plunging once more toward the edge of the cliff. What could he do? To guard against further sliding, he carefully dug his toes and heels into the hard clay. He spread his left arm out and pressed his stomach against the ground, to get as much traction as possible. Then, he let go the bush and, like a snake, carefully moved up the slope, half an inch at a time. When, finally, he reached the top, he sat down on a ledge and said a prayer of thanks.

Within a few minutes, he was making his way south again, following a rough trail along the lip of the canyon. Gradually, the path sloped downward. Soon the ground was level, and he made his way to the riverbank again. The artillery had virtually ceased. There was no noise except the rushing of the river and the steady clomping of his wet boots through the sand and gravel. He passed between a small Korean village and the river. Not a soul could be seen.

He stopped only occasionally to rest, and then for only three or four minutes at a time. The hours were slipping by quickly. By four o'clock, the sky in the east was light— dawn was approaching. Visibility increased alarmingly. He decided that he had better give up and get out of sight before he was spotted. He found a crevice similar to the one he had hidden in the afternoon before, camouflaged the entrance with some twigs and branches, and crawled inside and lay on the ground.

He began to think. According to his calculations, he had traveled along the twisting, winding river bed about nineteen miles. By now, he should have reached friendly lines. The fact that he hadn't was proof to him that the Chinese had pushed the lines south during the night. How much farther south would he have to go? Not far, he was sure. The Chinese could not have got *too* far. He could hear Chinese artillery and small-arms fire to the north and northeast, but nothing in the south. He became convinced that the Chinese had made only small gains and that he was, in fact, in the middle of no-man's land.

As he lay in the crevice, he took stock of his physical condition. He was shivering from the cold, his clothes were sopping wet, and his legs were bruised and battered from falling against rocks. Every muscle ached from the last few miles of hard travel. He inspected his hand and discovered that in climbing, he had pulled some more of the skin away. The wound on his right leg was beginning to pain. The muscle was drawing taut, and the leg was getting very stiff.

For a minute he allowed himself to think of his wife and children. He wondered what would happen to them when the "missing in action" report arrived. Then his thoughts returned to his escape. What if the Chinese launched another attack and moved farther south? He would be bypassed and would have to thread his way through the Chinese front lines all over again. His wounds needed medical attention. Perhaps a few hundred more yards would do it, he thought. The more he considered this, the more he convinced himself that he ought to keep moving. After a few minutes in the crevice, Shadduck threw caution to the wind, crawled out, and headed south once more.

He walked quickly because it was now almost completely light. About ten minutes later, as he was hurrying along the river's edge, he spotted six Chinese soldiers in green quilted uniforms coming over the crest of a hill about fifty yards away. He ducked into the brush, fell on his hands and knees, and crawled down to the edge of the water, praying that he hadn't been seen. A minute or two later, one of the Chinese soldiers pushed through the brush and leveled a rifle in Shadduck's face. He was trapped.

Without getting off the ground, he raised both hands above his head. The Chinese soldier pushed the bayonet toward his face. He jabbered in Chinese and waved the bayonet around several times. Shadduck pushed his head back into the sand, praying as hard as he could. Then, the Chinese stopped jabbering, and Shadduck lifted his head slightly, as if to get up. At that, the soldier went into another tantrum, waving the bayonet wildly, calling to his friends.

After twenty more Chinese had arrived, the soldier allowed Shadduck to get to his feet. Standing up shakily, he kept his hands high above his head. The soldiers motioned for him to climb up the riverbank to the trail. He struggled up the hillside, all the while waiting for a .30-caliber slug to rip into his back. The soldiers marched him down the trail to a second group of twelve or fifteen Chinese. Shadduck could tell by the garters they wore around their legs that they were officers. When they caught sight of him, they chattered loudly.

One of the officers stepped forward and said in English: "Gun?" Shadduck opened his flying jacket and flipped his shoulder-holster strap. The Chinese pulled the .45 from the holster and passed it around. They all examined it. One of them pointed it at Shadduck's head and shouted, "Kill. Kill."

He was not sure whether the officer was playing or serious. Then one of the officers said, in English: "We are Chinese peoples volunteers. Do not worry. We will not shoot you. We will not harm you. We will not take your personal belongings. Do not try to run away or you will be punished."

He could not believe it. If the Chinese soldiers were not going to kill him, it certainly represented a new situation—in fact, a drastic change in policy. The Communist high command must have cooked up a plot in which U.S. pilots were more useful to them alive than dead, Shadduck thought. Whatever it was, Shadduck was delighted to have been one of the first to benefit from the new policy.* He noticed that the soldiers almost outdid one another in trying to get across the point that he would not be harmed, and that his personal belongings would not be taken away.

Shadduck decided to put the new policy to the test. He made signs to indicate that he wanted to smoke, and the English-speaking soldier said, "O.K." With his left hand, he pulled a package of cigarettes from his pocket and he offered them to the officers standing nearby. They fell over one another refusing the offer. Apparently they did not want to be liable to charges brought by the informers and secret police in their midst that they had "taken" any of his possessions. Several of the officers kept repeating over and over in English, "We will not shoot you. We will not harm you. We will not take your personal belongings. We are Chinese peoples volunteers." They had obviously memorized the phrases.

Shadduck held out his burned hand and screwed up his face as if in pain. One of the officers called a Chinese medic. From a leather pouch with a red cross painted on the side, the medic took a jar of vaseline and a compress. He spread the vaseline on the burned portion of the hand, placed the compress on top, then wrapped Shadduck's hand with gauze. Shadduck nodded in thanks.

When the medic had finished, another Chinese officer searched Shadduck hurriedly. Then he summoned four enlisted men and pointed toward a hill. They nodded. It seemed clear to Shadduck that he was about to be escorted to the rear. A thought raced through his mind. Perhaps he could escape. Under the new policy they might not shoot him; they might even let him go. Without planning it further, he turned to one of the Chinese officers and asked, "May I go home now?" Before the officer could reply, Shadduck turned and started south.

He walked at a very slow pace. He wanted the Chinese to

* It was at this time that the Communists began collecting American pilots with the idea of brainwashing them so they could launch their phony charges of "germ warfare."

believe that he considered it the proper thing to do, just to walk off like that. He tramped up the crest of a hill. In the faint light, he could see U.S. troops, perhaps a half mile away, digging in on the top of another hill. His heart pounded wildly. Freedom was in sight!

He had gone seventy-five feet when one of the soldiers shouted, "Hey!"

Shadduck turned and pointed a finger at his chest.

"Who me?" he asked. He noticed that one of the officers had leveled his .45 at him, and two Communist soldiers had raised their rifles. They motioned for him to come back. Apparently the new policy did not include returning POW's. Shadduck turned and walked back to the group of "Peoples volunteers."

The four soldiers escorted Shadduck over a small hill to a command-post bunker. The officer in charge of the C.P. was very busy. When he saw Shadduck he told him by signs to empty his pockets. The officer searched through the contents: the Escape and Evasion kit, the silk handkerchief map, two cigarette lighters, two pipes, a watch, a Parker 51 fountain pen and pencil, two packages of cigarettes, wallet, a C-ration can opener, the letter from his wife, and an instruction booklet for a photographic light meter. Then he returned the stuff, called one of the guards, and motioned for him to escort Shadduck to another hill to the east.

As soon as they were out of sight of the other soldiers— and possible informers—the lone guard indicated that he was now ready to accept a cigarette. He would not allow Shadduck to come near him, so without thinking, Shadduck threw him the full package. The guard put a cigarette in his mouth, stuffed the package in the pocket of his quilted uniform, then motioned that he wanted a light. Again, without thinking, Shadduck threw him one of his lighters. The guard lit his cigarette, then stuffed the lighter in his pocket. When Shadduck insisted that they be returned, the guard pretended that he did not understand what he was talking about. "Hike," he said to Shadduck.

The guard led Shadduck to what appeared to be a company command post. There were five officers standing about, none of whom could speak English. One of the officers took Shadduck by the arm and directed him down the hillside about fifty yards to a large, half-covered foxhole in the side of the hill. The officer presented Shadduck to a Chinese soldier who spoke a little English. Shadduck guessed that he was an interrogator.

The soldier asked Shadduck his name, rank, serial number, age, marital status, number of children, native town, and organization. Then he asked what type of plane he had flown. Shadduck described the T-6 Mosquito, emphasizing that his plane had no guns, and that he just flew around over the lines looking. The interrogator asked about his civilian job and schooling. Shadduck replied that he was a dairy farmer and that he had graduated from high school and had attended college one year.

"You are a farmer and have been to college?" the Chinese asked.

"Yes," Shadduck replied.

"I do not believe it," the interrogator said. He was extremely skeptical. After a long explanation of night school and university extension courses, Shadduck convinced him. After that, the interview became less formal. The interrogator, in the spirit of the new policy, was cordial and quite friendly. Shadduck began to think that perhaps he could persuade him to turn his back while he slipped away into the bushes.

"I am wounded. I will not fight any more. I will be a liability to the U.N. They will just ship me home to my wife and children," Shadduck said. It was a test.

The Chinese did not respond.

"You will get home," he said, "but not now."

"But what will happen to me?" Shadduck asked.

"You will be escorted to the rear tonight for your own protection and then you will be given special training each day," the Chinese said.

Shadduck did not like the sound of that. "Special training" could mean anything.

The Chinese asked Shadduck to lay all his belongings on the floor of the foxhole. He examined each item very carefully. He took the ball compass from the Escape and Evasion kit and put it in his pocket. He asked Shadduck about the needle compass, and Shadduck tried to explain how it worked. The Chinese made signs to indicate that he did not like the needle compass, and put it back in the kit. Shadduck had a third, flat compass in his shirt pocket, but he did not show it to the Chinese.

The interrogator then noticed the instruction booklet for Shadduck's photographic light meter. For a long while he studied it intently, slowly turning each page. At length, he said:

"This seems to be an instruction book for the operation of a secret radio. Give me the radio."

Shadduck restrained a chuckle. He explained that he had no radio.

The Chinese frowned.

"Do not make jokes with me. Give me the radio," he said.

"I do not have a radio," Shadduck insisted. He tried without success to explain the operation of a photographic light meter. The Chinese searched Shadduck once more looking for the secret radio. He asked if it was in the aircraft. He would not give up. At length, the Chinese tucked the booklet away for future reference. He then took the Parker 51 fountain pen and put it in his pocket.

"I would like a cigarette," Shadduck said. "The guard took all of mine, as well as my lighter."

The interrogator frowned. Then he babbled excitely, half in English and half in Chinese. He got to his feet, shrieking and shouting. "Chinese soldiers do not steal from POW's" he insisted. Like the Chinese officers, the interrogator repeated the memorized phrases over and over. Shadduck refrained from pointing out that the interrogator himself had just stolen his compass and fountain pen. He just kept his mouth shut and listened.

Soon the interrogation was ended. The officer who had brought Shadduck to the foxhole escorted him back toward the C.P. When they were about halfway up the hill, all the Chinese in the surrounding area began firing their rifles into the sky and shouting what sounded to Shadduck like *"Fu ji le la. Fu ji le la."* Shadduck guessed what it meant: enemy aircraft. He looked up and saw a flight of four F-51's peeling off to make an attack. "Great Scott," he thought. He and the Chinese officer ran up the hill as fast as they could. They dove into the C.P. bunker just as the F-51's came over strafing and bombing. Shadduck lay in the bottom of the C.P. trembling. He could hear cries of pain everywhere as .50-caliber slugs ripped into foxholes and trenches. Then he heard napalm crashing through the trees, and he was very frightened.

In a few minutes the fighters went away. Shadduck and the Chinese officers in the C.P. sighed with relief. Then Shadduck noticed a Chinese soldier running up the hillside. The soldier pushed into the dugout and began screaming and shaking his fist in Shadduck's face. "Your fighters just strafed my fox-hole," he shouted over and over in English. A minute or two passed before Shadduck realized that the soldier was none other than the interrogator. Shadduck patiently explained that he had nothing to do with the air strike and that he was as frightened as the interrogator.

After the Chinese soldier stomped off, Shadduck and the officers in the C.P. lit up cigarettes. He noticed that the officers smoked American-made cigarettes. By signs he asked where they had obtained them. The officers told him—also by signs —that they captured them from the U.S. Third Division the night before when they took the hill just to the south. So the

Third Division troops are that close, Shadduck said to himself. I must make a break for it. He waited for the opportunity.

The Chinese soldiers fought mostly at night and stayed in their foxholes to avoid aircraft attack during the day. After a while they began to get sleepy. As was the custom, they lay on the floor and dozed off, but they did not take off their Russian 7.62 pistols. Shadduck decided that if he was ever going to escape, he had better try while they were sleeping. He formulated a quick plan: he would reach for a pistol and knock all the Chinese on the head, then he would make a break to the south.

Slowly he got up off the floor. He crouched over one of the officers, reaching for his pistol holster. At that moment, he heard footsteps outside the C.P., so he fell to the ground and pretended that he was asleep. A soldier came in and asked one of the officers a question. The officer and soldier talked a moment, then the officer turned over and went back to sleep. But the noise woke three or four of the other officers. One of them smoked again. Every time Shadduck got ready to move, another soldier barged into the C.P. to ask something of one of the officers. Finally, he gave up his plans for escape that afternoon. Later, when he saw the concentration of foxholes and guards on the side of the hill, he was glad he had not tried.

That evening Shadduck learned from the interpreter that the unit was to be moved out of the line and sent to the rear. A guard, consisting of the interpreter, a "medic," and two soldiers, was assigned to Shadduck, and just before dark, he was escorted to a small burned-out Korean village. There, three Korean civilians, hands tied behind their backs, joined them. Not long afterward, the three Koreans were led up a hill. Shadduck heard three shots, and then the guards returned without the Koreans. They had been murdered. Shadduck learned later they were "political" prisoners.

After a short hike, the group came upon a road that was clogged with long lines of Chinese soldiers. Their group sat down on the roadside, and one of the guards gave Shadduck a bowlful of cold rice. He was about to eat it when another of the guards covered the rice with a gooey, malodorous sauce that nearly made Shadduck sick at his stomach. He carefully scraped the sauce off and then ate the rice. When he asked for water, it was refused.

Meanwhile, he watched the procession of soldiers and equipment as it moved along the road. Apparently the entire division to which he had been attached was moving off to the northwest. All of the soldiers were walking. None rode in trucks. Shadduck noticed that the division artillery consisted of thirty-three American-made 105-mm. howitzers. Soon he was back on his feet, and the small group was marching along the road with the lines of soldiers.

They had not walked far when Shadduck heard an unexpected cry in the night:

"Hey, Shadduck!"

He looked over his shoulder and, among the soldiers and vehicles, saw his observer, Sergeant Gauldin, struggling along the road under guard and in company with another U.S. soldier. Shadduck waved, then attempted to make his way through the stream of men and artillery vehicles to Gauldin, but his guard interposed.

"No talking," the interpreter said.

Shadduck shrugged his shoulders. Gauldin nodded understandingly from a distance, then they all walked north once again.

At about three o'clock in the morning, on signal from a Chinese officer, the soldiers who were marching along the road veered off to the side and spread out on the hillside and sat down. Shadduck estimated that there were more than 1,500 troops, probably the bulk of a regiment. He noticed that they seemed to be waiting for something. While he was looking around, one of the guards gave Shadduck a handful of roasted peas. He ate them quickly. But again he was denied water.

Shortly afterward, a white horse galloped up the road. Its rider, who wore a long, flowing cape, pulled up short in front of the soldiers and dismounted. He spoke briefly to the officers, then got up on a large rock and began making a speech. There was not a sound from the large group of soldiers. Shadduck whispered to the interpreter: "What is he talking about?"

The interpreter turned pale. He frantically motioned for Shadduck to keep quiet. When the speaker finished, the troops stood up and cheered wildly. Seemingly indifferent to this ovation, the Chinese jumped on his white horse and rode up the road at a gallop. "O.K., now, tell me who that was?" Shadduck said to the interpreter.

The interpreter replied that the man was a political commissar. He had come to tell of the "wonderful" advances that the "Chinese peoples volunteer armies" had made the previous day, how the armies had "driven the U.N. forces far south toward Seoul," and how the Chinese would soon "push the warmongers back into the sea." Shadduck became very discouraged when he heard the news, because he knew every foot the Chinese advanced was one more foot he had to travel in order to reach friendly lines.

When the commissar had gone, the soldiers moved farther up onto the hillside and began to get settled for the day. The machine gunners climbed to the top of the hill and placed their guns in the most advantageous position. The other soldiers dug foxholes and carefully covered them with brush and trees. Shadduck and the "medic" made a foxhole by covering a drainage ditch with a rubber poncho. After they carefully placed bushes and shrubs over it, Shadduck thought to himself: This has got to be well camouflaged. I mean *very* well camouflaged.

By dawn, everyone was asleep in his hole. Shadduck slept for about two hours, then awoke with a start. His back ached from sleeping on the ground. The "medic" was still sleeping soundly. Shadduck peered out of the foxhole at the surrounding hillsides. Not a man was stirring. Now is the time to make a break for it, he thought. Slowly he inched his body from under the poncho. He was almost out when a voice shouted in English.

"Get back inside." It was the interpreter. He was watching from a nearby foxhole.

He crawled back under the poncho and lit one of his pipes. The "medic" woke up and asked for a puff on the pipe. Shadduck packed the bowl full of tobacco, then gave the pipe to the "medic." The latter puffed, grinned a toothy smile, then puffed again. Shadduck gave him the pipe. The "medic" was so delighted with the gift that he agreed to change Shadduck's bandage—the next day.

Three air strikes interrupted the stillness of the morning. When the planes came over, Shadduck lay in the bottom of his foxhole, holding his hands over his head, praying. The planes strafed the hilltops, knocking out several machine-gun positions. In the afternoon, he was allowed to make a fast trip to the latrine. On the way back, he spotted Gauldin and the other U.S. soldier in a foxhole, and stopped to chat for a moment. He discovered that except for a slight brush with the tail surfaces of the T-6, which scratched his back, Gauldin was not injured. After bailing out, he had landed in the Imjin River canyon, near Shadduck. The Chinese soldiers had surprised him in his hiding place. He was able to fire only two shots before a Chinese came from behind and knocked him cold with the butt of his rifle. Later, he had been taken to a Chinese C.P. and had experienced much the same sort of questioning and treatment as Shadduck. They were on the verge of discussing escape plans for the future when the interpreter yelled out and told Shadduck to get back in his foxhole.

At dusk, a soldier came around the hillside with a big tin washbasin heaped with hot rice. He ran from foxhole to foxhole, filling the small bowls that the soldiers held out. Most of the soldiers sat on the edge of the foxholes to eat, and afterward crawled back inside to sleep again. Shadduck ate a heaping bowl of rice. Once more he was not given water. A fine supper, he said to himself. Now, I must get in touch with Gauldin and plan the escape.

When it was dark and the Chinese were safe from enemy plane attack, all of the soldiers got out of their foxholes and assembled on the road once again. Then they marched southeast. After a few steps, Shadduck realized that all was not well with his right leg. It was stiff and sore. When the group turned off the road and started up a hill, the going became rough and Shadduck's leg very unstable. Soon he began to lag behind.

The guards were infuriated. One of them came up behind Shadduck and prodded him with the point of his bayonet. Gauldin dropped back to help Shadduck, but the guard motioned him away. The interpreter informed them that they could not be together. One of the guards threatened to shoot Shadduck if he did not speed up. With Gauldin shouting encouragement, Shadduck hobbled along as fast as he could. Finally, at three o'clock, the march stopped. The troops were once again dispersed on a hillside. As before, they dug in and carefully camouflaged their foxholes. The man on the white horse arrived and gave the daily pep talk.

Several of the officers decided that instead of digging a deep foxhole, they would cover over a ravine with ponchos. Accordingly, they tied four of the rubber sheets together and stretched them across a frame of limbs and poles. Then they littered the ponches with a mass of grass, twigs, brush, and shrubs. Shadduck looked on with interest. The officers ordered him to crawl inside, and Gauldin and the other soldier followed, along with four or five of the Chinese.

Shadduck whispered to Gauldin, "This is a hell of a place to be. It is too well camouflaged. A Mosquito pilot could spot it instantly from the air."

Gauldin agreed. But, should they tell the Chinese? They decided not to, even though they had as much at stake as any of them.

During the night, a front moved in and rain began to fall. The ponchos filled and then sagged, splashing water on the sleeping men. They cursed and laughed together. Shadduck slept on the outside and was very cold. He held his mouth open to let some of the water fall inside; it was his first taste of water since capture.

It rained all day, and consequently no planes came. Shadduck said a prayer of thanks. The interrogator questioned him a second time, asking much the same questions. He made Shadduck lay all his equipment on the ground and, after looking through it, confiscated everything except the flat compass hidden in his shirt pocket, the letter from his wife, the automatic pencil, ballpoint pen, the watch, and his remaining cigarette lighter and pipe.

As promised, the "medic" removed the bandage from his hand. Shadduck almost became sick when he saw the wound. It was a mass of pus. The "medic" dabbed at the pus with a swab, then took a pair of tweezers and began pulling off the charred skin. When he had cleaned the hand down to the raw flesh, he took out a bottle full of wet cotton balls. Shadduck discovered with almost unbearable pain that the balls had been doused in alcohol. He trembled as the "medic" wrapped the hand with a piece of gauze. Then, with his head on Gauldin's leg, he collapsed and slept.

Just before sundown, the unit broke camp and moved up into the mountains. After a short walk, they came to a large group of bunkers. Shadduck was ordered to crawl into one, and he squeezed through the tiny opening. The rooms themselves were warm and dry. The roofs were crisscrossed with heavy logs and covered with about four feet of dirt. For the first time, Shadduck felt safe from air attack. He lay down and slept.

About noon the following day, the rain stopped. A runner came into the dugout, bringing messages and a large overlay map of Korea, with the exact positions of the U.N. units marked across the top. The officers studied the map. Then one of them beckoned to Gauldin.

The officers said, "You are an observer, huh?"

Gauldin, who had previously informed them of that fact, nodded his head.

"Then you will check this map and tell us if the positions of the units are correct, O.K.?"

Gauldin tried to explain that he was only an aircraft observer, but the Chinese had already looked up the word "observer" in a World War II English-Chinese dictionary. They were certain that he was a senior militarist with a special knowledge of all U.N. troops, ships, tanks, aircraft, etc.

They asked him another question. Gauldin replied that he did not know the answer.

The Chinese soldier slapped him four times on each side of the face. Then he asked the question again. Gauldin shook his head negatively. Again the Chinese soldier slapped his face. Again Gauldin did not answer.

"Tell us the truth," the soldier said.

Gauldin replied that he was telling the truth. The soldier slapped him again.

"You are lying," he said.

For forty-five minutes the soldiers questioned Gauldin, slapped him, questioned him, and slapped him. Gauldin did not open his mouth. Finally, the beating stopped. One of the Chinese gave him a cigarette and a handful of tobacco, patted him on the back, and motioned for him to sit down. Gauldin was shaking, and Shadduck tried to help calm him. A few hours later, the questioning and beating resumed. This time it lasted only thirty minutes. By then, Gauldin had become numb and could absorb the blows with less difficulty.

Shadduck judged from the activity and map reading that the division was going back into combat that night. What would happen to them? He was sure that they would be sent far to the rear. He did not want that. For one thing, his leg was extremely weak, and he could not go on indefinitely walking around the Korean hillsides. If he did not march, they might kill him.

He knew both his hand and leg needed medical attention. But he wanted to stay near the front so that when circumstances permitted, he could escape to friendly lines. Then he had an idea: he would ask that he be sent to a medical-aid station or a hospital. That way, he might avoid further walking, get some medical attention, and prolong his time on the front.

He asked one of the officers, through the interpreter, if he could be sent to a hospital. The officer blinked at him unbelievingly. Shadduck sensed that the officer considered going to the hospital a disgrace, perhaps a fate worse than death itself. Shadduck reminded the officer that POW's were entitled to medical aid. He held up his messy hand. Then, when the officer laughed, Shadduck began to question the wisdom of his move. He had avoided death thus far. Perhaps in the hospital POW's were not protected by the new policy. Perhaps he would be taken out and shot, like the Korean civilians.

Finally, the officer said, "If you really want to go, you may." It was too late to back out. Shadduck bid Gauldin a reluctant good-by. It was the last he ever heard of the sergeant. Then he was escorted to the "hospital" about a half a mile away by a guard and the interpreter. The interpreter talked in Chinese for some minutes to an officer and then he said to Shadduck:

"This is your new *honcho*. Obey him and you will be taken care of." Then he went back to rejoin his division, which was already moving up to the front.

The "hospital" was not like any hospital Shadduck had ever seen. It consisted of about a hundred well-camouflaged dirt bunkers dug into both slopes of a valley about 250 yards wide. Each "ward" bunker housed from five to eight men. The hospital commandant, two officer assistants, and six nurses lived in one large, rather well-constructed bunker. One dugout served as the kitchen. It was equipped with a clay stove and an iron pot in which all the food for the "patients" in the hospital was cooked.

The "ward" to which Shadduck was assigned on his arrival measured five feet by twelve feet, a handsome-sized room, except that the distance from floor to ceiling was only thirty inches and, including Shadduck, eight men occupied the space. A small slit at each end of the room served as front and back doors. The floor was covered with two inches of straw over which a thin pad had been laid. The men—all of whom had leg and arm wounds—were cordial. One officer, a company commander, was especially friendly. Shadduck soon found out why: he wanted to smoke his pipe. In return he offered to share part of his poncho at night.

Three times a day, a Chinese soldier brought rice to the "ward" in a big pan. He carefully dished out each bowl, always licking the spoon clean between each serving. There was usually enough rice for one helping. However, sometimes a few received a second serving. After a while, Shadduck learned the way to become eligible for such a dividend—gobble down the first helping and be first to present the bowl again. The second bowl could be eaten in more leisurely fashion. It was in the "ward" that he had his first drink of water.

During his second day in the "hospital," an English-speaking political commissar came to talk with him, bringing along a paper questionnaire demanding such information as name, rank, serial number, home town. Shadduck filled out the form as requested, then sat outside the ward chatting with the commissar for hours, happy to have some distraction—something to keep his mind off his miserable surroundings. It was also comforting to find someone who spoke his own language.

The Chinese was his own age, twenty-seven. He traveled a great deal from camp to camp, but he assured Shadduck he would come as often as he wanted. He asked many questions about his farm, family, civilian job, education, etc. Shadduck answered all of the questions that did not deal with military information. The commissar talked at great length about "warmongering Harry Truman," "Madman MacArthur," the "Wall Street capitalists," and others who encouraged the Korean war in order to make money.

Shadduck soon perceived that the commissar was waging a not-too-subtle campaign to convert him to Communism.

He was being subjected to what would later become known as "brainwashing." The seducer promised all kinds of rewards if Shadduck embraced his doctrine. One day he even talked of sending him home, back to the United States—provided Shadduck would go home and tell the people that they were wrong to have entered the Korean War.

With this offer, Shadduck began thinking, Maybe this guy will let me walk back to friendly lines if I convince him I have seen the light. For a few days, he played along; he admitted he was tired of the war; he declared that indeed the warmongers were running it; of course, the people did not want to fight, etc. Soon, the commissar was completely convinced that Shadduck was a convert. He became very amiable, as did the Chinese patients in the ward.

Taking advantage of the man's misconception, Shadduck pressed him for all manner of favors. Pointing to a Chinese propaganda leaflet that showed a POW writing home to his wife extolling the virtues of Communism, Shadduck asked why he could not write his wife to let her know he was alive. The brainwasher hurried back with a piece of paper, on which Shadduck wrote, but with the full knowledge that the letter would never reach her.

He knew very well no letters from POW's held by the Chinese had ever been forwarded to the U.S. He suspected that the Chinese had an ulterior motive in permitting him to write his wife. He surmised—correctly as was later proved—that the commissar wished only to find out what was on his mind, what was bothering him. Once the weakness had been exposed, the Chinese would try psychologically to exploit it to their own advantage.

Shadduck began to complain about his medical care. He asked for a doctor, clean bandages, and medicines. With great elaboration, Shadduck told the commissar how the U.N. forces cared for Chinese POW's; how the wounded were evacuated by airplanes to hospitals, and within a matter of minutes after capture, received the finest medical care obtainable. The Communist was extremely interested in the details of the air evacuation of wounded POW's. Shadduck was able to give him considerable firsthand information since he had airlifted a great number of wounded POW's to U.N. hospitals. He was repeatedly promised medical attention, but it never materialized.

Finally, one day, Shadduck said, "O.K. I have been indoctrinated. Now when do I get to go home?"

"We will send you home when you are completely well," the brainwasher said.

"I feel well enough now," Shadduck said.

"No, we must get you completely well. Then we want to send you to China to get more schooling. Have you ever been to China?"

"No, I haven't," he said.

Shadduck broke out in a cold sweat. He had not even considered the possibility of being sent to China. His chances of ever escaping from there would be practically nil. To forestall any plans for his removal to China for "further indoctrination," Shadduck began to appear a less willing convert. He raised more questions and was cool to the commissar.

One day Shadduck tricked his mentor into admitting that Chinese soldiers in Korea were not "volunteer" forces but were there by order of Mao Tse-tung. The Communist was embarrassed by the slip. He became indignant and berated Shadduck in no uncertain terms. After that, he did not return, and the soldiers in the "ward" would not speak to Shadduck. He knew he was getting the silent treatment and began to worry. He did not want to overdo his role and wind up in front of a firing squad. He decided that if the commissar ever returned, he would take a "middle-of-the-road" position.

As Shadduck lay, day after day, in the smelly, fly-infested "hospital ward," staring at the smoke-smudged ceiling, his general physical condition became worse rather than better. His body was gaunt from loss of weight. A thick matty beard had grown over his cheeks and chin. His right eyelid, which had been burned in the plane, was sensitive, and his leg wound was very painful. Pus began to ooze from beneath the dirty bandage on his hand. On the fourth day, he called one of the nurses and asked for a clean bandage. She shook her head and said, "Nurses do not have authority to change bandages." They could not administer medicine; only the "doctor," whom Shadduck had yet to see, could do all these things.

On the fifth day, Shadduck's hand began to ache a great deal, and he became immensely worried. After his usual bowl of rice that night, he crawled out of the "ward" to watch the sunset. The arm pains became worse, so Shadduck began picking at the bandage. Dried pus had all but completely sealed the gauze, but he managed to pull it loose in a couple of places near the finger. As he did, two slimy, wormlike maggots crawled out and fell into his lap.

For a minute, Shadduck sat stunned. His mind whirled wildly with visions of his hand dropping off into his lap. Then, in a frenzy, he tore at the bandage, ripping it to shreds, pulling off large pieces of scab and skin with it. He looked in horror: maggots crawled all over the burned, rotting, pussy mess that was his hand. As fast as he could, Shadduck picked

the worms out. Some of them were stubborn: he had to pull
them out of holes in the top of his hand. Soon he became
aware that seven or eight wounded soldiers were standing
around watching him, laughing loudly. A "medic" ran up,
looked at the hand, and he, too, laughed heartily. With a
piece of straw, Shadduck dug the last two maggots from
between his fingers.

Several of the soldiers began yelling for a nurse, but by the
time one came on the scene, Shadduck, who was determined
not to put the rotten bandage back on his hand, had ripped
off a piece of his undershirt and had wrapped it around his
hand. The nurse disappeared and minutes later returned with
a roll of gauze—the first Shadduck had seen since the day of
his capture—and wrapped his hand. Shadduck felt relieved
but was still shaking when the company commander came out
of the "ward" with his tobacco pouch and pipe. The pipe helped
him calm his shattered nerves.

On the sixth day, the "doctor" came to Shadduck's "ward,"
trailed by a nurse carrying his bag, containing a jar of vaseline, several vaseline-impregnated compresses, rolls of gauze,
scissors, tweezers, and a dozen small packages labeled: "American Embassy Quick Service First-Aid Sulfadiazine Powder."
He also had a few waterproof cloth patches, a roll of muslin,
and several packages of Chinese sulphur flower, a yellow sulphur powder. Shadduck watched the doctor intently as he
moved from patient to patient.

The first patient was suffering from a severe wound on the
underside of his arm. The doctor removed the tightly wound
bandage, and a ball of maggots fell out and crawled all over
the patient and the floor of the ward. Using the old bandage,
the doctor brushed other maggots out of the soldier's wound.
He pulled the more reluctant maggots out with the tweezers,
and dumped a package of yellow sulphur into the wound.
Then, while the patient moaned, the doctor bound the wound
tightly with gauze.

By the time the "doctor" got to him, Shadduck had almost
taken the old bandage off. The "doctor" finished the job,
ripping off parts of the scab where the bandage had stuck.
Then, with the tweezers, he scraped off the remaining scab.
Shadduck looked down. In several places he could see the
bones of his fingers. After he had cleaned the pus off his hand,
the "doctor" wrapped it with a gauze bandage that he tied
very tight. Then he crawled out of the ward. As soon as he
was out of sight, Shadduck loosened the bandage, which he
believed the doctor had deliberately tied too tight. The Chinese soldiers chided him for touching the wrappings.

One night, after he had ventured out of the ward to relieve

himself, Shadduck noticed the dull glare of a searchlight playing off the clouds. He knew the Communists had no such lights. He surmised that it was U.N.—probably part of the Third Division. He knew the lights had tremendous range—as much as thirty-five miles when reflected from the clouds. The sight of these lights, so close and yet so far, led him to began thinking once more of escape. He stayed out of the ward that evening as long as he dared, memorizing the position of the light with regard to his own surroundings.

He knew from the previous calculations and observations that the "hospital" was located in the hills not far from the spot on the Imjin River where he had crashed. To escape, he need only make his way once more to the river and follow it south. The biggest hurdle would consist of slipping out of the "hospital" valley, which was literally a mass of bunkers filled with enemy soldiers. He could not hope to sneak through them. He would have to get the Communist soldiers used to the idea of his moving about the hospital area. Then one evening, he would walk near the "hospital" boundary and make a break for it.

The following day, he began a program of walking around the "hospital" area as much as possible. On the pretext of getting a drink of water, he picked up a cup and walked down to the kitchen bunker. He talked with the nurses and wounded in as many different bunkers as far away from his own as possible, always stalling, always carefully scrutinizing the surrounding countryside, noting especially the positions of enemy emplacements. After a few days, he was able to move around anywhere in the hospital area without causing alarm. Apparently the Chinese did not believe he had strength enough to escape.

One day he strolled down to a nearby dirt road ostensibly to inspect a disabled U.S. Army truck. Actually, he wanted to have a look up and down the road to see where the Chinese outposts were located. He looked over the truck and noted that the back had been napalmed and was completely melted. The Chinese had stripped the engine of all usable parts such as spark plugs, generators, fan belts. He was about to return to his ward, when from the hilltop, he heard a rifle shot, the traditional Chinese signal for an air raid. The warning was echoed from hilltop to hilltop.

Shadduck dove under the engine section of the truck. The fighters—F-51's—came in low and strafed the entire "hospital." The Chinese screamed in fright. Shadduck lay in the dirt under the truck quivering. Finally, the planes flew away.

One of the English-speaking Chinese came up to Shadduck and screamed:

"Why do your fighters strafe the innocent hospitals?"

"Because it is not marked with a Red Cross like a hospital should be," Shadduck replied. "Why don't you mark it?"

"We cannot do that," the Chinese said.

"Why not?" Shadduck asked.

"Because then they would know we were here," the Chinese said. The Oriental logic sometimes amazed him.

Shadduck's health grew steadily worse. On the sixth of May, his ninth day in the hospital, his hand began to ooze pus again, and he became weak and feverish. He made up his mind that if he did not escape from the hospital, he would soon die from his wounds. He decided that if everything was right for it, he would try to break out that evening after dinner. But later in the afternoon, a front descended over the valley, and a cold, lashing rain began to fall. Shadduck knew that in such weather, he could never get far. Once more he postponed the escape.

The following morning, he was glad that he had canceled the plan. His fever was worse. His hand and arm were very painful; his body ached all over. He was sicker than he had been at any time since his capture and was in extremely low spirits. He was very surprised when about noon the commissar, whom he had not seen for almost a week, came to the "ward."

Shadduck was glad to see him. He said, "I am very sick. If you do not get me medical care I am going to die."

Shaking his head, the Communist looked at Shadduck's wounds and felt his forehead. When he began to talk of Communism once more, Shadduck nodded eagerly as if he were ready to embrace it. He was ready to do almost anything to get to a hospital. After a short talk, the commissar said, "I promise that you will be taken to a real hospital. They are moving some of the seriously wounded to the rear tonight, and I will see that you are put on a stretcher so that you will not have to walk."

Shadduck dismissed the promises as more Communist chicanery. He was surprised when shortly after supper that night, a large number of two-wheeled litter carts were pulled into the "hospital" area. One of the litter carts stopped outside his "ward." Two Chinese soldiers ordered the "American flier" to come out and get in the litter cart. Shadduck crawled out of the bunker and climbed into the cart. A number of other wounded Chinese were loaded aboard the other carts.

The little carts bounced out of the hospital valley, climbed over a few hills, and soon came to a main road. A railroad track ran nearby. Shadduck recognized it instantly as the Seoul-Chowan highway. The litter carts procession turned up the highway northeastward toward Chorwan. Two Chinese took turns pulling Shadduck's cart. While one pulled, the other trailed behind to make sure Shadduck did not slip away. Once, during the night, the litter cart was forced off the road by low-flying B-26 bombers.

At about five o'clock in the morning, the parade of litter carts pulled off the main highway and followed a trail for a short distance to a small Korean village at the foot of a range of hills. The village appeared to be some kind of medical stopover station where injured soldiers traveling to the rear could hole up for the day when U.N. planes made the roads and open country untenable. The aid-station commandant, standing in front of a small mud hut, assigned each litter-borne patient to a house and then directed the litter-bearers up a hillside to some foxholes where they were to camp.

The road to the commandant's house was rocky and rough. Shadduck's litter-bearers were very tired, and they asked him if he would get out and walk the last few feet. Obligingly, he hobbled up near the house and sat down on a small rock. When the commandant saw him, he walked over and spoke to the guards. Then he became very angry. Shadduck could tell from the way he spoke that he was mad that an American POW who could actually hobble had been brought in a litter cart.

The commandant did not bother to examine Shadduck's wounds, or in any other fashion try to ascertain his degree of injury. Instead, he ranted and raved over Shadduck's having had a "free ride." Then, instead of assigning Shadduck to a house or room like the other wounded, he ordered him—presumably as punishment—to climb the hillside and spend the day in an open foxhole with the litter-bearers. Followed by his two guards towing the litter cart, Shadduck hurried up the hillside, as he wanted to get as far as possible from the commandant.

He crawled into an empty foxhole. The guards gave him a bowl of cold rice and then settled in a foxhole a few feet away. He ate hurriedly. A few hours later, a "medic" came up from the town below and ordered Shadduck to hold out his hand. When he did so, the "medic" ripped off the old cloth, which, by then, had practically grown to his skin, and as Shadduck gritted his teeth in pain, he dabbed at the pus with a rag that had been dipped in kerosene. When the "medic" got up to leave, Shadduck grabbed him by the jacket and pointed to his other wounds—the burn on his leg, his seared eyelash, the large boils on the back of his neck, and the numerous infected and raw spots on his body that had been caused by lice. The "medic" squinted at these briefly, then shrugged his shoulders and walked away.

As he crouched in the foxhole looking over the surrounding countryside, Shadduck began to worry considerably about his predicament. If this and his previous stay in the Chinese "hospital" were examples of Communist medical care, he was certain that he would never get well; he would only get worse. He was especially concerned about the commandant, who was very surly and angry. Did it mean he would no longer ride? Would he walk all the way to the hospital—wherever it was? Or would the commandant have him shot on the spot because he was not able to walk?

Once more he began to weigh his chances for escape. There were not many guards around, and he thought he might make a break after dark. Fortunately, he had flown over the road hundreds of times and knew exactly where he was, about forty miles due north of Seoul. To reach safety, he knew he need only follow the Seoul-Chorwan road directly south. He believed this would be fairly easy to do since there were washes and gullies running alongside the road. On a forced march he would probably make it to friendly lines in two days. He said to himself: "I am getting out tonight."

In the early afternoon, Shadduck noticed a Chinese soldier making his way up the mountainside. He went from foxhole to foxhole, peering at the sleeping soldiers. When he saw Shadduck, he immediately walked toward him. The Chinese appeared friendly. But when he offered a ready-made Chinese cigarette, Shadduck became very suspicious: this was not the way Chinese soldiers usually acted. While they smoked, the Chinese pulled out a broken, cheap wrist watch, pointed to Shadduck's fine watch, and indicated that he wanted to trade.

So that was it. The soldier had heard about the watch. Shadduck shook his head: "No."

The Chinese soldier insisted on the trade. Shadduck was firm, as he was sure the Chinese would not try to steal it, especially with all the other soldiers—and possible informers—around. The Chinese disappeared into the brush and returned within minutes with a large club. He whirled it over Shadduck's head, jabbering away, demanding a switch of watches.

As the threats became more vociferous, Shadduck left his foxhole and ran over to the foxhole in which his guard and litter-bearer slept. When he made signs to indicate he would wake the guard if the Chinese came any closer, the soldier gave up and walked off.

Shadduck had other visitors that afternoon. Chinese soldiers came by in large numbers to look him over. Some pulled on his long beard, others looked at his wounds and his burned trousers. All were fascinated by the second hand on his watch and sat, like children, staring at it for hours. Many expressed great amazement at the ballpoint pen. They wondered where the ink was stored. Most of them laughed and chatted in a friendly way, and Shadduck joked along with them, all the while waiting for nightfall—and a chance to slip away.

Late in the afternoon, Shadduck was taken back down to the village at the foot of the mountain. The commandant had formed up the procession of litter carts, and the patients had been placed aboard for the next leg of the journey to the hospital. But when Shadduck came into view, the commandant glowered and ordered him to stand at attention. While he did so, the parade of litter carts moved off without him over the trail toward the main road.

Shadduck knew that he was no longer en route to a hospital. The commandant who had deliberately separated him from the others, apparently had something else in mind. He was trying to deduce what it might be when the commandant appeared with three guards. He spoke to them rapidly in Chinese, then he turned to Shadduck and growled, "Hike." One of the guards moved in front of Shadduck; two brought up the rear. As they walked out to the main road, Shadduck knew that in his present situation, escape was impossible, so once more he postponed his plans.

A few miles up the road, the guards veered left, following a road to the northwest. Shadduck recognized the new route as the main road to the North Korean capital of Pyongyang. The group joined a Chinese regiment that was heading in the same direction. The going became much tougher for Shadduck because the regiment was moving along at double time, and the soldiers were literally trotting down the road. Shadduck sensed from the pace and from the manner in which the men about him talked that the unit was being moved far to the rear. He began to think, Am I on the way to China?

The soldiers in the unit were very curious about the American flier. They ran alongside him, pulling his beard or playfully jabbing their bayonets into his stomach or back, shouting, "Kill, kill." To them, Shadduck was a big source of merriment. Every time one of them devised a new way to scare him, they all burst into gales of laughter. The favorite trick consisted of firing a rifle directly over his head or immediately behind his ear. He tried to brace himself against the crack of the rifle, but the harder he braced, the farther he jumped and the harder the Chinese laughed.

A flight of F-80 jets, apparently returning from a bombing mission to the north, flew low over the road. The mile-long column of jogging soldiers veered off the road and took cover under nearby brush. Shadduck ran for a large, bushy tree,

where he hid with his three guards and a large number of
Chinese soldiers. When the planes passed over, the soldiers
pointed to Shadduck, as if he had been responsible, and once
more threatened playfully to shoot him. When one soldier
actually pumped a cartridge into the chamber of his rifle,
Shadduck jumped. The soldiers laughed.

A small Korean boy walked up under the tree and stared
wide-eyed at the prisoner. The boy, like the soldiers, pulled
his beard and felt his clothes. His expression seemed to say
that he had never seen anything like Shadduck in his life.
Shadduck watched the boy unblinkingly for a moment, then—
thinking he might give the soldiers a laugh and possibly incur
their favor—he shouted "B-o-o-o" at the Korean boy as loud
as he could. The boy literally leaped into the air and ran
away as fast as he could. The Chinese soldiers doubled up
on the ground in laughter. After that, Shadduck was their
friend—he made jokes, too.

Finally, the planes disappeared, and the long column of
men got out on the road and began jogging north again.
Several hours—and many miles—later, a lone B-26 flew up
the road from the south. The column once again veered off
the road and dove into the nearby bushes and ditches, and
just in the nick of time because the B-26 dropped a string
of six brilliant flares directly over the column. The Chinese
lay still. They were so frightened that they talked in a whisper.
The B-26, apparently searching for vehicles, ignored the
soldiers and flew down the road. When Shadduck heard the
bombs go off on the road up ahead, he relaxed.

After an hour's march, the Chinese unit to which Shadduck
and his guards had attached themselves slowed to a walk.
They were entering the area in which the B-26 had dropped
its bomb. Shadduck could see a long line of wounded soldiers slowly struggling south. Litter carts and hand-carried
stretchers, both regulation and makeshift, were racing here,
there, and everywhere collecting the wounded. The dead had
been piled high on several oxcarts. In a quick estimate, he
counted two hundred wounded and two hundred dead. He
was secretly delighted but dared make no outward sign of it.

Shadduck's guards struck up a conversation with some of
the Chinese soldiers who had survived the B-26 bombing.
After a minute or two, one of his guards pointed toward him
and told the Chinese that he was an American flier. The
wounded soldiers made slurring remarks. One who had been
hit in the leg hobbled toward Shadduck and beat him with
his fist. The other soldiers grabbed the wounded man and
pulled him away. Fortunately, within a few minutes, Shadduck's unit was ordered once more to jog on up the road.

But after several hours, Shadduck began to get very tired and sick. He was not used to running great distances, and his wounded leg ached. Every time he slowed down, one of his guards fired a shot over his head and shouted, "Hike!" Once he stumbled and fell, but he got up quickly, prodded by a bayonet in his back. Then he ran on, tripping over rocks and shrubs alongside the road.

He had been told by the English-speaking guard that he was, as he had guessed, en route to China. Shadduck was sick at the thought. First, he was not sure that he could walk all the way to China. Yet he knew that if he did not keep walking, he would probably be shot. Even if he did succeed in getting to China, he knew his escape problem would be infinitely more complicated. He could not carry enough food to walk back through Korea; he would starve or else be caught pilfering. For a while he considered making for the west coast of Korea, stealing a boat, and sailing to the safe islands. But how could he be sure the islands were still safe?

Finally, he decided that the only way out was to wait until they came to the Communist airfields near the Yalu, then break away and steal a MIG-15 jet. He would slip up alongside a MIG field, wait until one of the jets had been started, then he would race out, kill the pilot, and jump in. The cockpit would be unfamiliar, but the throttles at least would be recognizable. He would ram the power home and take off.

He had never flown a jet, much less a Communist jet, but he had flown many fighters in his Air Force career. The sensation of speed would not bother him. He would not try to raise the retractable landing gear. There were two good reasons for not doing so. One was that he could not be sure which lever operated the gear, and he did not want to take a chance on making a disastrous mistake. Second, with the landing gear down, the MIG's speed would be greatly reduced. Thus, if other MIG's took off in pursuit, he might be able, at a slower speed, to turn sharper than they and thus prevent his being shot down.

He would fly close to the ground so that they could not dive on him or come from underneath. Navigation would be easy: he would fly southwest until he came to the coast line of Korea, then follow it due south. When he got close to U.N. lines, he would execute a series of secret maneuvers that were signals used by U.N. pilots with dead radios to identify themselves to U.N. radar operators as friendly. Thus, he would probably not be intercepted. He would head straight for Suwon, the home of the 51st Fighter-Interceptor Wing, where U.S. F-86's were based.

If U.N. planes spotted him in the air, they would see his

open canopy and extended landing gear. Thus, they would
know it was no ordinary MIG. They would probably withhold fire and trail him. The antiaircraft at Suwon would probably mistake him for an F-86 at first—long enough for him
to get on the ground. Once he landed, no one would dare
fire. The U.N. had yet to capture an undamaged MIG.

Such escape plans diverted Shadduck's mind from the agony
of the forced march, but soon he stumbled and fell again.
Once more he struggled to his feet and pushed on, prodded
by the guards, who shouted, "Hurry up. No stopping. Keep
going. On your feet." Every few minutes or so they fired
a rifle near his ear. At last he fell and could not get up. He
asked the guards for permission to ride in one of the many
empty litter carts that were being pulled along with the unit.

The guards seemd sympathetic with the request—they knew
Shadduck's physical condition better than anyone else—but
they also appeared afraid to assume the responsibility for the
decision. They had been present the evening before when the
commandant of the stopover aid station had lashed out at
Shadduck for riding in the little cart. They were afraid, and so
they waited until four Chinese officers came up. The guards
put the question to them.

One of the officers, a tall, thin man who carried a heavy
walking cane, seemed particularly outraged by the request.
He looked at the guards and let fly a stream of expletives. Then
he turned on Shadduck and yelled, *"So-la!"*

Shadduck knew that meant "get up," so he tried very hard
to raise himself. He had almost propped himself up on one
knee when the officer with the stick let out a loud squeal and
ran toward him, swinging the stick. The first four blows
caught Shadduck on the head and neck. As he twisted away,
the stick slammed across his injured hand. For a half second,
he completely blacked out from the pain and collapsed in the
dirt. Then as the stick pounded again and again, he rolled
over and over, trying to get away.

Somehow in the confusion, Shadduck crawled to the feet
of his guard. He rolled behind the soldier and tried to get up.
The squealing officer charged in for a final assault. Just at
that moment, two other Chinese officers ran up and restrained
him. One of the officers was the commander of the unit with
which they had been marching. As the officers engaged in a
heated discussion, Shadduck, with a guard under each arm,
staggered down the road as fast as he could. His hand and
face were bleeding.

One of the guards, the one who could speak a little English,
said, "Do not worry, you are all right now. The officer who
beat you wanted to shoot you but the regimental commander

would not let him. You are O.K. now. We go only a little farther. Maybe thirty minutes." Shadduck passed out.

Soon, he was vaguely aware of entering a village. "We are here," the guard said. Through the fog, he saw a fat little Chinese soldier standing in front of a mud hut. He seemed to be a friend of the English-speaking guard.

"Ding-how," he heard the Chinese say, "you are my friend."

Shadduck blinked. The fat Chinese took him by the arm and walked him into the house. Once inside, he fell to the floor. His feet ached terribly. He fumbled with the laces of his boots, but could get only one off before he passed out again.

It was eleven o'clock in the morning when he awoke, alone in the hut. He tried to get up, but he was too stiff. He looked at his right leg; it was about twice its normal size. The scab on the burn was half torn off, and pus had run down his leg and caked on his socks and boots. In places the flesh had rotted, exposing the muscle.

His head felt as though it had been split wide open, and his hair and beard were matted with dried blood. The officer's stick had dug holes and cuts in his face and neck. When he started to unzip his jacket to look at his shoulder, he noticed that blood and pus were flowing out of the ends of the bandage on his right hand. So he held it aloft to keep the blood from dripping out. Then he crawled to a door, pushed it open, wormed out onto the ground, turned on his side, and urinated. Two Chinese guards came over, looked down at him, and shook their heads.

Shadduck made his way back inside the mud house and lay on the floor. Within a few minutes, the English-speaking guard came in and asked if he wished to wash. He was astounded. In all his sixteen days as a POW, he had never been asked that question. He nodded his head in the affirmative. Soon the guard returned with a basin full of warm water. Shadduck wondered vaguely if the water was indication of a change of attitude on the part of the Chinese.

While he washed, the English-speaking guard went away. A short time later the guard returned with the regimental commander and carefully pointed out each of Shadduck's wounds. He asked him to roll over, stand up, and then lie down. The commander examined the wounds for a long while; then he left the hut. A few minutes later he returned with the officer who had wielded the stick. For a moment Shadduck was uneasy. He relaxed when he realized that the regimental commander was not happy about the beating and had brought the other officer to show him the wounds that he had inflicted on Shadduck's body.

The officer spoke back in self-defense. The regimental commander became very angry and shook his fist in the officer's face, pointing to Shadduck and jabbering loudly. Shadduck had never in all his days in the military witnessed such a "chewing out." For a minute he thought the commander was going to beat the officer with his own stick. Finally, the two officers went away. Shadduck smiled; the scene had done much to lift his spirits.

Soon the commander returned to the hut. He talked for a moment with the guard and then he called in a soldier who carried a brief case. The soldier took out a pad and the commander began dictating. The guard explained to Shadduck that the commander was writing orders that would transfer Shadduck from the unit marching to China to a nearby hospital. Shadduck's heart beat wildly at the news. The commander affixed his seal to the completed orders, then gave the papers to a Chinese lieutenant who had come into the hut. The guard informed Shadduck that the lieutenant would escort him to the hospital.

Later that afternoon when the guard came back to the hut to say good-by, Shadduck thanked him for convincing the regimental commander that he ought to be sent to a hospital.

"There is one thing in return that I must ask you," the guard said.

"What is that?" Shadduck asked.

"This has been an unfortunate incident. Please do not ever mention to the North Koreans that you were beaten while a prisoner of the Chinese. The Chinese are supposed to set the example. If the North Koreans hear of this, they might do the same to their POW's. It is not likely that they will stop short of killing."

Shadduck assured the soldier that the North Koreans would never hear of it, at least not through him. Then, after the guard had gone, he took a series of short walks outside the hut to limber his stiff leg. The exercise reduced the swelling considerably, and by late afternoon he was able to put his boots back on.

After an early supper, the Chinese lieutenant, accompanied by a guard, came to the hut and told him to get ready to leave. As he stepped out of the hut onto the road, Shadduck noticed that a large number of officers and soldiers had gathered, apparently to see him off. He recognized the regimental commander, the English-speaking guard, and a number of other officers and men. The officer who beat him was not among them.

Following an irresistible impulse, Shadduck walked up to the regimental commander, drew his racked frame to attention, and saluted smartly. Then he stepped back and gave a thumbs-up signal. The commander was visibly moved. He returned Shadduck's salute and grinned from ear to ear. After the incident, Shadduck observed that the lieutenant and the guard treated him with increased respect. Since it seemed to impress the Chinese, he made up his mind that regardless of what happened in the future, he would always try to maintain a dignified military bearing.

The lieutenant, the guard, and Shadduck marched northwest down the dirt road. After a few miles, they abruptly turned and followed a road that led due south. The road was crowded with Chinese soldiers. As they walked along, the lieutenant paused from time to time to show off the "captured pilot." The soldiers stopped to examine him. They poked him in the ribs, felt his arms, pinched him, and made jokes about his beard and his burned-off trousers. Once, when they passed a group of convalescents, a Chinese soldier who was limping with the help of a cane, charged across the road and beat Shadduck across the back. Shadduck ducked behind the lieutenant. After that the wounded Chinese made no further effort to strike him.

The three men continued to walk south for several hours, until about ten o'clock that night, they came to a small, burned-out Korean village. The lieutenant directed Shadduck into a cave, which had been dug into a terrace near one of the burned huts. The lieutenant ordered the guard away; then he crawled into the cave behind Shadduck.

Shadduck had no idea why the officer had followed him into the cave. As they sat there alone, he began to worry. He did not like being alone with the Chinese, for under these conditions and when not worried about informers, they were much bolder. Had he orders to kill Shadduck? After a while, the officer struck up a conversation in Japanese. He offered Shadduck a cigarette and said, "I must be getting back to my unit. What time is it?"

Shadduck looked at his watch and gave him the time.

"Ah!" the lieutenant said. "What a beautiful watch. May I see it?"

Shadduck handed the watch to the lieutenant, who looked at it very carefully, then put it in his pocket. Suddenly Shadduck knew why the Chinese officer had come into the cave—he was out to steal his possessions.

"Hey. Wait a minute," Shadduck said. "You can't do that. Chinese do not steal from POW's. Give me my watch back."

The lieutenant offered Shadduck a small good-luck charm —a piece of iron with a tiny brass emblem embedded in it— as a trade. Shadduck shook his head; he needed his watch for planning escapes. Besides, he was not going to let it go for a piece of junk.

"Give me back my watch," he insisted.

The lieutenant increased his offer by three cigarettes, but Shadduck was not impressed. Then, acting on the slim chance that all the lieutenant really wanted was simply a souvenir of the "captured pilot," he took out his ballpoint pen and said, "You have pen. I keep watch." The lieutenant took the pen, looked at it briefly, then put it in his pocket. He added some Chinese coins worth approximately a half cent to the trade.

Shadduck again refused. He informed the lieutenant that the whole deal was off.

"Give me back both the watch and the pen," he said.

The lieutenant whipped out his Russian revolver and stuck it in Shadduck's ribs.

"Trade, O.K.?" he said.

"No," Shadduck replied.

The lieutenant cocked the pistol, and said:

"Trade, O.K.?"

Shadduck believed that he had pushed the Chinese as far as he could. He knew it was very dangerous, this arguing with the officer without witnesses. The lieutenant could easily kill him and claim the "American flier" had provoked the action. He hoped that he might postpone the trading until daylight, when other Chinese soldiers would be around and the lieutenant would be less bold.

"Tomorrow, maybe," Shadduck said.

The lieutenant smoked a cigarette but made no move to return the watch and the pen. Finally he announced: "Well, I must go and rejoin my unit. We are marching on to China. I do not want to be left behind. The people at this hospital will care for you from now on. You will see the *honcho* tomorrow." He slipped out of the cave and vanished into the night.

Shadduck lay in the cave seething over the indignity of this callous robbery and his own impotence. But gradually he became aware of the noise of rushing water. He crawled to the mouth of the cave, and in the moonlight he could see a large river nearby. He knew from its size that it could only be the Imjin. Where was he? He drew a small map on the dirt floor of the cave. As well as he could remember, he traced the direction of his travels of the last sixteen days. He then realized that he must have moved around in a big circle and was now back near the spot where he had been captured.

The sight and sound of the Imjin so close by once more

raised thoughts of escape. To reach friendly lines, he need only follow the river directly south, as before. If he could find a boat of some kind, or a log, and float down the river to the Yellow Sea, he might reach a safe island, a South Korean fishing vessel, or even the U.S. Navy. But it was after midnight, and he was dead tired from the long evening's march. He knew he would not get far before dawn. He decided to rest up that night, and then break out the next evening.

The following morning shortly after daybreak he awoke. The first thing he heard was the sound of American voices. What was up? Had U.S. troops come on the scene? Had he been rescued? These thoughts flashed through his mind as he scurried out of the cave. The questions were answered almost immediately in the negative. Chinese soldiers were everywhere. The American voices came from a small Korean hut about six feet distant from the cave. Shadduck walked over and peered through a large opening that had been blown through the mud wall.

It was dark inside, so Shadduck waited a moment for his eyes to adjust. The hut was very small, not more than eight feet square, and although the straw-thatched roof was still intact, three of the mud walls had been pushed out. Bamboo canes had been stacked along the open walls. One end of the room contained a broken-down clay stove, which was open in the back. The floor was covered with dirty straw and horse manure, an indication that the Chinese had once used the hut as a stable.

Lying in the manure on the floor, side by side, were four men wearing U.S. Army fatigues. Their faces, like Shadduck's, were heavily bearded and caked with dried blood. From their positions, and from the pus-stained bandages Shadduck could see that they were all badly wounded. One of the men had a dark, swarthy complexion. Shadduck recognized him as a Turkish soldier.

"Hey, GI's," Shadduck said.

The four men looked at him through bloodshot eyes.

"Who are you?" one of them said.

"I'm Lieutenant Shadduck, U.S.A.F.," he replied.

"Well, what are you doing here?" one of the soldiers asked.

"I was shot down in a T-6 and taken prisoner on April 23. What are you guys doing here?"

"We are from the Third Division. We were taken prisoners during the big push on the same day. The Turk here was attached to the Third Division."

Then Shadduck heard another American voice. It came from a hut about twenty feet away.

"That's another one of the fellows," one of the soldiers said. "He is wounded and alone and wants to come over here with us."

"There isn't much room in here," Shadduck said.

"That's O.K. We will make room for him," one of the soldiers said.

Shadduck walked toward the adjoining hut. On the way he noted that it was the only other hut in the Korean village that was still erect. The others—more than a hundred—had been burned or blown out. Many Communist soldiers were billeted in the demolished huts. Many more lounged about the caves and dugouts on the surrounding hillsides.

Shadduck introduced himself to the GI in the other hut. Like the others, he was an enlisted man from the Third Division. He was dirty, his beard was long, and his eyes were bloodshot. His right ankle was severely wounded, almost blown off. In fact, only skin and muscle held his foot to his leg. He had been hit and taken prisoner during the same Communist push, though a few days later than the others. Shadduck soon learned that his name was Jim and that he was twenty-four years old.

He was very grateful when Shadduck helped him from his hut to the hut where the other GI's were bedded down. The four soldiers pushed over on the dirty floor and made room for Jim. Then all five of the Americans talked about when and how they had been captured.

One of the boys, a nineteen-year-old Italian named Joe, said, "I have never seen such an attack. They came at night. They blew whistles and bugles. They screamed. Some guy was beating on a dishpan. They hollered and came in from every direction. You couldn't tell whether the guy next to you was your buddy or a gook." Joe was a sergeant. He had a very large shrapnel wound in his hip and a small piece of shrapnel in his left leg. Both wounds were infected.

The other GI's concurred with Joe's description of the battle. Shadduck told them how he had seen it building up from the air and then how he had been shot down, landed in the middle of the attacking Chinese, and had ultimately been captured. Most of the boys, he discovered, had been shunted around in much the same fashion that he had been. None had received medical care or proper food.

One of the boys, an eighteen-year-old private named Bill, was very seriously wounded. A large piece of shrapnel had entered his right side and lodged against his pelvic bone. He could move, but he could not stand. He told of being moved from place to place on a litter cart and of spending a few days in a large cave where a Russian doctor maintained an "operating room." The doctor had refused to operate on Bill. In fact, he had had no medical treatment in sixteen days. Like the others, his wound was infected.

"What is this place?" Shadduck asked. He swept his wounded hand toward one of the open walls.

"This is supposed to be a hospital," Bill replied. "Most of the soldiers you see out there are wounded. They live in those bunkers and caves. There are medics here and a few nurses. They say there is a doctor around, but we haven't seen him. As far as I know, we are the only Americans around here."

"What are we going to do?" Jim asked. He was beginning to moan. His ankle hurt very much.

"The first thing we are going to do is clean this place up," Shadduck said. He stood up and started outside. "All the able-bodied men follow me, and we will get some clean straw." Nobody moved, and for the first time Shadduck realized that none of the men could walk. Joe and the Turk were able to hobble around but only with great pain. Suddenly Shadduck was filled with a great sense of pity.

Shadduck was not strong himself, but he spent the entire morning cleaning up the hut. He found a large stick and pushed the manure and dirty straw from the dirt floor. Then he gathered clean straw and placed it under each man. When he put the staw under the Turk, he had a chance to look him over for the first time.

The Turk, he found, had seven .30-caliber machine-gun holes in his body—one in the thigh of each leg, one crease in the thigh of his left leg, one through the flesh of his left shoulder, one through the middle of his lung, one through the flesh of the stomach, and a shell lodged in the upper part of his hip in the back. Nevertheless, he seemed to be the healthiest man in the lot, and his wounds were not infected. He pulled the gauze patch off his chest and held Shadduck's hand over the hole to show that he could breathe through it. He grinned. He did not speak English.

Later in the morning a Chinese soldier came by the hut and threw a couple of small bags of millet onto the floor and grunted in English, "Food." Having got the living quarters as clean as he was able under the circumstances, Shadduck now began to think about eating, because they were all very hungry. He looked at the sausage-shaped bags of millet and talked with Joe.

"I guess we will need some water to cook this stuff with, huh?"

"We don't have any water here, Lieutenant," Joe said.

"Then I will get some," he said.

Shadduck went out of the hut and walked up to the nearest

Chinese soldier and asked for water. The soldier tilted his head back and roared with laughter. Then he turned his back and walked away. Shadduck realized that if they were going to have anything to eat, they would have to shift for themselves. He scoured the burned-out village looking for a well and a vessel in which to carry the water.

Luckily he found a gallon pail in a nearby ditch. He slung the handle over his good arm, then went on searching for a well. He found one, but when he looked down into it, he was disappointed—the sides were littered with rotten bags and debris. The water itself was covered by a thick, greenish scum, obviously polluted.

Nevertheless, he scooped up a bucketful and lugged it back to the hut.

"I have water," he told the GI's, "but it has to be sterilized. Does anyone have any Halazone tablets?" None did.

"Then I guess we will have to boil it," Shadduck said.

This was a formidable problem. There was no fire in the hut. The stove was a shambles, as was the fireplace. Then Shadduck went out, this time in search of a material with which to make a stove. He hobbled about the village until, in a foxhole, he found a burned-out ammunition can. A little farther on, he came across an old Korean pot with one side broken out. He dragged the two pieces of junk back to the hut and put the jar in one corner. Then he placed a circle of rocks inside the jar and set the ammo can on top. Inside the rock circle he planned to build his fire, which could then blaze up through the can.

He gathered some sticks. As he had no matches, his next problem was how to obtain a source of fire. He approached an old Korean who lived in one of the huts. The Korean was obliging and gave Shadduck two burning coals, which Shadduck placed in the lid of a tin can. He then ran back to the hut, laid the twigs among the rocks under the ammo can, and shoved in the red-hot coals.

The twigs did not catch fire, so Shadduck knelt down and blew a steady stream of sparks against the kindling. But still the fire did not catch. He puffed until he felt lightheaded.

Joe said, "I will always remember one thing about Lieutenant Shadduck—he sure was a windy guy." They all laughed, including the Turk, who had not understood a word.

Finally, the twigs caught. As they blazed up, Shadduck ran outside to gather more wood. The Turk, who possessed two strong, uninjured arms, broke the wood into small pieces. Soon the fire was burning briskly, flame and sparks shooting up through the burned-out ammo can. Shadduck found a piece of stiff wire, bent it into an "S" shape, and laid it across

the top of the can. This was the "grill." He put the gallon pail
of water on and waited for the water to boil. It took a long
time.

They were about ready to take the pail off the fire and mix
the millet when a Communist soldier entered the hut. He could
not speak English, but he made it plain that fires would attract
U.N. planes, and they were not permitted. Shadduck was trying to explain that they needed sterilized water to mix with
the millet so they could eat when the soldier ruthlessly jerked
the pail from his hand and poured the water over the fire. It
went out quickly.

"Oh my, oh my, oh my," Jim groaned. "What are we going
to do now?"

It was a problem of first magnitude. They could not eat
unless they were permitted to build a fire. Shadduck sat down
—by now he was very weak himself—and thought. Finally,
he said to the men, "We will have to build a fire anyway. But
we won't advertise it like we did this one."

Shadduck spent the afternoon gathering a large supply of
rice straw that lay about the village and surrounding fields.
He packed the straw to the hut, carrying it under his good
arm. Then, he carefully wove it in and about the widely
spaced bamboo poles that had been leaned against the open
sides of the hut. He believed that if he could completely wall
off the sides with rice straw, the Communist soldiers would not
see the fire burning—if he could get it going again. The straw
walls would also keep out the cold wind.

Shadduck could not carry much straw in one trip, and he
had to stop often to rest. Most of the GI's shouted encouragement, made jokes, and tried to keep their minds off their
wounds. Only Jim kept moaning. Finally, the job was completed. Shadduck took a pup tent from one of the men, unfolded it, and hung it up over the hut door to complete the
"walls."

Then he went to the Korean hut and begged two more
burning coals. He hobbled back to the hut and once more
went through the agonizing procedure of firing the twigs,
going to the well for a second bucket of dirty water, and starting the cooking all over again. However, within a few minutes,
another Chinese soldier burst into the hut, jabbered about the
fire, and dumped the pail of water on the coals and twigs. The
soldier stormed out, shaking his fists.

"We will just have to wait until dark when they can't see
the smoke," Shadduck said. He spent the last few minutes of
daylight gathering more rice straw, which he used to wall off
the open space behind the broken-out fireplace. That night,
with all sides of the hut carefully sealed, Shadduck begged

two more coals from the Korean and for the third time made a fire. When the water had boiled, he mixed a pail full of millet mush, this time without interference from the Chinese soldiers.

The meal was, for a gourmet, a failure. The men—the Turk excepted—almost retched. But since it was filling and had a certain nutritional value, Shadduck urged everyone to eat a lot of it to help build up strength. All except Jim followed his suggestion. Afterward, they talked for a long while, and by late evening Shadduck knew each of the men well.

The Italian sergeant Joe was, Shadduck believed, an extremely likable, but very hotheaded character. He differed with Shadduck on the matter of how they should conduct themselves with the Communists. Shadduck had come to believe firmly in the "friendly" approach, i.e., being civil and suppliant, yet at the same time maintaining a dignified military bearing, hoping that in return the Communists would see fit to supply minimum food and medical requirements. On the other hand, Joe believed they ought to treat the Communists with utmost contempt. He wanted to kill every Chinese soldier who came into the hut.

The Turk was friendly, but quiet. Unable to speak English, he did not join in the incessant GI chatter that went on from dawn to dusk. Mostly, he just sat in one corner of the hut and slept all day and all night. The only thing that seemed to perturb him in the least were aircraft. Whenever they heard the engine of a plane, no matter how high or how far away, he became almost panicky. Apparently his unit had once been accidentally strafed by friendly planes. He had seen firsthand the damage they were capable of inflicting. The Turk, like Joe, could struggle outside to relieve himself.

Shadduck made up his mind that Jim, the GI with the sleeping bag, was a "mama's boy." Though his ankle wound was severe, it was not as serious as the wounds of the others. He was actually in better health. Yet he was far more demanding than the others. He complained bitterly about the food; every two or three minutes he asked for water. He thoughtlessly defecated in his fatigues, without even waiting to be supplied with a "bedpan," a piece of broken crockery Shadduck had scavenged.

Dave, an eighteen-year-old private from Tennessee, was Shadduck's favorite of the five men. He came from a large family and seemed to have been raised to take care of himself. He was very badly wounded. A .30-caliber bullet had entered his leg about twelve inches above the knee and had shattered the bone. The leg had never been set. It caused excruciating pain whenever he moved, even slightly. Another bullet had paralyzed his right shoulder and disjointed the arm.

Dave never complained. He just lay on his side all day and stared at the wall of the hut, or else amused himself by trying to balance his lifeless right arm on its elbow. He never demanded food or water. When he did ask for help, especially with the bedpan, he was apologetic. He was forever offering encouragement to the other men. He told jokes and tried to be cheery.

Bill was very young, too, and while somewhat emotional, he appeared to have himself under control. He was friendly and talkative and, though very seriously wounded, was not demanding. He talked a lot about getting back to his home in the Midwest. He was inquisitive about such things as aviation techniques and tactics and talked on this subject whenever possible.

Late in the evening the fire died down and the GI's dropped off to sleep. The hut was too small for six men to lie down in at one time, so Shadduck went back to the cave to spend the night. After he had settled himself, he began to turn over the events of the day in his mind. The Imjin River, close at hand, marked an easy escape route, and it babbled invitingly of freedom. But he was sure that, if left alone, the GI's would die in a few days' time. It was obvious that the Communists would do nothing to help the wounded men. Shadduck knew he really had no choice.

The following morning he buckled down to the long job of pulling the men through—at least to get one well enough to take over his role as nurse. He prepared more of the cold mush for breakfast, removed the dirty bandages, and examined each man's wound. There was little he could do other than look, for he had no medicine or bandages. During the inspection he noticed that Jim's ankle was draining a clear white fluid. He believed that if Jim would put his foot in the sunlight, it would be beneficial. But when he made this suggestion to Jim, the latter said: "Oh, no, Lieutenant. It hurts too much."

"It's for your own good," Shadduck insisted.

"No. No. I can't do it," Jim said.

Shadduck dragged him into the sun anyway.

Not long afterward, a group of Chinese nurses came to the hut. They were dressed in the standard Chinese Army, green, quilted uniform. Shadduck recognized several of them as the nurses who had been with him at the first "hospital." He remembered the name of one girl who had once given him a clean bandage and a drink of water.

"Hello, Lin-Sho-Song," he said.

She was surprised when she saw him.

"Hello," she said in English.

Then she turned and jabbered loudly to the other nurses, who laughed and chatted gaily, apparently about their old friend "the American flier." Then suddenly they burst into song. This encouraged Shadduck to feel that he might prevail on them to provide him with bandages and medicine.

He listened attentively to the song. Occasionally he heard the word "Truman." He guessed that the ditty slandered the U.S., "Americans," "capitalists," and "Madman Truman." But he laughed anyhow because he wanted the girls to believe that he was friendly. He began singing with them, mimicking their words, not knowing what he was saying, but hoping that he could arouse some fellow feeling in them—at least enough to induce them to provide some medicine.

Later, when the song was over and they were laughing heartily, Shadduck asked them point blank for help. The nurses quieted down and then Lin-Sho-Song replied, "No can help." She painstakingly explained what she had told him in the first hospital: only the "doctors" had authority to change bandages and administer medicine. Besides, she said, "There is very little and we must use that for the people's volunteers." With that they went away.

As soon as they were out of sight, Joe turned to Shadduck and said, "What are you stringing along with the yellow bitches for? We should have killed them all." He was very angry. Shadduck once more tried to explain his belief, that a little joking and jesting with the Chinese might make them unbend somewhat, perhaps even to the point of giving medical supplies.

"You haven't got anything to lose, Joe," Shadduck said. "Not a thing in the world. And there is everything to gain." Joe would not hear of it. He simply refused to have anything to do with the Chinese.

Not long after the nurses had left, the commissar who had been with the nurses at the first "hospital" came to the hut. He was very friendly, beaming from ear to ear. Shadduck snapped to attention, saying, *"Ding-how,"* and *"Towshong."* ("I surrender.") The political soldier laughed. He told them he had come to show some of his friends the sweep second hand on Shadduck's watch and the mysterious ball-point pen. "Let me see them," he said.

Shadduck held out bare hands, shrugged his shoulders, and told the Communist about how the lieutenant had stolen the articles in the "trade." The Chinese became very angry.

"Why didn't you yell out and stop him?" he asked.

"Because he had a Russian-made pistol in my ribs," Shadduck said.

The commissar stormed indignantly out of the hut, promising that he would bring the whole affair to the attention of his commanding general. But neither he nor the commanding general ever mentioned it further.

"That ought to teach you to leave those birds alone," Joe said later.

"Take it easy, Joe," Shadduck said.

After the middle of the second day, it became clear to Shadduck that medical treatment for himself and the other POW's was simply unattainable and that he would have to improvise as best he could. He began by spending the remainder of the day scrounging through the hospital area, trying to find compresses, gauze, cloth, or anything at all that could be of use. An old Korean pot, which he found in a ditch, became useful as a container for mixing the mush. The gallon pail could then be reserved exclusively for boiling water. A glass jar was cleaned and set aside as a sort of canteen for storing the sterilized water.

Between gathering firewood, going to the well for water, boiling the mush, and shuttling back and forth with the bedpans, Shadduck became a very busy man. He really did not have time to do all the work properly, and the GI's soon nicknamed him "Just a minute" because he used the phrase so often. Shadduck himself was not well. His hand and leg were healing, but slowly. He had to take time out often to lie down in the sun and rest.

The hut and the surrounding areas were, like most Chinese Communist installations, literally alive with lice. There was no way to avoid the little bugs, no means of exterminating them. Shadduck and his men simply tolerated them as best they could. Shadduck was particularly annoyed by the vermin, as his skin was naturally sensitive, and he could not resist scratching occasionally. The result was that a large area of his skin was raw, a fact that added greatly to his general discomfort.

The lice were most active—or seemed to be—when he lay down to rest or to go to sleep at night. On those occasions they seemed to rush forth from every nook and cranny, and he would feel a crawling sensation all over his body. He soon developed a system to counteract the temptation to scratch: he would walk around in circles until he was almost asleep on his feet. Then he would collapse and go to sleep—hopefully before the crawling sensation began.

To keep the lice from accumulating on them in uncontrollable numbers, Shadduck insisted that all men set aside one period of each day to pick them off. He put a crock of water in the sun each morning. By early afternoon it was usually warm—at least enough to use for rinsing. As the men stripped down for the lice-hunting routine, Shadduck passed the warm bowlful of water around. On an average day, Shadduck pulled about two hundred lice from his body and clothing. The other men, Jim excepted, followed his example.

In the late afternoon of the second day, Jim was talking to his foot when two slimy maggots crawled out of the wound and dropped on the straw. At the sight of the worms, he went berserk. Shadduck could sympathize with him, as he remembered only too vividly the time when he first discovered the maggots in his hand. After Shadduck had calmed him down, Jim dug the maggots out of his wound with a piece of straw, and, unthinkingly, threw them on the floor. The maggots crawled on the other men.

"For Pete's sake," Joe shouted. "Get those damned maggots out of here, Jim. Stop throwing them on the floor."

To avoid further difficulty, Shadduck dragged Jim outside the hut and helped him dig most of the maggots from the wound. He realized that he had to find some means of separating Jim from the others. The thought that maggots were crawling on them might drive some of the men out of their minds. He scrounged through the village once more and returned dragging a smashed-up shutter. He placed this in one corner of the hut, spanning the broken clay fireplace. Then he laid Jim out on the shutter. Thus, in his crude bed set apart from the other men, he was free to pick the maggots and let them fall harmlessly down into the broken fireplace.

On the twelfth of May—Shadduck's fourth day in the new "hospital"—the political soldier returned to the hut with the news that the entire unit was to be moved to the rear. Shadduck was stunned.

"How far?" he asked.

"Not very far," the commissar said. But Shadduck was worried. He had encountered the Chinese concept of "not very far" before. It could mean several hundred miles.

"In that case," he said, "we will need litter carts."

The Chinese seemed annoyed.

"Why should you Americans always ride when we walk?" he said.

"These men are badly wounded," Shadduck said. "They can't walk."

"Very well, you will stay here," the soldier said.

"Now, wait a minute," Shadduck said. "Wait just a minute. You can't leave us here like this."

"If they can't walk with us, then they will be left behind," he insisted.

Shadduck looked at the men. He was not too worried about himself because he knew if worse came to worst, he could hobble. The Turk and Joe might be able to stumble along for some distance. But Jim, Billy, and Dave definitely needed a litter cart.

"Couldn't we at least get a couple of litter carts?" Shadduck asked.

"No," the commissar said. "Either you walk, or you stay here."

While the hospital unit packed up, Shadduck hobbled from one Chinese officer to the next, begging for litter carts. But his requests were completely ignored. When in the late evening a Chinese soldier came by the hut and threw five small bags of millet on the floor, Shadduck knew that the decision was final: they were to be left behind. By nightfall, the unit had moved on. A six-man unit remained behind to guard the POW's.

After a supper of mush, Jim began to moan. This aggravated the other men, who were in low spirits. Finally, Joe lost his temper.

"Will you shut up? You're driving us crazy with that moaning. You ain't the only one that's hurt here. Now, shut up!"

"Take it easy, Joe," Shadduck said. He made his way to the shutter that served as Jim's bed.

"You ought to try to stop moaning a bit, Jim. You need to conserve your strength."

"But why does it have to be me, Lieutenant?" Jim asked. "Of all the people there are in our country, they picked me to wind up in this place and be left to die like this. I didn't want to come to Korea. I just wanted to stay home with my mother. If I ever get out of this place, I will never leave her side again—ever."

"Listen, Jim, none of us wanted to come to Korea. None of us asked for this. I got a wife and three daughters in Chicago. My wife was just operated on, and she's in pretty bad shape. There is no place to put the kids. How do you think I feel, being here? Do you think I like this?"

Early the next morning, Shadduck got up and searched carefully through the entire abandoned hospital area for cast-off medical supplies or food. The guards watched in a disinterested fashion as he crawled from foxhole to foxhole. He was lucky: in one hole he found a small jar of vaseline-impregnated compresses. In a ditch he found several wooden splints, which he took back to the hut and hid under the straw floor, to serve as kindling.

The Chinese "medics" also left behind a large, steel, traction splint, the type generally used for setting broken legs and thighs. Shadduck dragged it to the hut and, after he had changed all the bandages with the newly found compresses, asked Dave if he would like to have the bulky splint on his leg.

He thought that if they could strap it on, they might succeed in fixing Dave's thigh in an immobile position, and thus enable him to move his body without suffering unbearable pain.

Dave was agreeable, so the other men moved to one side while Shadduck pulled the splint into position alongside Dave's leg. More than two hours were required to work the steel frame over the shattered thigh. The process was very painful for Dave. He gritted his teeth. Perspiration broke out on his forehead, but he did not cry out. The splint was tied into place with the straps, which wound around his legs and body. Actually, the splint did not do much good; such serious fractures require an elaborate plaster cast. But Dave did not let on. He just lay in the straw and suffered quietly.

In the afternoon, a Chinese infantry unit moved into the Korean village and occupied the foxholes and bunkers that had been abandoned by the medical unit. On the chance that he might beg some medical supplies or food, Shadduck approached one of the Chinese officers and indicated in an obsequious manner that he would like to talk with him. The Chinese spat in his face. That set the pattern for future relations with the unit. Except for an occasional warning to Shadduck when they believed he was straying too far from the hut, the Chinese infantry soldiers, like the six guards, simply ignored the American prisoners in their midst. Shadduck could only guess that they had all been left to die.

The millet lasted about five days. When it ran out, Shadduck took a small bowl and went from foxhole to foxhole, holding out the bowl. Most of the Chinese soldiers laughed; some even picked up dirt and poured it into the bowl. In one hole, Shadduck found two Chinese soldiers asleep. He saw that they had a small bag of ground millet. He thought of stealing it, but at the last minute, he changed his mind and shook one of the soldiers lightly, saying the Chinese word for food.

The soldier awoke in a bad humor. He lashed out at Shadduck with his arm and then, brushing a fly from his nose, picked up his Russian-made rifle, and drove the bolt home. By then, Shadduck was already scampering away as fast as his legs could take him. The soldier cursed Shadduck roundly but did not fire. Shadduck made up his mind then and there to look elsewhere for food.

He went to see the Korean who had given him the coals. The Korean produced a small bag of rice, but his price was very high—a pair of boots. Shadduck walked back to the hut and told the GI's about the deal. Billy spoke up first.

"Take mine, Lieutenant, I can't walk. My boots aren't doing me any good."

The rice lasted about two days, and then once more they were without food. Shadduck went back to the Korean, but this time he shook his head. He had no more food. While returning to the hut, Shadduck came across a Chinese soldier who permitted him to scrape a tiny bit of parched rice from the bottom of a pan. When he brought the burned rice to the hut, Joe was infuriated.

"I am going to kill those gooks," he cried, struggling to his feet.

"Joe, lie back down," Shadduck said.

"No. I am going to kill every damned one of them," Joe said.

"Joe," Shadduck repeated. His voice was calm. "Lie back down. That's an order." It was the first time he had pulled his rank.

"I am going to get him, and you're not going to stop me," Joe shouted.

Shadduck stepped across the row of GI's and with his left hand slapped Joe hard across the cheek.

"Now, lie back down, Joe. If you lose your head, you will get all of us killed."

Shadduck pushed him to the floor, then he sat down on his chest. Joe was furious. He beat on Shadduck with his fists. Later, he apologized for his conduct.

"That's O.K., Joe," Shadduck said. "I don't like them any better than you do, but we don't want to aggravate them."

The following morning, Shadduck found a large, frayed wicker basket, slung it under his good arm, set off up the hillside, and spent the morning picking weeds and dandelions. When the basket was overflowing, he returned to the hut, pressed the weeds in the iron pot, poured in some of the sterilized water, and put wood on the fire. The heaping pile of weeds boiled down to a tiny portion of mushy green stuff. Shadduck carefully divided it and served it for lunch.

Jim complained. After the first bite, he said: "Lieutenant, this is the worst stuff I have ever tasted. I wouldn't even feed this to a bunch of chickens, much less human beings."

Underneath Shadduck became very angry. He had worked all morning picking the weeds, and he was in no mood for complaints. But he held his temper.

"I don't like it either, Jim, but you ought to eat it for your own good. There is nothing else to eat here. If you eat this, you might keep your strength up."

Two days later, a Korean civilian walked by the hut with a bag of rice. Shadduck stopped him with the idea of negotiating for the food. The Korean pointed to Shadduck's leather jacket, but Shadduck shook his head—that was too much.

The Korean insisted. Then Shadduck realized that he was helpless and had no bargaining power. He took off his jacket and gave it to the Korean. The rice lasted five meals, and then they went back on weeds again.

Several days later a North Korean colonel came into the hut saying he had heard about the "American flier" and was anxious to see him. When Shadduck stood up and gave his customary salute, the colonel seemed impressed. The two men conversed for some minutes in Japanese. When the colonel finally turned to leave, Shadduck grabbed him by the sleeve and asked him for tobacco. The Korean took out a pack of American cigarettes and gave it to Shadduck.

There was only one cigarette in the package, but it was like finding a rare gem. Thus far their tobacco supply had been made up of very strong, raw, Korean leaf, which the Turk begged from any and all who came near the hut. The tobacco was kept in a "community" can. Several times a day they poured a bit of the tobacco into paper torn from a Sears Roebuck catalogue a Korean boy had found nearby and given to them. They passed the cigarette around, everybody taking a couple of drags, which were usually followed by coughing and gagging on the strong smoke.

Shadduck carefully lit the American cigarette, took the usual two drags and then passed it on. He was amazed at how mild it was. Dave, Billy, Jim, and the Turk also took two drags. Joe refused to smoke the cigarette. He did not approve of the way Shadduck had saluted and talked with the Korean colonel.

Shadduck said, "Look. We got the cigarette, didn't we? What harm did it do? We might even have gotten some medicine—and we might yet."

They smoked the cigarette until it was about one quarter of an inch long. Then they extinguished the fire and spilled the remaining strands of tobacco into the "community" tobacco can.

Shadduck knew that he was working very hard, perhaps too hard for his own good, but in a way he was glad of it. The work kept his mind off his wife and family. It kept him from feeling sorry for himself. Even so, he never once stopped thinking of escape. He was convinced that if he and the five men with him were to come out of North Korea alive, they would someday have to get back to friendly lines. In short, he knew that ultimately he would *have* to escape.

He did not tell the others, but almost every move he made was designed to assist in the ultimate escape. When he went about the camp, searching for food and medicine, or whatever other junk he could find, he walked with an exaggerated limp. He did this because he did not want the Chinese to think that he was getting well enough to be moved to the rear—to begin the walk to China again. That would take him away from the front. Moreover, he believed that if the Chinese became convinced that he was lame and feeble, they would grow lax in their surveillance of his movements, a prerequisite to his plan for escape.

At first, Shadduck remained pretty much in the vicinity of the hut. Then—as he had done at the first hospital—he gradually enlarged his radius of activity. Soon he took to limping about the entire village. The Chinese guards watched him closely at first; but, little by little, as he expected, they became relaxed and unconcerned about his movements. Once Shadduck hobbled more than a quarter of a mile to the bank of the Imjin River. He took off his clothes and bathed, ostensibly the purpose of his trip, but all the while, he carefully scrutinized the surrounding countryside, especially the area near the banks of the river to the south.

One day, Billy called Shadduck to his side and handed him a small Bible that he had been carrying in his fatigues.

"Lieutenant," he said, "the light is bad here and I can't see. How about reading to me from this?"

Shadduck thumbed through the Bible. Then he turned to the other GI's.

"How about you guys—do you want to hear this?" He held up the Bible.

They all said yes.

Shadduck turned to an appropriate passage—the Twenty-third Psalm. He began reading: "The Lord is my Shepherd, I shall not want. . . ." He read for more than an hour. When he finished, the men fell into a discussion of religion. Joe identified himself as a Catholic. Jim was a Lutheran. Billy was a Methodist. Inevitably, an argument broke out about which religion was best. Shadduck interrupted.

"Now, wait a minute. We can't have any of that," he said.

"What's your religion?" Joe asked.

"Well," Shadduck said, "I guess you can't say I have any one religion, or that I belong to any one sect. I got my religion in the service. I grew up among men of all religions. I went to the chapel where men of all faiths attend. I believe in God, but I believe in the right of every man to love and honor God as he wishes. And that is the way it is going to be here. If not, then I'll knock off reading the Bible."

They quickly agreed to maintain routine Air Force chapel conditions wherein the religion would be nonsectarian. Thereafter, Shadduck established a regular Bible-reading hour for each day, a period that became very popular. If he missed the appointed hour because he was busy gathering food or emptying the bedpans, the GI's were quick to remind him of it. When he sat down, leaning against the bamboo wall, and pulled out the Bible, the men were very attentive.

On Sundays—they kept track of the days by scratching a mark on the mud wall of the hut—Shadduck held a formal Sunday-school lesson. It was different from the daily reading of the Bible in that the Sunday session was conducted in a very formal atmosphere and was usually followed by a lengthy question and answer period. Chaplain Shadduck made a point of trying to tidy up the hut a bit before the Sunday sessions.

One Sunday during the question and answer period, Billy said, "Lieutenant, I have always been a religious guy. I have gone to church every Sunday of my life when I was able. I have read the Bible. Now, if I have always been so good, then why has the Lord put me in this place to suffer like this?"

Shadduck replied, "Billy, what makes you think you're so bad off? You know, things could be a lot worse than they are. For example, to take the worst, you could be dead. You're not dead. You're very much alive. In fact, you are so much alive, you are able to contemplate God and his mysterious ways. Isn't that something in itself?"

Billy nodded. Shadduck went on.

"Yes, you could be a lot worse off. You could have had your guts blown out. You might have had half of your head shot off, or maybe an arm, or leg. Sure, you're hurt bad, and you can't move around much, but, at least, you're not getting worse. You're not dying."

Shadduck did not entirely believe that because he knew Billy was very badly wounded. More likely than not, he was on the downgrade, not the upgrade. But the little discussion had an amazing effect on Billy's morale. He began to think of all the ways he might be worse off, and he began to feel better. The Sunday-school lessons also began to affect the others: Shadduck could tell because the men looked forward to them so eagerly.

Once while they were in the midst of a Bible lesson, they heard the noise of a U.N. plane overhead. Shadduck peeped outside the bamboo wall. "Jeepers!" he exclaimed. "Look at that!" The plane swooped down low over the burned-out village, machine guns rattling. Several other planes followed behind. The Turk became very frightened and hid under the straw. Shadduck and the GI's were far from being at ease. "Boy, just don't drop a can of napalm down here," Joe said.

The planes came back the following day and then the day after. They seemed to have found a favorite target on the ridge top behind the village. The attacks were exceedingly disconcerting because in order to get a straight run on the ridge top, the planes flew directly over the hut. Invariably the pilot began firing his machine gun just as he passed over the rooftop. They all feared that one of the pilots might someday begin firing too soon and strafe the hut.

One evening after a strafing attack, Shadduck as usual limped up on the grassy hillside behind the hut to empty the bedpan. While he was out, he looked up at the ridge top several hundred feet away and wondered what was there that made so fine a target. Then the thought suddenly occurred: perhaps he could make a signal to the planes! He looked around for possible material, and his eyes fell upon several stacks of yellow rice straw. He noticed that the straw stood out in vivid contrast against the background of the new spring grass.

Shadduck gathered several stalks of straw and began arranging them across the hillside in the shape of letters. He was afraid that if he worked too long he might attract the attention of the guards, so after a few minutes he returned to the hut. But on the following night he returned to the hillside and dragged several more stalks into place. On the third night he completed the sign. The letters were about fifteen feet high, and as wide as the rice straw, about thirty inches. They spelled out "6-P-W." Later Shadduck added an arrow pointing to the hut.

When Shadduck finally told the others about the sign, they were very excited. He explained that it not only served as a warning to U.N. pilots not to strafe their hut but also was, in effect, a kind of SOS. He particularly stressed the latter aspect of the sign. Sooner or later, he told them, one of the pilots would spot the sign, and when he did, he would send in a helicopter to pick them up. This was hope, and the sign raised morale considerably.

But no amount of Bible reading or rescue talk helped Jim. Shadduck soon discovered that he was impervious to encouragement and refused to try to help himself. He continued to complain about the food, to ask for water every five minutes. He moaned, talked to his foot, and screamed whenever he saw a maggot crawl out of his wound. Shadduck's major problem became that of trying to keep up Jim's morale, of trying to instill in him a desire to help himself stay alive.

One day Jim was particularly stubborn about eating. He would not touch his food. Finally Shadduck lost his patience and snapped out: "Jim, I order you to eat that food." It was the second time that Shadduck had pulled his rank. It made no impression on Jim.

"O.K., Jim. No water for you until you eat," Shadduck said. This was a stern measure for Jim. He could not go long without water. He surprised Shadduck by holding out for more than three hours. But finally he broke down and said, "O.K., Lieutenant, I'll eat now."

Meantime, Jim's wound was getting worse. One day, Shadduck noticed that a dark black and blue line was creeping up the side of his leg. He knew that it was blood poisoning. This presented a very delicate situation because Shadduck did not want Jim to know that his wound was getting worse. He was afraid the boy would give up entirely. All along his strategy had been to try to convince him that he was getting better. Shadduck could think of no way to deal with the new problem.

He was extremely concerned, as he knew the blood poisoning could easily be fatal. He lay on the straw at night worrying about what he should do. Finally he decided to approach the Chinese and ask them to operate. The following morning he explained the situation to a Chinese officer. The officer seemed sympathetic and promised that he would "soon" have Jim transferred to a hospital where the leg could be amputated.

This was encouraging, but now Shadduck was faced with a larger problem! Should he tell Jim? He felt that he must; first, because he wanted Jim to know in advance that he would be leaving the group. Second, he wanted Jim to be familiar with the severity of his wound so that when he got to a Chinese hospital, he would not arbitrarily oppose the amputation.

That evening, Shadduck reversed all his previous "stories," and told Jim the truth about his wound. He showed him the dark line creeping up his leg and told how he had made arrangements to have him taken to a rear area hospital. Jim's morale dropped out of sight, and he moaned and cried all night. The GI's yelled at him to shut up.

The next day Shadduck sought out the Chinese officer to ask when he would send Jim to a hospital. He was very worried because the blood-poisoning line had moved even higher up Jim's leg. The officer told Shadduck that he had changed his mind. He would not permit Jim to be taken to the rear. The POW's, he said, would have to attend to their wounds the best way they could.

Shadduck was stunned. He stumbled back to the hut in a fog. He suddenly realized that if Jim's leg was coming off, he, Shadduck, would have to take it off. He shuddered at the thought. Later he explained the whole situation to Jim. Then he asked if he would mind if he made a try at taking off the leg? Jim said no; he no longer cared what happened. He just lay on the shutter bed moaning.

Shadduck thought about the operation all morning. It would not be easy. His own right hand was still useless. He decided he would take the leg off at the knee, while the Turk and Joe, who had fairly strong arms, held Jim down. Then he would singe the ends of the nerves and blood vessels, to keep him from bleeding to death. He almost became sick when he thought about it, and he prayed that he would have the courage and strength to go through with it.

When he was finally ready, he went back to the Chinese officer to borrow a knife to use in the operation. But the officer said, "We cannot let you have a knife. That is a weapon." He even refused to let Shadduck use the knife under close supervision. He would not do anything to assist the Americans. Shadduck turned and walked slowly back to the hut, mentally kicking himself for the way in which he had handled the entire matter.

Jim went to pieces when he learned the news. He cried and wailed until all of the men yelled for him to shut up. He called for his mother. He asked for water over and over. He drank all of the clean water and then insisted on having some that had not even been boiled. Shadduck said no.

"But, Lieutenant, I have to have some water," he said.

"I don't care," Shadduck said. "You've got to wait until it's been sterilized. It'll be ready in about half an hour. I've got to go pick some weeds. Please be quiet and try to get some rest."

While Shadduck was out in the field, a Korean boy who had taken to hanging around the POW's sauntered into the hut. Jim ordered him to go to the well and fill the glass bottle with water. The Korean boy took the bottle and soon returned with the water, which Jim drank. When Shadduck returned from the field and discovered what had happened, he lost his temper.

"What're you trying to do, deliberately kill yourself?"

"No, Lieutenant. I am not trying to kill myself. I just want to get back to my mother. I just want everybody to leave me alone."

The following morning, Jim moaned and cried more than usual. Then he became sick and threw up all over himself, the shutter, and the broken-out fireplace. Shadduck cleaned up the mess, and said, "Jim, please shut up."

For once, Jim did as he was told. He stopped moaning and closed his eyes. He did not make another sound. After several hours, Shadduck began to worry about him. He noticed that flies had collected on his lips. He made his way to the shutter bed, looked at Jim's glazed eyes, felt his pulse, and knew that he was dead.

Though while alive Jim had caused all of them misery and inconvenience, his death had a profound effect on the men. They became hysterical. Billy shouted, "See. See. This is what is going to happen to all of us. We are all going to die just like this." Shadduck moved from one man to the next, trying to calm them down. Finally, he took out the Bible and hurriedly read aloud in an attempt to drown out the wailing and crying. More than two hours were required to restore peace and quiet to the hut.

Shadduck then faced the problem of arranging a funeral for Jim. He knew none of them had strength to dig a grave, so he went to the Chinese and asked if they would detail a few soldiers to attend to the matter. As usual the Chinese refused to have anything to do with the POW's.

Shadduck returned to the hut and removed all of Jim's personal effects except one dog tag. Then he wrapped the body inside a rubberized poncho, and with the help of the Turk and Joe, dragged it outside and put it in the little cave in the hill behind the hut. It was the cave in which Shadduck had spent his first night in the "hospital." They placed some boards and rice straw over the entrance and covered the lot with dirt. When they had finished, Shadduck read an appropriate passage from the Bible.

"Jim killed himself," Shadduck told the other GI's, "and I don't want anybody else to do that."

It was a dismal afternoon. Shadduck read more passages from the Bible, but inevitably the talk returned again and again to Jim. Shadduck perceived that nothing short of a miracle would snap the men out of their despondent mood. He was about to suggest that they begin the afternoon lice-picking session when suddenly the stillness was disturbed by the distant rumble of big guns.

"Artillery," Joe said.

"It couldn't be," Billy said. "The lines are down near Seoul. It must be the Chinese practicing somewhere."

As the late afternoon wore on, the deep rumble persisted. The men laid their ears to the ground, and speculated on what it might mean.

"The U.N. must be advancing north," Shadduck said after a careful consideration of the situation. "The lines are getting closer. The Chinese must be retreating." He did not say it, but he thought: If the Chinese retreat, they will move the American POW's to the rear. The GI's—especially Dave and Billy—cannot even make it to the edge of the camp. They will either die of their wounds or the Chinese will shoot them.

Not long afterward, a long line of Chinese troops came into view marching northward up the road that skirted the Imjin River. Shadduck could see that the troops were very tired and many of them were wounded. Obviously the Chinese were retreating in large numbers. The troops billeted in the area around the hut went down to the road to talk with the retreating soldiers. Shadduck could tell that they were concerned about the changing battle situation. He became certain that within a few days—perhaps hours—a crisis would befall the American POW's.

The new situation did not help the already low morale in the hut. Hope of escape, which had been instilled by the "6-P-W" sign, rapidly dissipated when the men discussed the consequences that might befall them as a result of the advancing U.N. front. Billy was certain that if he was forced to leave the hut, he would die within a matter of minutes. Dave, for the first time, broke down and cried. He knew that with his shattered leg he could never move. It was shortly after supper that evening that Shadduck made up his mind to escape. It had become plain that he had to make a break for the U.N. lines and go after a rescue unit. It was now or never.

Shadduck spent the remaining minutes of daylight hurriedly stockpiling supplies, including three days' supply of firewood and a full pail of water from the well. Then, acting on a hunch, he walked down and stood alongside the road along which the Chinese were retreating, begging for food and medicine. One soldier stopped, looked at Shadduck, then took off his rucksack and gave him a five-pound bag of barley. Another soldier—a medic of some kind—dug into his Red Cross bag and gave Shadduck a handful of compresses, a tube of vaseline, five rolls of gauze, two packages of "American Embassy Sulfa Powder," and a double handful of good tobacco. As Shadduck raced back to the hut with his supplies, he was almost delirious with joy. He believed a miracle—the miracle he needed—had occurred.

That evening, Shadduck prepared a meal of barley mush. After the steady diet of dandelion greens it was a welcome change as well as a morale booster. Later, with the new medical supplies, he changed all the bandages and then lit up and passed around a cigarette.

This was the moment, he decided, to tell the men that he had determined to escape and how he proposed to do it. He pointed out how lately he had been taking more and more time each evening to empty the bedpan and how he had elected a disposal place at the nearest approach of the camp's perimeter to the river. From the disposal point a small trail ran down a steep hill to the water, along which he could move silently and unobserved.

There was only one exposed place on the trail, and that was where it crossed a highway. If he could get across that undetected, he would be in the clear before enough time had elapsed for the guards to become suspicious. Once he reached the river, he had only to follow it southward until he reached friendly lines. He told them he expected to reach the U.N. lines by the third day. But he cautioned them not to lose hope, even if help did not arrive for six or seven days.

"The lines might change again," he said. "Besides, I might get captured. In that case, it might take a couple more days for me to escape again." He told them that the minute he reached friendly lines, he would instruct the Fifth Air Force to send in a flight of fighters to circle over the hut as a signal that he had made it.

"On second thought," he whispered, "I will have the fighters circle twice. I will tell them to come in once, fly around the hut three times, then go away, and come back again and fly around the hut three more times. If possible, Joe, when the plane comes over the first time, slip out in the field back there and let them see you. That way, the pilot can make sure you are still in the hut and that it is the right one."

"Right, Lieutenant," Joe said.

"And then," Shadduck said, "the helicopters will come in right behind the fighters. Joe, you be sure and get everybody ready and carry them out into the field when the chopper comes."

"O.K.," Joe said.

The GI's were enthusiastic about the new plan, and they discussed it in low tones for more than an hour. Only the Turk did not understand what was going on. He sat in his corner as usual, quietly smoking. Shadduck appointed Joe, the senior man, to take care of the others. Joe was impetuous, but he had one asset that outweighed everything else—he was able to walk. Shadduck believed that Joe—with the Turk's help—could attend to the nursing and cooking. Joe assured Shadduck that he could handle the situation, especially with the three-day stockpile of firewood and the newly acquired supply of barley.

The longer the men discussed the plan, the more excited and optimistic they became. Shadduck was pleased because that was just what he had hoped for. The thought of possible rescue almost completely offset Jim's death. The men had become very alert and talkative, offering ideas and suggestions. Joe got out his shelter half and gave it to Shadduck to carry along as a blanket. Bill provided the frying pan from his mess kit. Shadduck buckled the pan on his belt and strapped the shelter half on his back.

He turned to Joe. "If the Chinese want to know where I am, tell them that one of the Chinese officers came to the hut and took me north. It will take them a couple of days to check the story."

"Right, Shad," Joe said. "Good luck. And—say. Just in case. How about taking down my address?" One of the GI's produced the broken stub of a pencil and a rumpled piece of paper. Shadduck carefully jotted down the full names, serial numbers, and addresses of each of the men—"just in case."

He checked to make sure he had Jim's personal effects in his pocket.

"One more thing, Lieutenant," Joe said. "If they can't get into here with a copter to get us out, ask them to drop some medical supplies and something to eat."

"Right, Joe," Shadduck said. He started out the back door of the hut. Just then the Turk grunted and walked over.

He had been watching the goings-on with interest. When Shadduck had strapped on the shelter half and started out the door, he had finally grasped what was afoot. He grabbed Shadduck by the arm and whispered: "No. No. Many Chinese, No. No."

Shadduck smiled. "That's O.K., Turk," he said. "It will be all right. So long, fellows."

It was nine thirty when he stepped out into the black of the night and, bedpan in hand, started walking slowly toward the bluff. It had begun to rain, a very lucky break, Shadduck knew, for in his thirty-two days behind enemy lines, he had rarely seen a Chinese or North Korean soldier move about in the rain. The odds were good that no guard would follow him to the bluff and also that none would come to the hut that night for a nose count.

When he reached the bluff, Shadduck tossed the refuse over the side and immediately set off down the trail at a fast, but not hasty, pace toward the Imjin River. He slipped down a hillside, then hurried through the pitch dark to a small wheat field alongside the road. The traffic on the highway had been curtailed by the rain, but Shadduck could hear a few soldiers tramping along. He did not want to bump into them in the darkness, so he lay in the field a long time, waiting until he was certain the way was clear.

Finally, he got up and, bending over to reduce his silhouette, started across the yellowish gravel. At that instant, the bright beam of a flashlight swept up the road and flickered across his body. Had he been spotted? He wheeled and raced back across the road and dove into the wheat field. He lay quietly as two Chinese soldiers walked up the road apparently unconcerned. They either had not seen him or had dismissed him as a Korean. Another lucky break.

After a while he got up and once more made for the road. This time he crossed it without incident. The way to the river was clear. However, to avoid enemy perimeter outposts he kept on the low ground, stumbling along in the dark, barely able to see the way. Once he stepped off into a deep ditch. He landed on his shoulder and spun over and over. Rocks and stones clattered loudly into the draw behind him, but he was not injured. Fortunately the rain had drowned out the noise.

Within a few minutes he reached the river. He tried to cross to the opposite bank, where he knew there were fewer soldiers, but the current was too swift. Without further ado, he turned south, running from rock to rock, ducking behind bluffs and trees whenever they were available, pushing on through the driving rain.

Soon the river flowed into one of the many canyons along its route. In searching for a way out, Shadduck found a small trail that had been hacked in the side of the steep canyon wall. He debated a long while over whether or not he ought to use it. He soon realized that the only other alternative was to get into the water, which ripped through the gorge at a very fast rate, swooshing noisily through rocks and rapids. He did not think he could survive in the water, so even though he was leery of it, he chose the trail.

Shadduck followed the trail around a bend in the canyon. Suddenly he became aware of a dim glow ahead that looked like the reflection of a fire. But how could anyone keep a fire going in this rain? Shadduck thought. He moved toward the glow. Then he saw that it was indeed a fire, burning in the edge of a cave in the canyon wall just off the trail. He could also see the dark forms of several men huddled in the cave. It was an enemy outpost, a check point on the trail.

This was very bad. The check point blocked the only way out of the canyon. What could he do? Shadduck sat down on the trail and hung his legs over the side of the cliff, peering down at the rushing river. Should he jump? Or should he go back? For the first time, he began to lose his confidence. He knew that if he were caught trying to escape, he would be shot on the spot. There was still time to sneak back.

Suddenly he heard the noise of a B-26 bomber in the distance. The guards in the cave heard the plane at the same instant. Shadduck saw them douse the fire. The B-26 flew over the canyon and dropped its bombs in the distance. The Communist guards did not relight the fire. Had the B-26 hastened their bedtime? Shadduck eased to within thirty feet of the cave. He could hear the men talking. Then, one by one, he saw them drop off to sleep. Another stroke of luck, Shadduck thought. Now, maybe I can get by.

He sat on the ledge in the driving rain for another hour to make sure the men had gone to sleep. Then he lay down, and inched forward, being very careful to pick up and place out of the way each little loose rock or stone. He passed within ten feet of the mouth of the cave. Even above the roar of the rain and rush of the river water, he could hear the men snoring. He kept crawling until he was about fifteen feet south of the check point, then he got up and ran without stopping for more than a half a mile.

Several miles farther south the river flowed out of the canyon into the flatlands. Shadduck slowed his pace. He knew from experience that there were more Communist troops in the valleys than in the canyons. He continued following the bank until he came to a point where the Imjin, joined by a branch flowing from the east, made an abrupt turn and flowed southwest, toward the Yellow Sea. He knew the junction well and that he had only to continue following the river to reach friendly lines. He kept to the north bank.

Within an hour, it began to get light, and he began to search for a good place to hide out for the day. He did not want to make the mistake of moving in daylight again. The north bank of the Imjin was extremely rugged, mottled with numerous crevices and cracks. After a while he crawled between two rocks and lay down with the idea of staying all day. But after looking around a bit, he abandoned his position and moved to another hide-out that was higher and drier. He spread the shelter half over him and lay down, well hidden from view.

He was very tired, but he was not able to sleep. For one thing, he was too wet and cold. His teeth chattered. Then he began to think about the GI's he had left in the hut. Soon the guards would come by to make the routine morning count. Would Joe remember what he was supposed to say? Could he take care of the other boys? The more he thought about them, the wider awake he became. Then, once more, the urge to move on gripped him.

It was now completely daylight and raining very hard. Travel in such weather would not be hazardous—especially if he could get to the south bank of the Imjin, where he was less likely to encounter enemy soldiers. Just then, his eye fell upon a battered old Korean skiff that had been pulled up on the sandy river beach and wedged between two rocks. He considered the boat providential, and without further hesitation, he slipped from his hiding place and made his way down to the skiff.

A chain had been draped across the sand to anchor it. He dragged the chain into the boat—with a fearful rattle— then pushed it back out into the swiftly flowing river. He used an old paddle to steer along in the current toward the south bank, but a back current forced the boat away from the shore. He was beginning to feel very conspicuous, so he paddled as close to the beach as he could, jumped out of the skiff, and left it to drift on downriver. The water was shallow, and he easily waded ashore.

The south bank of the river was steep but not impassable.

For more than eight hours Shadduck walked along it, pushing through brush, stopping occasionally to drink from a spring or to rest against a rock. In the late afternoon he came to a place where the lower bank turned into a sheer cliff. He was forced to leave the water's edge and climb up a few feet to a rough trail. He had walked along the trail but a few hundred feet when he became aware that a double-skirted, barbed-wire entanglement had been placed along the bank below the trail. Barbed wire meant enemy troops!

He followed the trail for several hundred feet, looking for a way to climb to the top of the bank. Then, with a start, he saw a thin wire stretched across the trail, about two inches off the ground. His eye followed the wire to a land mine, half-buried in the dirt a few feet off the trail. He looked back along the trail and saw that he had stepped over three of the trigger wires. Had he walked into a trap? With both eyes on the lookout for other wires, he ran off at a fast pace.

He had gone but twenty feet when a loud explosion rocked the countryside. The grass around Shadduck was neatly mowed, and branches were clipped from a treetop over his head. A violent object struck him in the back of the neck. He spun around crazily and fell to the ground. After all this, he thought, I have been hit by an enemy hand grenade. He lay in the path a long while, waiting for another grenade to fall or the rush of enemy soldiers.

To his surprise he found himself still continuing to live. Moreover the aching in the back of his neck became less severe. Still he could feel warm liquid flowing down the back of his wool shirt collar. At length, he rolled over and with his good hand, felt the back of his neck to ascertain the extent of the wound. It was soft and mushy. Then he looked at his hand. It was covered, not with the blood he had braced himself to expect, but with a thick, black, oozing mud. Quickly he scraped more of the slime from his neck. Then, he realized that he had not been wounded at all! He had been struck by a mud ball.

He stood up and looked around. Just off the trail, he noticed that a three-foot hole had been blown into the ground, and he realized he had set off a land mine! Fortunately no Chinese troops had come running to the scene. He scolded himself for being so careless and quickly crawled up the steep riverbank to get away from the area. When he reached the top of the bank, he cut directly inland, passing through woods, fields, and rice paddies. It was still raining very hard.

Late in the afternoon, he came upon a small Korean village. He hid in the underbrush and watched it for a long time. He saw no one walking about, nor were there signs of enemy troops. Nevertheless, he set a course that would skirt wide around the town and bring him back to the river farther south. He had almost completed the detour and was making his way back to the river when he spotted three more mud houses set off by themselves. He ducked behind a tree.

Shadduck watched the houses intently for more than an hour. He knew he was getting very close to the Chinese front lines, and he was determined not to be caught by a careless mistake. As he watched the house, he saw an old woman, a man, a younger woman, and several children of varying ages. The three huts apparently made up the main dwellings of a farm. There was no indication of the presence of Chinese troops.

The longer he watched the houses, the more he became aware of the fact that he was very tired and hungry. A thought crept into his mind: Was it possible that these Koreans were friendly? Would they give him something to eat, and perhaps some information as to the whereabouts of the Communist troops? At first, he rejected the idea of approaching the house as foolhardy. But then the thought of food returned. Finally, he decided he would chance it.

Some minutes later, an old man walked out of one of the houses toward the well, which was not far from the tree where he was hiding. Shadduck stepped from behind the tree and walked toward the old man. He held a sharp rock in his good hand under the shelter half—just in case. When the Korean saw Shadduck, he started. Shadduck held up his injured hand and by signs tried to indicate that he was friendly and in need of help. The Korean nodded as though he understood and motioned for Shadduck to follow him to the house.

When they reached the house, the Korean opened the door and stepped aside, indicating Shadduck should enter. But he refused, as he was not sure of the loyalty of the native. Instead, he stepped under a small side porch to get out of the rain. The Korean made signs to indicate that it was dangerous for Shadduck to remain out in the open. But Shadduck did not want to risk being captured inside the house. He elected to remain outside where, if surprised, at least, he could run.

When the Korean realized that Shadduck would not go inside, he spoke to the young girl, who had come outside to look at Shadduck. She scurried away and returned with a bowl of cold rice. Shadduck picked the rice up in his fingers and pushed it into his mouth. Bits of it stuck on his beard. Within seconds, he had finished the bowl and returned it to the girl. Then he gobbled down a plate of chopped onions the old man had prepared.

While he was eating, a young boy came to the house.

Shadduck was pleasantly surprised when he discovered that he could speak Japanese. He plied him with questions about the Chinese troops. In reply the boy told Shadduck that there were no Chinese in the immediate vicinity but that they were retreating and the front lines were only a few miles to the south. He advised Shadduck to stay near the river and go around the main force of the enemy, rather than try to sneak though the lines. While they talked, the old man kept urging everyone inside the house.

The boy became interested in Shadduck's wound. He examined his hand very carefully and asked how he had injured it and where he had come from. Shadduck told him that he was an American aviator and that he had been shot down thirty-three days previously. The boy became very excited when he heard this. He pulled up his trousers and showed Shadduck a large wound in his leg. He said that he had been strafed by a U.N. plane. But he was not bitter. In fact, when he saw the condition of Shadduck's hand, he went inside the house and got some strips of cloth and a jar of vaseline. He dabbed the last bit of vaseline in the jar on Shadduck's wound. Then he bound it with the cloth strips.

Shadduck was immensely impressed by the kindness of the Koreans, especially the boy. It was obvious that there was no more vaseline in the house, and that the boy needed it for his own wound; yet he had given the last of it to him. This act of kindness was soon followed by another—the boy gathered up a few scraps of tobacco and carefully rolled six cigarettes. He gave all of them to Shadduck. Later the young girl returned with a freshly cooked bowl of rice and gave it to him. He ate hungrily.

Meanwhile, the old man continued to worry about Shadduck's being out in the open. After a while, he went into the house and came out with a bucket of hot coals. He motioned to Shadduck to follow him. Shadduck did not know what the old man had in mind, but by then, he had made up his mind to trust the Koreans, so he trailed along behind. About twenty-five yards from the house, the Korean stopped and pulled apart a group of bushes. Shadduck saw that the shrubs camouflaged the entrance to a cave. The old man crawled inside. Shadduck followed, burrowing along a narrow tunnel.

The tunnel was about six feet long. It opened into a rather large, well-built room, about eight by five feet. The walls and floor of the room were covered with a fine straw matting. The old man put the coal bucket in the middle of the floor, then he made signs to indicate that Shadduck ought to try to dry his clothes. The boy built racks near the fire on which to place his shoes and socks. The girl brought two more steaming bowls of rice. Soon Shadduck, stuffed with food and drowsy from the warmth of the cave, dropped off to sleep.

When he awoke the following morning, the boy brought him another bowl of rice. He ate quickly and gave the bowl back to the Korean, who returned to the house and refilled it. After the second bowl, Shadduck lit up a cigarette and began to think about what he was going to do. He was still mulling it over when the boy crawled back inside the cave shouting, "Americans. Americans. Come. Come."

Shadduck dressed hurriedly. He crawled out of the cave and stood up on a mound of earth that provided a good view to the south. The sunlight was dazzling. Nevertheless, about two miles away, he could see fifty-odd U.N. troops approaching very cautiously. His heart pounded fast. At last, he had reached safety! He watched as the U.N. troops inched forward. Then suddenly, out of the corner of his eye, he saw a large group of Chinese soldiers about a hundred yards away. They were retreating north at a fast trot.

Shadduck was caught completely by surprise. He dropped behind the mound, kicking himself for letting down his guard. You're not rescued yet, he said to himself. The boy yelled for him to get back in the cave. By the time he had said it a second time, Shadduck was halfway inside. As he crawled hurriedly down the tunnel he made up his mind not to come out again until he could hear American voices. The boy, however innocently, had almost led him into a trap.

About an hour later, the boy returned to the cave, crying, "Americans. Americans. Come. Come." But this time Shadduck refused to budge. He sat near the pot of coals and questioned the boy about the number of men, how they were dressed, what sort of weapons they carried. The boy's answers indicated that the troops were U.N. But Shadduck was not convinced until the boy pulled a brand-new C-ration spoon from his pocket. It was still wrapped in cellophane. That did it.

Nevertheless, Shadduck decided to wait a few more minutes just to make sure all the Chinese had been cleaned out of the area. He did not want to make another last-minute mistake. While he waited, he thanked the boy for his assistance, and promised a reward for the family. Shadduck took a five-dollar bill he had found among Jim's personal effects, wrote his name on it, and gave it to the boy with instructions not to part with it until the proper authorities had made contact with him and presented the reward.

When Shadduck crawled out of the cave the second time, he saw that the U. N. troops were about seventy-five yards away. When they spotted him, they spread out and lay on the ground. Several of them pointed submachine guns at him. Shadduck held his arms out to the side, and slowly walked toward them yelling, "Hey, GI's. Hey, GI's." One of the soldiers got up and advanced slowly. When he realized that Shadduck was an American, he rushed toward him shouting. Then the others followed. They were Greeks.

They embraced Shadduck warmly, slapped him on the back, showered him with C-rations, candy bars, and crackers. One soldier stuck a cigarette in Shadduck's mouth and lit it. He puffed away, ate some of the salty crackers, but declined the candy. He asked to be taken immediately to an American liaison officer. On the way, a U.N. fighter flew low over the troops. Instinctively, Shadduck dove under a bush. The Greek soldiers, who had not moved, laughed. "U.N.," they said, helping Shadduck to his feet. "U.N."

The Greek soldiers—a patrol from the U.S. Seventh Cavalry Division—escorted Shadduck through the woods to a concealed jeep. An American officer was working busily at a radio set mounted in the rear when the group walked up. The officer turned, looked at Shadduck, did a double take, and shouted:

"My gosh! Who in the world are you?"

"Melvin Shadduck, U.S.A.F.," was the reply.

"Well, what are you doing here?" the officer asked.

"Shot down behind the lines on April 23, was a POW, and escaped," Shadduck said.

"April 23? That's thirty-four days ago. Geeze. You need a shave and a haircut. Get in the jeep, and I'll take you back to regimental headquarters."

Shadduck said good-by to the Greek soldiers, then climbed into the front seat. The officer drove speedily over a rough trail. Soon he stopped before a large tent.

"Well, here we are," he said. "Pile out."

The officer walked around and helped Shadduck out of the jeep. Several GI's who were standing around the entrance of the headquarters tent stared bug-eyed at the bearded airman. The officer hurried Shadduck into the tent, impatiently pushed his way around several officers, and finally presented Shadduck to the Army colonel who commanded the regiment.

"Holy cow, Shadduck, sit down here," the colonel said, dragging up a camp chair. "Tell us all about it."

"Well, sir," Shadduck said, "before I do that, I want to tell you that there are three injured Americans and a Turk still up in the POW camp I broke out of. They are waiting for me to come back and get them."

"Holy cow," the colonel said. He walked over to a map. "Show me where they are."

Shadduck walked to the map and put his forefinger on the exact position of the hut.

"Right here," he said.

The colonel marked off the distance. Then he said, "That's forty miles from here, and every mile of it behind enemy lines."

"I told them I would send a chopper and snatch them out," Shadduck said. "We have to hurry. It may already be too late."

"Well, this calls for some thinking," the colonel said. "Did you say they were injured?"

"Yes," Shadduck said. "Not one of them could walk a mile. Two of them can't walk at all." He was thinking of Dave and Billy.

"Well, how will they be able to get into the helicopter? There won't be much time. You can't snatch POW's out of a POW camp without getting shot at."

"One of the POW's, Joe, a sergeant, will pull them out of the hut onto the hill," Shadduck said.

"Well, that sounds pretty iffy to me," the colonel said. "Suppose he can't get them out there?"

"Well, then, I don't know what," Shadduck said.

The colonel was thinking hard. He called in several officers and they huddled over his desk in conference. Finally, the colonel said to Shadduck:

"We'll do it with tanks."

"Tanks?" Shadduck said.

"Yes, tanks," the colonel said. "We have them right here— nine of them—and we can be sure of getting the men on board."

"Yes, but it's forty miles behind enemy lines. You can't send tanks clear through the Chinese front and then hope to get back!" Shadduck said.

"Good God!" the colonel said. "You sure don't know much about how tanks can slither through a fluid front."

The details were quickly arranged. A small Army liaison aircraft was assigned to the Tank Task Force, to help direct the vehicles to the exact spot. Shadduck talked to the pilot and told him how he should circle the hut as a signal to Joe that help was on the way. Within a matter of minutes, the tanks formed up in single file and drew to a halt near the regimental C.P.

"Well, let's get going," Shadduck said, when he saw the tanks.

"You're not going anywhere," the colonel said.

"I want to go along and make sure my buddies get out," Shadduck said.

"You're in no condition to go anywhere," the colonel said. "Don't worry about the boys. If they are still there, we will get them out."

Shadduck stood watching helplessly as the nine tanks churned off through the woods. He yelled, "Good luck"; but the tankers had already "buttoned up" for the dash through Chinese lines. Shadduck turned to the Colonel and said, "There go some guys with a lot of guts."

"You're a little thin," the colonel said, "but I suspect you're not short on guts yourself, Shadduck."

Shadduck was taken to a medical-aid station. His wounds were dressed, his body sprayed with DDT to kill the lice and other vermin, and he was given a good meal and new clothing. After an additional lengthy conference with the regimental G-2, in which he turned over all useful information in his possession, Shadduck was sent to the rear area. Late that evening, he arrived at a hospital in Seoul.

Meantime, the Tank Task Force, in what was probably the most unusual mission of the Korean war, raced through enemy territory to reach the four POW's. The liaison aircraft arrived first. The pilot spotted the "6-P-W" sign and, as per the prearranged signal, circled over the hut three times. Joe hobbled out into the field and waved. The plane flew away and then returned and circled the hut three times again. Then it moved off, in order not to draw attention to the hut, and via radio, guided the Task Force to the scene.

It was not an easy rescue. The tanks pulled up in front of the hut with guns blazing. Joe and the boys were almost delirious with joy. Amid the hail of bullets—for the Chinese were firing, too—the tankers loaded the three Americans and the Turk inside their vehicles. This was somewhat complicated in Dave's case, because he still had the splint around his thigh. Billy could only be moved with the greatest care.

Once the precious cargo had been loaded aboard, the tanks turned around and headed back toward friendly lines. The Army liaison plane directed them through short cuts and guided them around strong enemy positions. Both Dave and Billy gritted their teeth and winced from the pain. The tanks were not gentle. Late that evening, the machines broke through the lines, and returned safely to the regimental C.P.

Immediately upon arrival, the four wounded men were transferred to waiting helicopters and flown south to the Army hospital in Seoul. Shadduck, who had beaten them there by only half an hour or so, met them at the door. When the GI's caught sight of him, they yelled out, "Hey, Shad! Hey, Shad!"

Shadduck ran to the side of their stretchers and grasped

their hands. They all broke down in tears—even the Turk. Joe kept saying over and over, "You made it, Lieutenant! You made it! It was a miracle! A real miracle!"

Finally, Shadduck broke in: "I've made arrangements here for all of us to be billeted in the same room. I figure we couldn't get along without being able to talk and argue."

"Right, Lieutenant," Billy said.

"And by the way," Shadduck said as the stretcher-bearers carried his charges down the hall toward their private room, "how was that tank ride?"

"Lieutenant," Joe said, "that was the roughest ride I ever had. But you know something? It was the *best* ride I ever had, too."

Dave, Joe, and Billy underwent immediate surgery and were soon evacuated by air back to the U.S. In due time, they fully recovered and were returned to civilian life. The Turk had healed so well that he was able to rejoin his outfit in Korea within a matter of days. After medical treatment, Shadduck recovered from his hand and leg wounds. Eventually he was returned to the States, where he joined his wife and family in Chicago. No trace of his observer Gauldin was ever found.

Shadduck was happy to find that when his wife had received the "missing in action" report, it had had the opposite effect from what he had feared. A deeply religious person, in her moment of anxiety, she turned to God. Prayer seemed to give her new strength and determination to pull through her illness.

Shadduck finished out the Korean war in the United States as an instructor at the Strategic Air Command Survival School, in Reno, Nevada. Now he is back on his dairy farm in Minnesota among friends and family.

He had the unique distinction of being the only U.S.A.F. pilot of the Korean war who successfully planned and executed an unaided escape, after being captured, from behind enemy lines. This modest man has never shown interest in an official award or decoration, which he so richly deserves. Apparently he is content with his memories of the days when he was the Tiger of the Imjin, and the enduring gratitude of the four survivors of the grim ordeal on its upper reaches.